8th Student Research Workshop (RANLPStud 2023)

Macau, China
4-6 September 2023

ISBN: 978-1-7138-9041-6

Printed from e-media with permission by:

Curran Associates, Inc.
57 Morehouse Lane
Red Hook, NY 12571

Some format issues inherent in the e-media version may also appear in this print version.

Printed with permission by Curran Associates, Inc. (2024)

For permission requests, please contact the Association for Computational Linguistics at the address below.

Association for Computational Linguistics
209 N. Eighth Street
Stroudsburg, Pennsylvania 18360

Phone: 1-570-476-8006
Fax: 1-570-476-0860

acl@aclweb.org

Additional copies of this publication are available from:

Curran Associates, Inc.
57 Morehouse Lane
Red Hook, NY 12571 USA
Phone: 845-758-0400
Fax: 845-758-2633
Email: curran@proceedings.com
Web: www.proceedings.com

RANLPStud 2023

Proceedings of the 8th Student Research Workshop

associated with

The 14th International Conference on Recent Advances in Natural Language Processing RANLP'2023

4–6 September, 2023

STUDENT RESEARCH WORKSHOP
ASSOCIATED WITH THE INTERNATIONAL CONFERENCE
RECENT ADVANCES IN
NATURAL LANGUAGE PROCESSING'2023

PROCEEDINGS

4–6 September 2023

Series Online ISSN 2603-2821

Designed by INCOMA Ltd.
Shoumen, BULGARIA

Preface

The RANLP 2023 Student Research Workshop (RANLPStud'23) is a special track of the established international conference Recent Advances in Natural Language Processing (RANLP'23).

The RANLPStud is being organised for the 8th time and this year is running in parallel with the other tracks of the main RANLP 2023 conference. The target of RANLPStud'23 is to be a discussion forum and provide an outstanding opportunity for students at all levels (Bachelor, Masters, and Ph.D.) to present their work in progress or completed projects to an international research audience and receive feedback from senior researchers.

The RANLPStud'23 received a good number of submissions, this year fifteen (15) papers were submitted to the event coming from Asia, The Americas (North and South) and Europe, a fact which was reflecting the great number of events, sponsors, submissions, and participants at the main RANLP conference.

We have accepted 5 excellent student papers for oral presentations, one of them has received the Best Paper Award and 7 submissions are presented as posters.

We did our best to make the reviewing process in the interest of our authors, by asking our reviewers to give as exhaustive comments and suggestions as possible, as well as to maintain an encouraging attitude. Each student submission was reviewed by at least two Programme Committee members, who are specialists in their field and were carefully selected to match the submission's topic.

This year, as usual, we invited both strictly Natural Language Processing (NLP) papers, and submissions at the borderline between two sciences (but bearing contributions to NLP).

The topics of the accepted submissions include: Computational Social Science and Social Media; Computer-aided Language Learning; Dialogue and Interactive Systems; Discourse and Pragmatics; Ethics and NLP; Information Extraction; Information Retrieval and Text Mining; Intent Recognition and Detection; Interpretability and Analysis of Models for NLP; Language and Vision; Language Generation; Language Resources and Corpora; Linguistic Theories; Machine Translation and Computer-aided Translation Tools; Multilingual NLP; Multimodal Systems; NLP Applications – Biomedical, Educational, Healthcare, Financial, Legal, Semantic Web, etc.; Opinion Mining and Sentiment Analysis; Phonetics, Phonology, and Morphology; Question Answering; Semantics; Stylistic Analysis; Sublanguages and Controlled languages; Syntax: Tagging, Chunking, and Parsing; Temporal Processing; Text Categorization; Text Simplification and Readability Estimation; Text Summarisation; Text-to-Speech Synthesis and Speech Recognition; Textual Entailment.

We are thankful to the members of the Programme Committee for having provided such exhaustive reviews and even accepting additional reviews, and to the conference mentors, who provided additional comments to participants.

The RANLPStud 2023 Organisers

Momchil Hardalov, AWS AI Labs, Spain
Zara Kancheva, IICT, Bulgarian Academy of Sciences, Bulgaria
Boris Velichkov, FMI, Sofia University "St. Kliment Ohridski", Bulgaria
Ivelina Nikolova-Koleva, IICT, Bulgarian Academy of Sciences, and Ontotext, Bulgaria
Milena Slavcheva, IICT, Bulgarian Academy of Sciences, Bulgaria

Organizers:

Momchil Hardalov, AWS AI Labs, Spain
Zara Kancheva, IICT, Bulgarian Academy of Sciences, Bulgaria
Boris Velichkov, FMI, Sofia University "St. Kliment Ohridski", Bulgaria
Ivelina Nikolova-Koleva, IICT, Bulgarian Academy of Sciences, and Ontotext, Bulgaria
Milena Slavcheva, IICT, Bulgarian Academy of Sciences, Bulgaria

Programme Committee:

Cengiz Acarturk (Jagiellonian University, Poland)
Svetla Boytcheva (Ontotext, Bulgaria)
Necva Bölücü (CSIRO, Australia)
Daniel Dakota (Indiana University, USA)
Mattia Di Gangi (AppTek GmbH, Germany)
Souhila Djabri (Universidad de Alicante, Spain)
Momchil Hardalov (AWS AI Labs, Spain)
Tracy Holloway King (Adobe Inc., USA)
Dmitry Ilvovsky (National Research University, Higher School of Economics, Russia)
Sonia Kropiowska (University of Wolverhampton, UK)
Sandra Kübler (Indiana University, USA)
Michał Marcińczuk (Wrocław University of Science and Technology, Poland)
Alexandra Mayn (Saarland University, Germany)
Elena Murgolo (Orbital14 S.r.l., Italy)
Tsvetomila Mihaylova (Aalto University, Finland)
Ivelina Nikolova-Koleva (Bulgarian Academy of Sciences and Ontotext, Bulgaria)
Alistair Plum (University of Luxembourg, Luxembourg)
Raheem Sarwar (Manchester Metropolitan University, UK)
Milena Slavcheva (Bulgarian Academy of Sciences, Bulgaria)

Table of Contents

Papers Accepted for Oral Presentation

Detecting ChatGPT: A Survey of the State of Detecting ChatGPT-Generated Text
Mahdi Dhaini, Wessel Poelman and Ege Erdogan 1

Unsupervised Calibration through Prior Adaptation for Text Classification using Large Language Models
Lautaro Estienne 13

Controllable Active-Passive Voice Generation using Prefix Tuning
Valentin Knappich and Timo Pierre Schrader 23

Age-Specific Linguistic Features of Depression via Social Media
Charlotte Rosario 33

Trigger Warnings: A Computational Approach to Understanding User-Tagged Trigger Warnings
Sarthak Tyagi, Adwita Arora, Krish Chopra and Manan Suri 44

Papers Accepted for Poster Presentation

Evaluating Hallucinations in Large Language Models for Bulgarian Language
Melania Berbatova and Yoan Salambashev 55

Leveraging Probabilistic Graph Models in Nested Named Entity Recognition for Polish
Jędrzej Jamnicki 64

Crowdsourcing Veridicality Annotations in Spanish: Can Speakers Actually Agree?
Teresa Martín Soeder 68

Weakly supervised learning for aspect based sentiment analysis of Urdu Tweets
Zoya 78

Exploring Low-resource Neural Machine Translation for Sinhala-Tamil Language Pair
Ashmari Pramodya 87

Prompting ChatGPT to Draw Morphological Connections for New Word Comprehension
Bianca-Madalina Zgreaban and Rishabh Suresh 98

Detecting ChatGPT: A Survey of the State of Detecting ChatGPT-Generated Text

Mahdi Dhaini **Wessel Poelman** **Ege Erdogan**
Technical University of Munich
Department of Computer Science
Germany
{mahdi.dhaini,wessel.poelman,ege.erdogan}@tum.de

Abstract

While recent advancements in the capabilities and widespread accessibility of generative language models, such as ChatGPT (OpenAI, 2022), have brought about various benefits by generating fluent human-like text, the task of distinguishing between human- and large language model (LLM) generated text has emerged as a crucial problem. These models can potentially deceive by generating artificial text that appears to be human-generated. This issue is particularly significant in domains such as law, education, and science, where ensuring the integrity of text is of the utmost importance. This survey provides an overview of the current approaches employed to differentiate between texts generated by humans and ChatGPT. We present an account of the different datasets constructed for detecting ChatGPT-generated text, the various methods utilized, what qualitative analyses into the characteristics of human versus ChatGPT-generated text have been performed, and finally, summarize our findings into general insights.

1 Introduction

LLMs have been showing remarkable abilities in generating fluent, grammatical, and convincing text. The introduction of ChatGPT (OpenAI, 2022) has been widely regarded as a significant and controversial milestone for LLMs. Models such as GPT-3 (Brown et al., 2020) and PaLM (Chowdhery et al., 2022) already demonstrated the power of LLMs in many natural language processing (NLP) tasks. ChatGPT is the first model that has seen widespread adoption outside NLP research.

The increased performance of LLMs raises important questions regarding their potential societal impact. The risks of LLMs are numerous, from confidently presenting false information to generating fake news on a large scale (Sheng et al., 2021; Weidinger et al., 2022). ChatGPT is no exception in this regard (Zhuo et al., 2023).

Instances of the misuse of ChatGPT have already been documented in various domains, including education (Cotton et al., 2023), scientific writing (Gao et al., 2022), and the medical field (Anderson et al., 2023). Given this context, the detection of machine-generated text is gaining considerable attention. This detection is part of a larger push towards responsible and appropriate usage of generative language models (Kumar et al., 2023).

In addition to academic interest, a growing number of commercial parties are trying to solve this task. Recent work from Pegoraro et al. (2023) gives an overview of commercial and freely available online tools. They come close to the current work. However, we limit our scope to academic work and provide additional background information on methods, datasets, and qualitative insights.

Many approaches, datasets and shared tasks[1] have been put forth recently to tackle the *general* (i.e., not specific for ChatGPT) task of detecting machine-generated text (Jawahar et al., 2020). Given the enormous use and cultural impact of ChatGPT, we limit our review to datasets and methods developed directly for ChatGPT. We discuss these methods in the context of the controversial position ChatGPT is in, namely that it is a closed-source system with very little information available regarding its training setup or model architecture at the time of writing. We outline what general methods exists for this task and review recent work that directly focuses on datasets and methods for ChatGPT.

Given the peculiar place ChatGPT is in, we also consolidate qualitative insights and findings from the works we discuss that might help humans to detect ChatGPT-generated text. These include lin-

[1] For instance, AuTexTification or CLIN33 Shared Task.

Proceedings of the Student Research Workshop associated with RANLP-2023, pages 1–12, Varna, Bulgaria, Sep 4–6, 2023.
https://doi.org/10.26615/issn.2603-2821.2023_001

guistic features or writing styles to look out for. Lastly, we present outstanding challenges for this detection task and possible future directions.

2 Related Work on Detecting Machine-Generated Text

LLMs have become a driving force in many language processing-related benchmarks and tasks (Radford et al., 2018; Brown et al., 2020; Chowdhery et al., 2022). LLMs can solve complex NLP tasks and generate convincing and trustworthy-looking text. However, they are also prone to generating false and misleading information, generally referred to as *hallucinating* (Lin et al., 2022). Additionally, misuse of these models can pose significant risks in academia, journalism, and many other areas. Currently, human judges are decent at spotting machine-generated text from older LLMs such as GPT-2 (Ippolito et al., 2020; Dugan et al., 2020, 2023). Still, the increasing abilities of LLMs give rise to the need for more sophisticated detection tools and models.

A recent survey by Crothers et al. (2023) provides a thorough overview of risks, approaches, and detection methods. They discuss interesting aspects such as the effect of domains on the detection task, adversarial attacks, and societal impacts of generated texts. Work done by Jawahar et al. (2020) inspects the field of machine-generated text detection. It outlines three main detection methods: a classifier trained from scratch, zero-shot detection by a language model, and a fine-tuned language model as a classifier. Recently, detection methods from computer vision have also been tried on language models, such as watermarking (Kirchenbauer et al., 2023a,b) or trying to find model-identifying artifacts in generated content (Tay et al., 2020). To use and evaluate these methods, fine-grained access to the source model is required in training and inference time. Both these preconditions are not the case with ChatGPT at the time of writing.

When discussing detection methods, an essential factor to consider is access to the log probability output of a model. This is the probability distribution over the vocabulary of a model for the next token to be generated. Numerous successful detection methods evaluate the average log probability per token combined with a threshold in a zero-shot setting (Gehrmann et al., 2019; Ippolito et al., 2020; Mitchell et al., 2023). This method is model agnostic and generally performs quite well. At the time of writing, users of ChatGPT do not have access to these probabilities. Without this access or knowledge about model internals, detection methods are limited to using just the generated text in a binary classification setting, with the options being *human* or *machine*. These methods use simple classifiers trained on n-grams (Solaiman et al., 2019; Ippolito et al., 2020) or fine-tuned pre-trained language models (Uchendu et al., 2020; Ippolito et al., 2020; Zellers et al., 2020).

Another group of detection tools we want to mention are the *human-machine collaboration systems*, as Jawahar et al. (2020) labels them. These tools do not necessarily classify a passage directly but assist a human in making that decision. The previously mentioned work by Gehrmann et al. (2019) visualizes tokens in different colors, depending on where a given token ends up in the top-k most probable tokens from the model. This can also assist a human judge in spotting which part of a larger text might be machine-generated, such as possibly rephrased or copied sections for example. As mentioned, this method requires access to output probabilities, so it is not usable for ChatGPT. Another tool to help humans in the detection task is to outline the linguistic properties and characteristics of machine-generated text. This was one of the main goals of the *Real or Fake Text?* (RoFT) game created by Dugan et al. (2020, 2023). This game asked players to decide if a machine partially wrote a piece of text, and if yes, where the transition point from human to machine is in the text. This resulted in a considerable dataset of annotations and indicators humans look for in detecting machine-generated text.

Another area of research that might help humans to make this decision is explainable AI. As we will see, some papers we discuss use explainability methods, such as SHAP (Lundberg and Lee, 2017), in their approaches. These methods help to better understand how detectors make their predictions. Such methods can help provide insights on the input features that most contribute to a prediction, which, in turn, can facilitate analyses of the differences between human and ChatGPT writing styles.

As far as we know, the previously mentioned work by Crothers et al. (2023) and Jawahar et al. (2020) come closest to ours. They discuss detection methods and datasets but not ChatGPT. The work from Pegoraro et al. (2023) does mention ChatGPT, among other models, but focuses mainly on online detection tools.

Our contributions are the following:

- We provide an overview of *general* approaches to machine-generated text detection.
- We outline research that specifically addresses the detection of ChatGPT-generated text and how this relates to the general approaches.
- We show the datasets that are created and used for this detection task.
- We summarize the qualitative analyses that these recent works provide and try to give general insights.

3 Review of Approaches for Detecting ChatGPT-Generated Text

3.1 Datasets

Table 1 shows datasets that can be used to perform analyses or train models to distinguish between human and ChatGPT written text. We describe how they were collected and provide further information on their domains and public availability.

3.1.1 Guo et al. 2023 (HC3)

Available in both Chinese and English, the Human ChatGPT Comparison Corpus (HC3) contains question-answer pairs collected from different datasets such as OpenQA (Yang et al., 2015) and Reddit ELI5 (Fan et al., 2019). These questions are then given to ChatGPT with context-sensitive prompts (e.g., asking ChatGPT to answer *like I am five* for the Reddit ELI5 dataset) so that each question has one human-generated and one ChatGPT-generated answer.

3.1.2 Yu et al. 2023 (CHEAT)

The ChatGPT-written Abstract (CHEAT) dataset contains human- and ChatGPT-generated title-abstract pairs for computer science papers, with the titles and human-written abstracts fetched from IEEE Xplore. Artificial abstracts are generated in three ways:

- *Generate*: ChatGPT is directly prompted to write an abstract given the title and keywords.
- *Polish*: ChatGPT is given human-written abstracts and is told to "polish" them.
- *Mix*: Text from human-written and polished abstracts are mixed at the sentence level.

The CHEAT dataset also covers adversarial scenarios as the *Polish* and *Mix* methods correspond to methods a malicious user might try to evade detection.

3.1.3 He et al. 2023 (MGTBench)

The Machine Generated Text Benchmark (MGT-Bench) uses three question-answering datasets: TruthfulQA (Lin et al., 2022), SQuaD1 (Rajpurkar et al., 2016), and NarrativeQA (Kočiský et al., 2018). Questions are randomly sampled from each dataset, and ChatGPT is prompted to answer them with the appropriate context (e.g., with a relevant passage and instructions for NarrativeQA).

Although our primary focus is ChatGPT, MGT-Bench contains text generated by different language models and thus can be used to benchmark detection methods across models.

3.1.4 Liu et al. 2023 (ArguGPT)

The ArguGPT dataset contains prompts and responses from various English learning corpora, such as WECCL (Zhi-jia, 2008), TOEFL11 (Blanchard et al., 2013), and hand-picked from graduate record examinations (GRE) preparation material. The texts are from essay writing assignments about a given topic or standpoint. GPT models are prompted to write responses, but their output is processed for grammatical errors and to remove obvious signs of ChatGPT-generated text (e.g., "As a large language model…").

3.1.5 Vasilatos et al. 2023

The dataset used in Vasilatos et al. (2023) for detection builds on Ibrahim et al. (2023), a dataset of questions with metadata and student answers from various university courses. ChatGPT is directly prompted with the questions three times to obtain three human and ChatGPT answers for each question.

3.1.6 Mitrović et al. 2023

Attempting to build a classifier to detect ChatGPT-generated restaurant reviews, Mitrović et al. (2023) build on the Kaggle restaurant reviews dataset[2] and prompt ChatGPT to generate reviews of various kinds (e.g., "write a review for a bad restaurant"). Additionally, ChatGPT is prompted to rephrase the human-written reviews to create an adversarial set.

[2] https://www.kaggle.com/competitions/restaurant-reviews/overview

Dataset (name)	Domain	Public	OOD	Size and Setup
Guo et al. 2023 (HC3-English)	Multi-domain	✓	×	*Q&A* Questions: 24,322 Human-A: 58,546 ChatGPT-A: 26,903
Guo et al. 2023 (HC3-Chinese)	Multi-domain	✓	×	*Q&A* Questions: 12,853 Human-A: 22,259 ChatGPT-A: 17,522
Yu et al. 2023 (CHEAT)	Scientific	×	✓	*Abstracts* Human: 15,395 ChatGPT: 35,304
He et al. 2023 (MGTBench)	General	✓	×	*Q&A pairs* Human: 2,817 ChatGPT: 2,817
Liu et al. 2023 (ArguGPT)	Education	✓	×	*Essays* Human: 4,115 ChatGPT: 4,038
Vasilatos et al. 2023	Education	Human*	×	*Q&A* Questions: 320 Human-A: 960 ChatGPT-A: 960
Mitrović et al. 2023	General	Human*	✓	*Reviews* Human: 1,000 ChatGPT-query: 395 ChatGPT-rephrase: 1,000
Weng et al. 2023	Scientific	Human	×	*Title-Abstract pairs* Human: 59,232 ChatGPT: 59,232
Antoun et al. 2023a	General	✓	✓	*Q&A* HC3-English OOD-ChatGPT: 5,969
Liao et al. 2023	Medical	Human	×	*Abstracts and records* Human: 2,200 ChatGPT: 2,200

Table 1: Datasets used in ChatGPT-generated text detection, with public availability information (if a dataset is available, it can be accessed by clicking on its *Public* column entry). The *Human* entry in the *Public* column signals that only human-written text datasets are made public. The *OOD* (out-of-domain) column signals if a dataset contains examples generated in a different way than the main part (e.g., rephrasing of human-written text). *Authors state it will be made available at a future date.

3.1.7 Weng et al. 2023

Weng et al. (2023) expand on Narechania et al. (2022)'s dataset of title-abstract pairs fetched from top data visualization venues by prompting ChatGPT to write abstracts given the titles. Compared to another dataset of title-abstract pairs, CHEAT (Yu et al., 2023), Weng et al. (2023)'s dataset contains more examples but lacks the adversarial samples included in CHEAT.

3.1.8 Antoun et al. 2023a

Antoun et al. (2023a) extend HC3 (Guo et al., 2023) by translating its English part to French using Google Translate and add further French out-of-domain (OOD) examples to make models trained on this data more robust. The OOD dataset consists of direct French responses by ChatGPT and BingChat to translated questions from the HC3 dataset (as opposed to translating the answers as done originally), question-answer pairs from the French part of the multi-lingual QA dataset MFAQ (De Bruyn et al., 2021), and sentences from the French Treebank dataset (Le Monde corpus). Finally, the dataset also contains a small number of adversarial examples written by humans with access to ChatGPT to obtain a similar style to that of ChatGPT.

3.1.9 Liao et al. 2023

Focusing on the medical domain, Liao et al. (2023) build on two public medical datasets: a set of medical abstracts from Kaggle[3] and radiology reports from the MIMIC-III dataset (Johnson et al., 2016). ChatGPT is given parts of an example medical abstract or a radiology report for the machine-generated samples and is prompted to continue writing it. The authors state that text continuation can generate more human-like text compared to rephrasing or direct prompting.

3.2 Methods

In this section, we report on the various methods proposed for detecting ChatGPT-generated text. The scope of this review does not include the evaluation or comparison of the results obtained from these methods. This limitation primarily arises from the absence of a common experimental setup and the utilization of different datasets and metrics. Table 2 provides an overview of these recent approaches.

Some previous works have utilized transformer-based models to classify text generated by ChatGPT and human-written text, as demonstrated by Mitrović et al. (2023). Their approach consists of two components: a detection model and a framework to explain the decisions made by this model. They first fine-tune an uncased version of DistilBERT (Sanh et al., 2019) and then employ SHAP to provide local explanations in the form of feature importance scores to gain insights into the significance of different input features of the model's results. As a baseline comparison, they implement a perplexity-based classifier that categorizes text based on its perplexity score, where GPT-2 is used for calculating perplexity scores. Their results show that the DistilBERT-based detector outperforms the perplexity-based classifier. However, its performance decreases when considering the rephrased dataset by ChatGPT.

In Liao et al. (2023), different models are proposed to detect medical text generated by ChatGPT: a fine-tuned BERT model (Devlin et al., 2019), a model based on Classification and Regression Trees (CART), an XGBoost model (Chen and Guestrin, 2016) and a perplexity classifier that utilizes BioGPT (Luo et al., 2022) for calculating text perplexity. Predictions by the BERT model are explained by visualizing the local features of the samples, where it can be seen that using conjuncts is an essential feature for the model classifying a medical text as machine-generated.

Liu et al. (2023) fine-tune RoBERTa to detect argumentative essays generated by different GPT models, including ChatGPT, and evaluate its performance on document, paragraph, and sentence-level classification. The essays are broken down into paragraphs and sentences for paragraph and sentence-level classification. They train and compare the performance of SVM models using different linguistic features. These models serve as a baseline to compare with the RoBERTa model and to understand which linguistic features differentiate between human and ChatGPT-generated text.

Guo et al. (2023) implement a machine learning and deep learning-based detector. They utilize a logistic regression model trained on the GLTR Test-2 dataset (Gehrmann et al., 2019) and two deep classifiers based on fine-tuning the pre-trained transformer model RoBERTa. One deep classifier is designed explicitly for single-text detection, while the other is intended for QA detection. The authors construct various training and testing datasets versions to assess the models' robustness. They create full-text, sentence-level, and mixed subsets of the collected corpus. Each subset has both a raw version and a filtered version where prominent indicating words referring to humans (such as "Nope" and "Hmm") or ChatGPT words (such as "AI assistant") are removed. The evaluation of the models reveals that the RoBERTa-based models outper-

[3] https://www.kaggle.com/datasets/chaitanyakck/medical-text

Paper	Dataset	Approaches	Explainability	Code
Mitrović et al. 2023	Mitrović et al. 2023	DistilBERT PBC	SHAP	×
Liao et al. 2023	Liao et al. 2023	BERT PBC XGBoost CART	transformer-interpret	×
Liu et al. 2023	Liu et al. 2023 (ArguGPT)	RoBERTa-large SVM	×	✓*
Guo et al. 2023	Guo et al. 2023 (HC3)	GLTR RoBERTa-single RoBERTa-QA	×	✓
Antoun et al. 2023a	Antoun et al. 2023a Guo et al. 2023 (HC3)	CamemBERT CamemBERTa RoBERTa ELECTRA XLM-R	×	✓
Vasilatos et al. 2023	Ibrahim et al. 2023	PBC	×	×

Table 2: Methods proposed in the literature for detecting ChatGPT-generated text. PBC: Perplexity-based classifier. Publicly available models can be accessed by clicking on the ✓character. *Authors indicate it will be made available at a future date.

form GLTR in terms of performance and exhibit more robustness against interference. Moreover, the RoBERTa-based models are not influenced by indicating words.

Building upon the work of Guo et al. (2023), Antoun et al. (2023a) propose an approach for developing robust detectors able to detect ChatGPT-generated text in different languages, with a focus on French. Their approach consists of fine-tuning pre-trained transformer-based models on English, French, and multilingual datasets. They train RoBERTa and ELECTRA (Clark et al., 2020) models on the English dataset, CamemBERT (Martin et al., 2020) and CamemBERTa (Antoun et al., 2023b) on the French datasets and XLM-R (Conneau et al., 2020) on the combined English and French dataset. They evaluate the robustness of these models against adversarial attacks, such as replacing characters with homoglyphs and adding misspelled words. Considering in-domain text, their results show that French models perform well in detecting machine-generated text. Still, they were outperformed by the English models, while XLM-R provides the best and most resilient performance against adversarial attacks for both English and French. However, this performance decreases when evaluated on out-of-domain text.

Another method proposed for detecting ChatGPT-generated text is a metric-based approach proposed by Vasilatos et al. (2023) to detect machine-generated student assignments by calculating perplexity scores using GPT-2. They show that having category-wise thresholds (derived from dataset metadata) results in better detection performance than only having one threshold value.

3.3 Analysis of Human and ChatGPT-Generated Text

The textual characteristics of ChatGPT-generated text as well as its syntactic and linguistic features, are of significant focus in the works we reviewed. These linguistic and stylistic features are compared to the human-written texts in the datasets. In this section, we summarize and provide an overview of the findings of such analyses for the different domains and datasets we reviewed.

- **Medical domain:** Medical texts generated by ChatGPT have lower text perplexity and are more fluent, neutral, positive, and logical but more general in content and language style, while medical texts written by humans are more diverse and specific (Liao et al., 2023).

- **English argumentative essays:** ChatGPT produces syntactically more complex sentences than English language learners, but ChatGPT-authored essays tend to have lower lexical diversity (Liu et al., 2023).

- **Multi-domain question answering:** ChatGPT writes in an organized and neutral way, offers less bias and harmful information, and refuses to answer questions where it believes it does not know. ChatGPT answers are formal, less emotional, and more objective than human answers (Guo et al., 2023).

- **Scientific abstracts:** ChatGPT has a better choice of vocabulary, can generate more unique words, uses more connecting words, and has fewer grammatical errors (Yu et al., 2023).

- **Language-agnostic characteristics:** The linguistic and syntactic characteristics of ChatGPT-generated text tend to be language-agnostic. Text generated in different languages, such as English, French, and Chinese, shows similar characteristics where ChatGPT tends to produce didactic and impersonal text without errors. Such errors can indicate human text, like grammatical, spelling or punctuation mistakes (Antoun et al., 2023a; Guo et al., 2023).

3.4 General Insights

Based on trends and regular mentions we encountered during the creation of our review, we now report some general insights on the state of detecting ChatGPT-generated text.

Role of explainable AI: Explainability techniques such as SHAP are helpful with detection models. These techniques provide insights into the most important features and words that contribute to classification, thus allowing a better understanding of the writing styles of humans and ChatGPT. This is also valuable in debugging detectors as they can highlight the main words contributing to the misclassification and thus enable better analysis of such models.

Humans versus ChatGPT in detection task: Another insight is that humans are worse at detecting machine-generated text by ChatGPT compared to ChatGPT itself. With additional training, humans would achieve better results.

Robustness of detectors: The robustness of detectors improves when they are trained on datasets that are extended to include also perturbed data, such as homoglyphs and misspellings. This might help the detectors focus more on writing style than writing errors. When evaluated on out-of-domain texts, the performance of detectors tends to decrease, especially when adversarial text is included.

Impact of text length on detection: The shorter the text length, the more challenging and less reliable detection becomes. Models trained on datasets containing full text and question-answer subsets (including answer contexts) do not perform well when evaluated on short texts such as sentences or smaller QA subsets.

Lack of special prompts in ChatGPT-generated text: Some conclusions and analyses in the reviewed papers have been made based on considering text generated by ChatGPT using its most general style and state, i.e., without using any special prompts that could ask ChatGPT to pretend to be a certain writer or to write in a special style. This could be an interesting area of investigation for future work, where new datasets are constructed, and the robustness of detectors against this type of text is tested.

Perplexity-based detectors: perplexity-based detectors depend on using open-source LLMs like GPT-2 and BioGPT to calculate perplexity scores. As ChatGPT generates the target text, calculating these scores using ChatGPT could benefit a lot in this task, as seen with other models using this method. However, this is not possible due to the unfortunate fact of it being a closed-source model.

Cost of constructing machine-generated datasets: Constructing and utilizing large-scale ChatGPT-generated datasets is important for drawing more generalized and precise conclusions. Therefore using ChatGPT's API is essential for this sake. However, the costs of doing so can be prohibitive.

Multilinguality: Our sample of papers has English dominance and performance for other languages is worse. Just as in NLP in general (Artetxe et al., 2020), we call for more work in this area. This could help explain why some detectors are less reliable in detecting machine-generated text when the text is translated into different languages.

4 Conclusion and Future Work

The impressive capabilities of ChatGPT in producing high-quality and convincing text have brought attention to the risks associated with its improper usage across different domains. Consequently, the reliable detection of ChatGPT-generated text has become an important task. To address this concern, numerous datasets and detection methods have been proposed. In this paper, we provided a concise overview of the diverse datasets created, proposed methods, and qualitative insights of comparing human-written text with text generated by ChatGPT.

We see a wide variety of approaches and datasets in the papers we discussed. On the one hand, this is good to see since many factors, such as the domain, language, or format, influence the detection task. On the other hand, we also see a big diversity in experimental and dataset setups. Some works use adversarial examples, and others do not. Some allow the rephrasing of human text by ChatGPT, while others use purely human versus machine-generated text. Some works include the prompts and ChatGPT versions they used to generate the data; others do not. These, among other differences, make comparisons difficult, which is one reason we do not include scores in this survey. This also highlights important future work, namely to test *methods across datasets* and *datasets across methods*.

Another factor to consider is the domain of the text. The datasets we have discussed are in diverse domains and cover at least two important ones affected by ChatGPT's risks: health and education. One notable domain we did not encounter is (fake) news. Although this is a big NLP field on its own, we expected more attention for it in the context of ChatGPT. Future work can definitely help in this area. The format of the text is related to the domain and is another important factor to consider. For example, the shared tasks we mentioned provide tweets, news articles, or reviews as their formats. A systematic look at format and domain influence concerning ChatGPT could be valuable future work.

Multilinguality is another open problem. As with virtually all NLP tasks, we have seen that English is, unfortunately, the dominant language in the datasets. Experiments and gathering datasets across different languages are important future directions. The current task could also draw inspiration from the field of machine translation. It has a long and ongoing history of trying to detect (badly) translated text, so-called *translationese* (Baroni and Bernardini, 2006), which could be used or adapted to detect general machine-generated text.

Lastly, an important factor we have not seen discussed much is the temporal aspect of ChatGPT. Outputs might change over time, especially since it is a closed-source system. This calls for repeated tests over time to ensure detection methods are not regressing in their performance. Machine-generated text detection is also a cat-and-mouse game; since models are optimized to mimic human language, detection becomes harder and harder.

5 Limitations

A limitation of our work is that recent methods proposed for detecting ChatGPT-generated text are pre-prints published in arXiv, due to the rapid pace of work in this area. Additionally, we limit our scope to academic papers and exclude online non-academic tools as we do not know how those tools were trained or how they work internally.

This is also a big problem when discussing ChatGPT in general. Since it is a closed-sourced system without detailed information about its training and dataset, it is impossible to know if the results are reproducible. Models can change at any moment in the background, models can be decommissioned, or the price of access can change drastically. We are well aware of and concerned about these developments, but given the significant opportunities and risks ChatGPT poses, we believe a survey like this one is valuable.

Acknowledgements

We thank Florian Matthes and the Software Engineering for Business Information Systems (SEBIS) chair at TUM for their funding and support. We also thank the anonymous reviewers for their helpful and insightful comments.

References

Nash Anderson, Daniel L Belavy, Stephen M Perle, Sharief Hendricks, Luiz Hespanhol, Evert Verhagen, and Aamir R Memon. 2023. AI did not write this manuscript, or did it? Can we trick the AI text detector into generated texts? The potential future of ChatGPT and AI in Sports & Exercise Medicine manuscript generation. *BMJ Open Sport & Exercise Medicine*, 9(1):e001568.

Wissam Antoun, Virginie Mouilleron, Benoît Sagot, and Djamé Seddah. 2023a. Towards a Robust Detection of Language Model Generated Text: Is ChatGPT that Easy to Detect? (arXiv:2306.05871v1).

Wissam Antoun, Benoît Sagot, and Djamé Seddah. 2023b. Data-Efficient French Language Modeling with CamemBERTa. (arXiv:2306.01497v1).

Mikel Artetxe, Sebastian Ruder, Dani Yogatama, Gorka Labaka, and Eneko Agirre. 2020. A Call for More Rigor in Unsupervised Cross-lingual Learning. In *Proceedings of the 58th Annual Meeting of the Association for Computational Linguistics*, pages 7375–7388, Online. Association for Computational Linguistics.

Marco Baroni and Silvia Bernardini. 2006. A New Approach to the Study of Translationese: Machine-learning the Difference between Original and Translated Text. *Literary and Linguistic Computing*, 21(3):259–274.

Daniel Blanchard, Joel Tetreault, Derrick Higgins, Aoife Cahill, and Martin Chodorow. 2013. TOEFL11: A corpus of non-native english. *ETS Research Report Series*, 2013(2):i–15.

Tom Brown, Benjamin Mann, Nick Ryder, Melanie Subbiah, Jared D Kaplan, Prafulla Dhariwal, Arvind Neelakantan, Pranav Shyam, Girish Sastry, Amanda Askell, Sandhini Agarwal, Ariel Herbert-Voss, Gretchen Krueger, Tom Henighan, Rewon Child, Aditya Ramesh, Daniel Ziegler, Jeffrey Wu, Clemens Winter, Chris Hesse, Mark Chen, Eric Sigler, Mateusz Litwin, Scott Gray, Benjamin Chess, Jack Clark, Christopher Berner, Sam McCandlish, Alec Radford, Ilya Sutskever, and Dario Amodei. 2020. Language Models are Few-Shot Learners. In *Advances in Neural Information Processing Systems*, volume 33, pages 1877–1901. Curran Associates, Inc.

Tianqi Chen and Carlos Guestrin. 2016. XGBoost: A Scalable Tree Boosting System. In *Proceedings of the 22nd ACM SIGKDD International Conference on Knowledge Discovery and Data Mining*, KDD '16, pages 785–794, New York, NY, USA. Association for Computing Machinery.

Aakanksha Chowdhery, Sharan Narang, Jacob Devlin, Maarten Bosma, Gaurav Mishra, Adam Roberts, Paul Barham, Hyung Won Chung, Charles Sutton, Sebastian Gehrmann, Parker Schuh, Kensen Shi, Sasha Tsvyashchenko, Joshua Maynez, Abhishek Rao, Parker Barnes, Yi Tay, Noam Shazeer, Vinodkumar Prabhakaran, Emily Reif, Nan Du, Ben Hutchinson, Reiner Pope, James Bradbury, Jacob Austin, Michael Isard, Guy Gur-Ari, Pengcheng Yin, Toju Duke, Anselm Levskaya, Sanjay Ghemawat, Sunipa Dev, Henryk Michalewski, Xavier Garcia, Vedant Misra, Kevin Robinson, Liam Fedus, Denny Zhou, Daphne Ippolito, David Luan, Hyeontaek Lim, Barret Zoph, Alexander Spiridonov, Ryan Sepassi, David Dohan, Shivani Agrawal, Mark Omernick, Andrew M. Dai, Thanumalayan Sankaranarayana Pillai, Marie Pellat, Aitor Lewkowycz, Erica Moreira, Rewon Child, Oleksandr Polozov, Katherine Lee, Zongwei Zhou, Xuezhi Wang, Brennan Saeta, Mark Diaz, Orhan Firat, Michele Catasta, Jason Wei, Kathy Meier-Hellstern, Douglas Eck, Jeff Dean, Slav Petrov, and Noah Fiedel. 2022. PaLM: Scaling Language Modeling with Pathways. (arXiv:2204.02311v5).

Kevin Clark, Minh-Thang Luong, Quoc V. Le, and Christopher D. Manning. 2020. ELECTRA: Pre-training Text Encoders as Discriminators Rather Than Generators. (arXiv:2003.10555v1).

Alexis Conneau, Kartikay Khandelwal, Naman Goyal, Vishrav Chaudhary, Guillaume Wenzek, Francisco Guzmán, Edouard Grave, Myle Ott, Luke Zettlemoyer, and Veselin Stoyanov. 2020. Unsupervised Cross-lingual Representation Learning at Scale. In *Proceedings of the 58th Annual Meeting of the Association for Computational Linguistics*, pages 8440–8451, Online. Association for Computational Linguistics.

Debby R. E. Cotton, Peter A. Cotton, and J. Reuben Shipway. 2023. Chatting and cheating: Ensuring academic integrity in the era of ChatGPT. *Innovations in Education and Teaching International*, 0(0):1–12.

Evan Crothers, Nathalie Japkowicz, and Herna Viktor. 2023. Machine Generated Text: A Comprehensive Survey of Threat Models and Detection Methods. (arXiv:2210.07321v4).

Maxime De Bruyn, Ehsan Lotfi, Jeska Buhmann, and Walter Daelemans. 2021. MFAQ: a multilingual FAQ dataset. In *Proceedings of the 3rd Workshop on Machine Reading for Question Answering*, pages 1–13, Punta Cana, Dominican Republic. Association for Computational Linguistics.

Jacob Devlin, Ming-Wei Chang, Kenton Lee, and Kristina Toutanova. 2019. BERT: Pre-training of Deep Bidirectional Transformers for Language Understanding. (arXiv:1810.04805v2).

Liam Dugan, Daphne Ippolito, Arun Kirubarajan, and Chris Callison-Burch. 2020. RoFT: A Tool for Evaluating Human Detection of Machine-Generated Text. In *Proceedings of the 2020 Conference on Empirical Methods in Natural Language Processing: System Demonstrations*, pages 189–196, Online. Association for Computational Linguistics.

Liam Dugan, Daphne Ippolito, Arun Kirubarajan, Sherry Shi, and Chris Callison-Burch. 2023. Real or Fake Text?: Investigating Human Ability to Detect Boundaries between Human-Written and Machine-Generated Text. *Proceedings of the AAAI Conference on Artificial Intelligence*, 37(11):12763–12771.

Angela Fan, Yacine Jernite, Ethan Perez, David Grangier, Jason Weston, and Michael Auli. 2019. ELI5: Long Form Question Answering. In *Proceedings of the 57th Annual Meeting of the Association for Computational Linguistics*, pages 3558–3567, Florence, Italy. Association for Computational Linguistics.

Catherine A. Gao, Frederick M. Howard, Nikolay S. Markov, Emma C. Dyer, Siddhi Ramesh, Yuan Luo, and Alexander T. Pearson. 2022. Comparing scientific abstracts generated by ChatGPT to original abstracts using an artificial intelligence output detector, plagiarism detector, and blinded human reviewers. page 2022.12.23.521610.

Sebastian Gehrmann, Hendrik Strobelt, and Alexander Rush. 2019. GLTR: Statistical Detection and Visualization of Generated Text. In *Proceedings of the 57th Annual Meeting of the Association for Computational Linguistics: System Demonstrations*, pages 111–116, Florence, Italy. Association for Computational Linguistics.

Biyang Guo, Xin Zhang, Ziyuan Wang, Minqi Jiang, Jinran Nie, Yuxuan Ding, Jianwei Yue, and Yupeng Wu. 2023. How Close is ChatGPT to Human Experts? Comparison Corpus, Evaluation, and Detection. (arXiv:2301.07597v1).

Xinlei He, Xinyue Shen, Zeyuan Chen, Michael Backes, and Yang Zhang. 2023. MGTBench: Benchmarking Machine-Generated Text Detection. (arXiv:2303.14822v2).

Hazem Ibrahim, Fengyuan Liu, Rohail Asim, Balaraju Battu, Sidahmed Benabderrahmane, Bashar Alhafni, Wifag Adnan, Tuka Alhanai, Bedoor AlShebli, Riyadh Baghdadi, Jocelyn J. Bélanger, Elena Beretta, Kemal Celik, Moumena Chaqfeh, Mohammed F. Daqaq, Zaynab El Bernoussi, Daryl Fougnie, Borja Garcia de Soto, Alberto Gandolfi, Andras Gyorgy, Nizar Habash, J. Andrew Harris, Aaron Kaufman, Lefteris Kirousis, Korhan Kocak, Kangsan Lee, Seungah S. Lee, Samreen Malik, Michail Maniatakos, David Melcher, Azzam Mourad, Minsu Park, Mahmoud Rasras, Alicja Reuben, Dania Zantout, Nancy W. Gleason, Kinga Makovi, Talal Rahwan, and Yasir Zaki. 2023. Perception, performance, and detectability of conversational artificial intelligence across 32 university courses. (arXiv:2305.13934v1).

Daphne Ippolito, Daniel Duckworth, Chris Callison-Burch, and Douglas Eck. 2020. Automatic Detection of Generated Text is Easiest when Humans are Fooled. In *Proceedings of the 58th Annual Meeting of the Association for Computational Linguistics*, pages 1808–1822, Online. Association for Computational Linguistics.

Ganesh Jawahar, Muhammad Abdul-Mageed, and Laks Lakshmanan, V.S. 2020. Automatic Detection of Machine Generated Text: A Critical Survey. In *Proceedings of the 28th International Conference on Computational Linguistics*, pages 2296–2309, Barcelona, Spain (Online). International Committee on Computational Linguistics.

Alistair E. W. Johnson, Tom J. Pollard, Lu Shen, Liwei H. Lehman, Mengling Feng, Mohammad Ghassemi, Benjamin Moody, Peter Szolovits, Leo Anthony Celi, and Roger G. Mark. 2016. MIMIC-III, a freely accessible critical care database. *Scientific Data*, 3(1):160035.

John Kirchenbauer, Jonas Geiping, Yuxin Wen, Jonathan Katz, Ian Miers, and Tom Goldstein. 2023a. A Watermark for Large Language Models. (arXiv:2301.10226v3).

John Kirchenbauer, Jonas Geiping, Yuxin Wen, Manli Shu, Khalid Saifullah, Kezhi Kong, Kasun Fernando, Aniruddha Saha, Micah Goldblum, and Tom Goldstein. 2023b. On the Reliability of Watermarks for Large Language Models. (arXiv:2306.04634v3).

Tomáš Kočiský, Jonathan Schwarz, Phil Blunsom, Chris Dyer, Karl Moritz Hermann, Gábor Melis, and Edward Grefenstette. 2018. The NarrativeQA Reading Comprehension Challenge. *Transactions of the Association for Computational Linguistics*, 6:317–328.

Sachin Kumar, Vidhisha Balachandran, Lucille Njoo, Antonios Anastasopoulos, and Yulia Tsvetkov. 2023. Language Generation Models Can Cause Harm: So What Can We Do About It? An Actionable Survey. In *Proceedings of the 17th Conference of the European Chapter of the Association for Computational Linguistics*, pages 3299–3321, Dubrovnik, Croatia. Association for Computational Linguistics.

Wenxiong Liao, Zhengliang Liu, Haixing Dai, Shaochen Xu, Zihao Wu, Yiyang Zhang, Xiaoke Huang, Dajiang Zhu, Hongmin Cai, Tianming Liu, and Xiang Li. 2023. Differentiate ChatGPT-generated and Human-written Medical Texts. (arXiv:2304.11567v1).

Stephanie Lin, Jacob Hilton, and Owain Evans. 2022. TruthfulQA: Measuring How Models Mimic Human Falsehoods. In *Proceedings of the 60th Annual Meeting of the Association for Computational Linguistics (Volume 1: Long Papers)*, pages 3214–3252, Dublin, Ireland. Association for Computational Linguistics.

Yikang Liu, Ziyin Zhang, Wanyang Zhang, Shisen Yue, Xiaojing Zhao, Xinyuan Cheng, Yiwen Zhang, and Hai Hu. 2023. ArguGPT: Evaluating, understanding and identifying argumentative essays generated by GPT models. (arXiv:2304.07666v1).

Scott M Lundberg and Su-In Lee. 2017. A Unified Approach to Interpreting Model Predictions. In *Advances in Neural Information Processing Systems*, volume 30. Curran Associates, Inc.

Renqian Luo, Liai Sun, Yingce Xia, Tao Qin, Sheng Zhang, Hoifung Poon, and Tie-Yan Liu. 2022. BioGPT: Generative Pre-trained Transformer for Biomedical Text Generation and Mining. *Briefings in Bioinformatics*, 23(6):bbac409.

Louis Martin, Benjamin Muller, Pedro Javier Ortiz Suárez, Yoann Dupont, Laurent Romary, Éric de la Clergerie, Djamé Seddah, and Benoît Sagot. 2020. CamemBERT: A Tasty French Language Model. In *Proceedings of the 58th Annual Meeting of the Association for Computational Linguistics*, pages 7203–7219, Online. Association for Computational Linguistics.

Eric Mitchell, Yoonho Lee, Alexander Khazatsky, Christopher D. Manning, and Chelsea Finn. 2023. DetectGPT: Zero-Shot Machine-Generated Text Detection using Probability Curvature. (arXiv:2301.11305v2).

Sandra Mitrović, Davide Andreoletti, and Omran Ayoub. 2023. ChatGPT or Human? Detect and Explain. Explaining Decisions of Machine Learning Model for Detecting Short ChatGPT-generated Text. (arXiv:2301.13852v1).

Arpit Narechania, Alireza Karduni, Ryan Wesslen, and Emily Wall. 2022. VitaLITy: Promoting Serendipitous Discovery of Academic Literature with Transformers & Visual Analytics. *IEEE Transactions on Visualization and Computer Graphics*, 28(1):486–496.

OpenAI. 2022. ChatGPT: Optimizing Language Models for Dialogue.

Alessandro Pegoraro, Kavita Kumari, Hossein Fereidooni, and Ahmad-Reza Sadeghi. 2023. To ChatGPT, or not to ChatGPT: That is the question! (arXiv:2304.01487v2).

Alec Radford, Jeffrey Wu, Rewon Child, David Luan, Dario Amodei, and Ilya Sutskever. 2018. Language Models are Unsupervised Multitask Learners.

Pranav Rajpurkar, Jian Zhang, Konstantin Lopyrev, and Percy Liang. 2016. SQuAD: 100,000+ Questions for Machine Comprehension of Text. In *Proceedings of the 2016 Conference on Empirical Methods in Natural Language Processing*, pages 2383–2392, Austin, Texas. Association for Computational Linguistics.

Victor Sanh, Lysandre Debut, Julien Chaumond, and Thomas Wolf. 2019. DistilBERT, a distilled version of BERT: Smaller, faster, cheaper and lighter. (arXiv:1910.01108v4).

Emily Sheng, Kai-Wei Chang, Prem Natarajan, and Nanyun Peng. 2021. Societal Biases in Language Generation: Progress and Challenges. In *Proceedings of the 59th Annual Meeting of the Association for Computational Linguistics and the 11th International Joint Conference on Natural Language Processing (Volume 1: Long Papers)*, pages 4275–4293, Online. Association for Computational Linguistics.

Irene Solaiman, Miles Brundage, Jack Clark, Amanda Askell, Ariel Herbert-Voss, Jeff Wu, Alec Radford, Gretchen Krueger, Jong Wook Kim, Sarah Kreps, Miles McCain, Alex Newhouse, Jason Blazakis, Kris McGuffie, and Jasmine Wang. 2019. Release Strategies and the Social Impacts of Language Models. (arXiv:1908.09203v2).

Yi Tay, Dara Bahri, Che Zheng, Clifford Brunk, Donald Metzler, and Andrew Tomkins. 2020. Reverse Engineering Configurations of Neural Text Generation Models. In *Proceedings of the 58th Annual Meeting of the Association for Computational Linguistics*, pages 275–279, Online. Association for Computational Linguistics.

Adaku Uchendu, Thai Le, Kai Shu, and Dongwon Lee. 2020. Authorship Attribution for Neural Text Generation. In *Proceedings of the 2020 Conference on Empirical Methods in Natural Language Processing (EMNLP)*, pages 8384–8395, Online. Association for Computational Linguistics.

Christoforos Vasilatos, Manaar Alam, Talal Rahwan, Yasir Zaki, and Michail Maniatakos. 2023. HowkGPT: Investigating the Detection of ChatGPT-generated University Student Homework through Context-Aware Perplexity Analysis. (arXiv:2305.18226v2).

Laura Weidinger, Jonathan Uesato, Maribeth Rauh, Conor Griffin, Po-Sen Huang, John Mellor, Amelia Glaese, Myra Cheng, Borja Balle, Atoosa Kasirzadeh, Courtney Biles, Sasha Brown, Zac Kenton, Will Hawkins, Tom Stepleton, Abeba Birhane, Lisa Anne Hendricks, Laura Rimell, William Isaac, Julia Haas, Sean Legassick, Geoffrey Irving, and Iason Gabriel. 2022. Taxonomy of Risks posed by Language Models. In *Proceedings of the 2022 ACM Conference on Fairness, Accountability, and Transparency*, FAccT '22, pages 214–229, New York, NY, USA. Association for Computing Machinery.

Luoxuan Weng, Minfeng Zhu, Kam Kwai Wong, Shi Liu, Jiashun Sun, Hang Zhu, Dongming Han, and Wei Chen. 2023. Towards an Understanding and Explanation for Mixed-Initiative Artificial Scientific Text Detection. (arXiv:2304.05011v1).

Yi Yang, Wen-tau Yih, and Christopher Meek. 2015. WikiQA: A Challenge Dataset for Open-Domain Question Answering. In *Proceedings of the 2015 Conference on Empirical Methods in Natural Language Processing*, pages 2013–2018, Lisbon, Portugal. Association for Computational Linguistics.

Peipeng Yu, Jiahan Chen, Xuan Feng, and Zhihua Xia. 2023. CHEAT: A Large-scale Dataset for Detecting ChatGPT-writtEn AbsTracts. (arXiv:2304.12008v1).

Rowan Zellers, Ari Holtzman, Hannah Rashkin, Yonatan Bisk, Ali Farhadi, Franziska Roesner, and Yejin Choi. 2020. Defending Against Neural Fake News. (arXiv:1905.12616v3).

Xu Zhi-jia. 2008. A Review of Spoken and Written English Corpus of Chinese Learners. *Journal of Longyan University*.

Terry Yue Zhuo, Yujin Huang, Chunyang Chen, and Zhenchang Xing. 2023. Red teaming ChatGPT via Jailbreaking: Bias, Robustness, Reliability and Toxicity. (arXiv:2301.12867v4).

Unsupervised Calibration through Prior Adaptation for Text Classification using Large Language Models

Lautaro Estienne
ICC, CONICET-UBA, Argentina
Faculty of Engineering, University of Buenos Aires, Argentina
lestienne@fi.uba.ar

Abstract

A wide variety of natural language tasks are currently being addressed with large-scale language models (LLMs). These models are usually trained with a very large amount of unsupervised text data and adapted to perform a downstream natural language task using methods like fine-tuning, calibration or in-context learning. In this work, we propose an approach to adapt the prior class distribution to perform text classification tasks without the need for labelled samples and only a few in-domain sample queries. The proposed approach treats the LLM as a black box, adding a stage where the model posteriors are calibrated to the task. Results show that these methods outperform the un-adapted model for different number of training shots in the prompt and a previous approach where calibration is performed without using any adaptation data.

1 Introduction

In the last years, Large Language Models (LLMs) like GPT-3 (Brown et al., 2020), FLAN-T5 (Chung et al., 2022), InstructGPT (Ouyang et al., 2022) have proven to be useful for a large variety of complex natural language understanding tasks, showing outstanding performance on many benchmarks related to reading comprehension, summarization, information retrieval, and generative question-answering, among others (Narayan et al., 2018; Zellers et al., 2019; Khattab et al., 2022; Omar et al., 2023). LLMs are pre-trained on a large amount of unsupervised text data following a cost function that is usually self-supervised (autoregressive, denoising, etc.) (Yang et al., 2019; Chung et al., 2022; Devlin et al., 2018).

Notably, LLMs achieve competitive results in a zero-shot scenarios, i.e., without being adapted to the downstream task of interest (Wei et al., 2021; Chung et al., 2022; OpenAI, 2023). Nevertheless, when data is available for adaptation, significant gains can be achieved over the zero-shot scenario. In these cases, the adaptation is done, for example, through (full or selective) fine-tuning (Devlin et al., 2018; Chung et al., 2022), in-context learning (Brown et al., 2020; Wei et al., 2021), or post-processing of the model's outputs (Zhao et al., 2021; Jiang et al., 2021), depending on the size of adaptation dataset, whether this data is labelled or not, and the amount of computational resources available.

In this work, we propose an approach to adapt LLMs to text classification tasks using unlabelled in-domain data. That is, we assume we have examples of the type of text that needs to be classified, but we do not have the actual class of these examples. We propose a light-weight method inspired by the theory of calibration which, for the datasets we experimented with, required only a few dozen of in-domain samples to achieve optimal performance. We call this method **UCPA** (**U**nsupervised **C**alibration through **P**rior **A**daptation). We compare our proposed approach with a previously proposed approach which does not rely on any in-domain data (Zhao et al., 2021) and show that the additional information provides significant performance improvements. Further, we compare our method, theoretically and empirically, with supervised calibration of the posteriors using logistic regression. We show that our approach performs similarly to supervised calibration, without the need for labelled data. Finally, another version of the method is presented where we assume that, even though no labelled data is available, the class priors can be estimated from knowledge of the task. We call this variant **SUCPA** (**S**emi-**U**nsupervised **C**alibration through **P**rior **A**daptation) since some information about the task is needed to estimate the priors.

Proceedings of the Student Research Workshop associated with RANLP-2023, pages 13–22, Varna, Bulgaria, Sep 4–6, 2023.
https://doi.org/10.26615/issn.2603-2821.2023_002

2 Related Work

Large Language Models (LLMs) LLMs are language models with a large number of parameters, in the order of billions, trained with a massive amount of text to minimize a cost function that can vary from model to model. Models like GPT-2 (Radford et al., 2019), GPT-3 (Brown et al., 2020) or LLaMA (Touvron et al., 2023) are decoder-only transformer-based (Vaswani et al., 2017) architectures trained with an autoregressive loss. In contrast, models like BERT (Devlin et al., 2018) or T5 (Raffel et al., 2019) are trained to denoise the input to obtain the output.

Fine-tuning Pre-trained LLMs can be adapted to a specific task of interest using finetuning techniques like Parameter Efficient Finetuning (PEFT) (Liu et al., 2022), soft-prompt (Lester et al., 2021) and Reinforcement Learning from Human Feedback (RLHF) (Ouyang et al., 2022). Despite the attempt of some methods to reduce the number of trainable parameters without sacrificing performance, finetuning is generally an expensive way of adapting a LLM to a certain task since it requires significant amounts of in-domain data, as well as computational resources to load and train the LLM.

In-context Learning Given the large computational and data requirements of the fine-tuning approach, alternative approaches to adapt LLMs to a certain task of interest have been proposed. In-context learning refers to the practice of prepending instructions about the task of interest before the text to be classified, summarized or continued in some other way. Besides these instructions, examples (usually called "shots") on how to perform the task can be added to the prompt. The GPT-3 paper (Brown et al., 2020) showed that close to the state-of-the-art performance in many tasks could be obtained by providing instructions in the prompt without any further adaptation to the task. This work led to the study of good prompt design practices (Zhao et al., 2021).

Calibration There is a large body of literature regarding calibration of classifiers' outputs (Filho et al., 2021), with some recent applications to Natural Language Processing Tasks (Jagannatha and Yu, 2020; Braverman et al., 2019). Recently, a work from Zhao et al. (2021) used the concept of "content-free" input to perform an ad-hoc unsupervised form of calibration for different tasks carried out by a LLM. Our work can be seen as a generalization and formalization of this work, where we derive the approach as unsupervised calibration with an affine expression where the parameters are obtained through the minimization of the cross-entropy.

3 UCPA: Unsupervised Calibration through Posterior Adaptation

An LLM produces posterior probabilities $P(n|\mathbf{h}, \mathbf{q}, \mathbf{e})$ for the next token, n, given the history of previously generated words or tokens, $\mathbf{h}$, and the query, $\mathbf{q}$, and preface, $\mathbf{e}$, which together form the prompt $(\mathbf{e}, \mathbf{q})$. The bolded variables indicate sequences of one or more tokens, while n is a single token. In our case, the preface contains instructions on the classification task to be solved (Chung et al., 2022) and, optionally, a set of training examples for in-context learning (Brown et al., 2020).

When using a LLM to do classification, we need to use the model to obtain $P(y|\mathbf{q}, \mathbf{e})$ from a prompt $(\mathbf{e}, \mathbf{q})$, where $y \in \mathcal{Y}$ and $\mathcal{Y} = \{y_1, \ldots, y_K\}$ is the set of possible classes. To do this, we first define an *ad-hoc* label name w_k for every label $y_k \in \mathcal{Y}$. Then, we prompt the LLM, which we will call θ, with the word sequence given by $\mathbf{e}$ followed by $\mathbf{q}$ to get a score

$$s_k = P_\theta(w_k|\mathbf{q}, \mathbf{e}) \tag{1}$$

for the class y_k. Finally, the probability distribution $P(y|\mathbf{q}, \mathbf{e})$ is computed by normalizing this score to get a probability distribution over the classes:

$$P(y = y_k|\mathbf{q}, \mathbf{e}) = \frac{s_k}{\sum_{k'} s_{k'}} \tag{2}$$

Note that there may be cases in which the label name is represented with more than one token (see Table 1 for a complete list of datasets used and the label names of each one). In those cases the probability $P_\theta(w_k|\mathbf{q}, \mathbf{e})$ can be computed as

$$P_\theta(w_k|\mathbf{q}, \mathbf{e}) = \prod_{m=0}^{M_k-1} P_\theta(w_k^{m+1} \mid \mathbf{q}, \mathbf{e}, w_k^{1:m}) \tag{3}$$

where $w_k^{1:m} = [w_k^1, \ldots, w_k^m]$ and $w_k^{1:0}$ is an empty string. The posteriors on the right-hand side are obtained directly from the LLM.

Using the definition of conditional probability, the posterior $P(y|\mathbf{q}, \mathbf{e})$ can be written as:

$$P(y \mid \mathbf{q}, \mathbf{e}) = P(y \mid \mathbf{e}) \frac{P(\mathbf{q} \mid y, \mathbf{e})}{P(\mathbf{q} \mid \mathbf{e})} \tag{4}$$

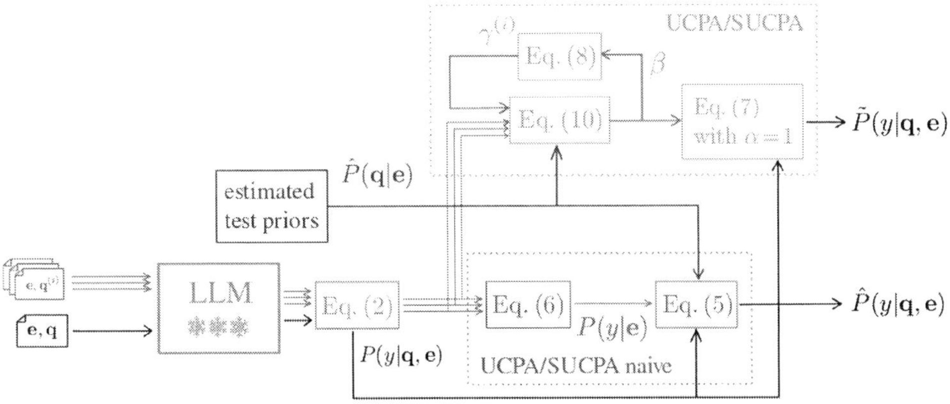

Figure 1: Schematic of the proposed approach. The test sample $(\mathbf{e}, \mathbf{q})$ is processed by the LLM and plugged to Equation (2) to produce the posterior $P(y \mid \mathbf{q}, \mathbf{e})$. In addition, a set of in-domain queries $\{\mathbf{q}^{(1)}, \ldots, \mathbf{q}^{(N)}\}$ is used to reestimate the priors in a "naive" (bottom) or iterative (up) way. Lastly, estimated test priors $P(\mathbf{q} \mid \mathbf{e})$ are used to produce adapted posteriors $\tilde{P}(y \mid \mathbf{q}, \mathbf{e})$ or $\hat{P}(y \mid \mathbf{q}, \mathbf{e})$. For the UCPA approach, $P(\mathbf{q} \mid \mathbf{e})$ is assumed uniform, whereas for SUCPA, specific knowledge of the task is used to estimate that prior.

The factor $P(\mathbf{q} \mid y, \mathbf{e})/P(\mathbf{q} \mid \mathbf{e})$ is the ratio between the likelihood of the query given the preface and the class name, and the likelihood given only the preface. This likelihood ratio (LR) reflects the increase in the likelihood of the query obtained by adding the class name to the response.

The quantity $P(y|\mathbf{e})$ can be understood as a prior probability in the sense that it is not conditioned on the query: it is the probability of the class given only the preface. This prior depends strongly on the task of interest. While the LLM might have a tendency to predict a certain class given the preface, this may not be the most likely class for the task of interest. As we mentioned in Section 1, adapting the model to the application of interest is key for obtaining relevant responses from the LLM. While the preface $\mathbf{e}$ is, in fact, a way to adapt the LLMs outputs to the task of interest, it may not be sufficient to fully adapt the posteriors since not all the information about the task can be represented in a short text explanation.

In this work we propose to improve the posteriors computed from the LLM's scores by explicitly adjusting the priors to the task of interest. This is done by assuming the following expression for the in-domain posterior:

$$\hat{P}(y \mid \mathbf{q}, \mathbf{e}) = \delta \; P(y \mid \mathbf{q}, \mathbf{e}) \frac{\hat{P}(y \mid \mathbf{e})}{P(y \mid \mathbf{e})} \tag{5}$$

which can be interpreted as taking away the effect of the mismatched prior $P(y|\mathbf{e})$ from the LLM-derived posterior $P(y|\mathbf{q}, \mathbf{e})$, replacing it with the in-domain prior $\hat{P}(y|\mathbf{e})$, and then rescaling by δ to make sure the resulting distribution adds up to one. To obtain $\hat{P}(y|\mathbf{q}, \mathbf{e})$ we need to compute the posterior, which is obtained directly from the LLM using Equation (2), and the two priors.

The prior $\hat{P}(y|\mathbf{e})$ is the prior we expect for our task of interest. We may or may not know this distribution. In this work we compare results under two assumptions: 1) that we do not know anything about the prior distribution in which case we simply assume a uniform distribution $\hat{P}(y_k|\mathbf{e}) = 1/K$ for all k, and 2) that, even though we do not have labelled data, we do have a good estimate of the frequencies of the classes we expect to see in practice. In our experiments, for this second scenario we compute $\hat{P}(y_k|\mathbf{e}) = N_k/N$, where N_k is the number of training samples of class k. In practice, though, these priors could be estimated from knowledge of the task rather than from in-domain labelled data. Arguably, this second scenario is no longer unsupervised, so we will call this method Semi-Unsupervised Calibration through Prior Adaptation (SUCPA), while the method that uses uniform priors will be called Unsupervised Calibration through Prior Adaptation (UCPA).

The prior $P(y \mid \mathbf{e})$ is the prior for y that is implicit in our LLM. It is the distribution of classes that the model would output for this task, across all possible relevant queries we may provide. Hence, we estimate this prior by simply running the LLM on (unlabelled) training data $Q^{\text{train}} = \{\mathbf{q}^{(1)}, \ldots, \mathbf{q}^{(N)}\}$ and averaging the resulting posteriors:

$$P(y|\mathbf{e}) \approx \frac{1}{N}\sum_{i=1}^{N} P(y|\mathbf{q}^{(i)}, \mathbf{e}) \quad (6)$$

The method above is a heuristic that relies on an assumption (Equation (5)) that may or may not hold, as well as on the approximation of the prior above. When using this expression to obtain the prior we call the method "UCPA/SUCPA-naive". As we will see, this heuristic works quite well in our experiments. Further, as we explain in Section 4, we can also obtain the prior in a more principled way using an expression derived from linear logistic regression.

3.1 Content-free Prompts

The approach proposed by Zhao et al. (2021) can be seen as a special case of the UCPA-naive method. In that work, calibrated posteriors are computed using Equation (5), where the training set Q^{train} is composed of one or more "content-free" inputs, in the sense that they do not contain any relevant meaning, and they are created manually by the user. For example, the authors experiment with using "[MASK]", "N/A", and the empty string.

4 Supervised Affine Calibration and Semi-UCPA (SUCPA)

A standard way to adapt the posterior probabilities from a classifier to a certain domain of interest is to calibrate them using in-domain labelled data. Calibration refers to the process of transforming the scores of a system to optimize the quality of the scores as posteriors. This is usually done by choosing a certain parameterized form for the transform and training those parameters to minimize a proper scoring rule like the cross-entropy (Filho et al., 2021). One instance of this approach is linear logistic regression.

Linear logistic regression assumes that the logarithm of the calibrated posteriors are given by:

$$\log \tilde{P}(y_k|\mathbf{q}, \mathbf{e}) = \gamma + \alpha_k \log P(y_k|\mathbf{q}, \mathbf{e}) + \beta_k \quad (7)$$

where $P(y_k|\mathbf{q}, \mathbf{e})$ is given by Equation (2), α and β are parameters, and the value of γ is determined so that $\sum_{k=1}^{K} \tilde{P}(y_k|\mathbf{q}, \mathbf{e}) = 1$. That is,

$$\gamma = -\log \sum_{k'=1}^{K} P(y_{k'}|\mathbf{q}, \mathbf{e})^{\alpha_k} e^{\beta_{k'}} \quad (8)$$

The α_k and β_k parameters are estimated by minimizing the cross-entropy on a training set $\mathcal{C}^{\text{train}} = \{(\mathbf{q}^{(1)}, y^{(1)}), \ldots, (\mathbf{q}^{(N)}, y^{(N)})\}$ where $\mathbf{q}^{(i)}$ and $y^{(i)}$ are the query and the class of sample i:

$$\mathcal{L} = -\frac{1}{N}\sum_{i=1}^{N} \log \tilde{P}(y^{(i)}|\mathbf{q}^{(i)}, \mathbf{e}) \quad (9)$$

In this work we take α_k to be a scalar, independent of the class. This is what is usually done for calibration (Brummer and Van Leeuwen, 2006; Guo et al., 2017; Platt et al., 1999). In particular, temperature scaling (Guo et al., 2017), one of the most widely used calibration methods, corresponds to taking $\beta_k = 0$ for all k and α_k a single scalar.

If we restrict the calibration transformation to have $\alpha_k = 1$ and set the derivative of the cross-entropy to zero, we can derive the following expression for β_k:

$$\beta_k = \log\frac{N_k}{N} - \log\left[\frac{1}{N}\sum_{i=1}^{N} P(y_k|\mathbf{q}^{(i)}, \mathbf{e})e^{\gamma^{(i)}}\right] \quad (10)$$

where $\gamma^{(i)}$ is given by Equation (8) with $\mathbf{q} = \mathbf{q}^{(i)}$. Note that this is not a closed-form expression for β_k but rather a system of equations since the right-hand side contains all the β_k within the $\gamma^{(i)}$.

We can now compare Equation (5) and Equation (7). Taking the logarithm of Equation (5) for one specific class k we get:

$$\log \hat{P}(y_k|\mathbf{q}, \mathbf{e}) = \gamma' + \log P(y_k|\mathbf{q}, \mathbf{e}) + \beta'_k \quad (11)$$

where $\gamma' = \log \delta$ and

$$\beta'_k = \log \hat{P}(y_k|\mathbf{e}) - \log P(y_k|\mathbf{e}) \quad (12)$$

The form of this expression is identical to that of Equation (7) when taking $\alpha_k = 1$ for all k. Both γ and γ' are determined so that the posterior on the left-hand side adds to one. Hence, if $\beta_k = \beta'_k$, the two posteriors would be identical.

Comparing the expressions for β_k and β'_k we can see that they coincide if we take $\hat{P}(y_k|\mathbf{e}) = N_k/N$ as we assume in our experiments for the SUCPA approach, and if we take $\gamma^{(i)} = 0$, since in that case the second term in β_k coincides with Equation (6). Of course, $\gamma^{(i)}$ is not necessarily zero. Yet, as we will see in the experiments, making this assumption has little effect on the results. Nevertheless, we can also estimate the β_k that satisfies Equation (10) exactly using an iterative approach where we first set $\gamma^{(i)} = 0$ and compute

β_k for all k, plug those values into Equation (8) to get a new value for $\gamma^{(i)}$ and plug that back into Equation (10), repeating these steps until convergence. We find that this algorithm leads to identical results as running linear logistic regression with $\alpha_k = 1$. In the following, we will refer to the UCPA (and SUCPA) approach described in section 3 as "UPCA-naive" (and "SUCPA-naive"), whereas the iterative version of this method will be called simply UCPA (and SUCPA). Figure 1 summarizes both approaches for both the UCPA and SUCPA variants.

5 Experimental Set Up

We evaluate the proposed approach on the n-shot text classification task following a similar procedure as Zhao et al. (2021). We use four datasets for which the task is classification of a single text into known categories: binary sentiment analysis using SST-2 (Socher et al., 2013), 6-way question classification using TREC (Voorhees and Tice, 2000), 4-way news classification using AGNews (Zhang et al., 2015), and the 14-way ontology classification using DBPedia (Lehmann et al., 2015). Table 1 shows the number of test samples, class priors and prompt used for each dataset.

We used the standard train and test partitions for all datasets. For AGNews and DBPedia we selected 1000 random samples from the test set since their test splits were too large for computation in our infrastructure. This approach was similar to the one used by Zhao et al. (2021) where they selected 300 test samples (see their github repository[1]). Also following this work, we used GPT-2 XL which has 1.5B parameters and consists of a decoder-only transformer architecture (Vaswani et al., 2017). The checkpoint was downloaded from the `huggingface` website[2], and the code used to run experiments is available on github[3].

For each dataset, a set of n shots were selected by random sampling the train split and added to the preface (see Table 1). Then, the Q^{train} set was generated by random sampling 600 samples from Q^{train} after discarding the samples added to the preface. The $\mathcal{C}^{\text{train}}$ set to train the calibrator was the same as Q^{train} with the difference that $\mathcal{C}^{\text{train}}$ contains the labels and Q^{train} does not. For some of the experiments we further subset the training set to smaller sizes. When doing this, we use 10 different seeds to generate the subsets to assess the variation in results due to varying training sets. For each training set we obtain posteriors on the test set and generate 100 bootstrap samples (Tibshirani and Efron, 1993; Keller et al., 2005). The curves in the figures 2 and 3 show the mean performance on the pooled performance estimated from all training sets and test bootstraps and confidence intervals plotted one standard deviation away from the mean.

We show results in terms of error rate (1-accuracy), equivalently to Zhao et al. (2021). Further, in the final results, we also include the cross-entropy performance. Cross-entropy is a proper scoring rule which means that it evaluates the performance of the provided scores as posterior probabilities (Gneiting and Raftery, 2007). In the figures we show normalized cross-entropy, where the cross-entropy is divided by the cross-entropy of a naive system that always outputs the prior distribution, ignoring the input sample. A normalized cross-entropy larger than 1.0 indicates that the system is so badly calibrated that its performance is worse than that of a naive system (Brummer, 2010; Ferrer, 2023).

6 Effect of the Training Set Size

Figure 2 shows the error rate for all datasets as a function of the number of training samples used to perform domain adaptation for the 0-shot scenario (no examples added to the preface). This set is used either to train the calibration model (in which case the class labels are used), to compute Equation (6) for UCPA/SUCPA-naive, and to compute Equation (10) for UCPA/SUCPA. For SUCPA, the training labels are used to compute N_k/N which is used to obtain $\hat{P}(y|\mathbf{e})$ and in Equation (10). For UCPA, the training labels are never used and N_k/N is assumed uniform over the classes. The figure also shows the results for the baseline system which takes the posteriors from Equation (2) without any prior adaptation. Finally, we show the performance of a naive baseline that always chooses the most likely class in the training data.

We first note that, as explained in Section 4, SUCPA and linear logistic calibration with $\alpha = 1$ gives identical performance. We found the same results for the case of 1, 4 and 8-shot learning, indicating that our iterative algorithm for estimating the β_k that satisfies Equation (10) is working as ex-

[1]`https://github.com/tonyzhaozh/few-shot-learning`

[2]`https://huggingface.co/gpt2-xl`

[3]`https://github.com/LautaroEst/efficient-reestimation`

Dataset	Class Priors	Test Samples	Prompt Template
TREC	0.28: Description 0.23: Number 0.19: Entity 0.16: Location 0.13: Person 0.02: Abbreviation	500	*"Classify the questions based on whether their answer type is a Number, Location, Person, Description, Entity, or Abbreviation.* *Question:* `[example 1]` *Answer Type:* `[label 1]` ... *Question:* `[example n]` *Answer Type:* `[label n]` *Question:* `[query]` *Answer Type:"*
SST-2	0.50: Negative 0.50: Positive	1821	*"Review:* `[example 1]` *Sentiment:* `[label 1]` ... *Review:* `[example n]` *Sentiment:* `[label n]` *Review:* `[query]` *Sentiment:"*
AGNews	0.27: Technology 0.26: Business 0.25: Sports 0.22: World	1000	*"Classify the news articles into the categories of World, Sports, Business, and Technology.* *Article:* `[example 1]` *Answer:* `[label 1]` ... *Article:* `[example n]` *Answer:* `[label n]` *Article:* `[query]` *Answer:"*
DBpedia	0.09: Artist 0.09: Nature 0.08: Athlete 0.08: Plant 0.08: Company 0.07: School 0.07: Village 0.07: Animal 0.07: Transportation 0.07: Politician 0.07: Album 0.06: Book 0.06: Building 0.05: Film	1000	*"Classify the documents based on whether they are about a Company, School, Artist, Athlete, Politician, Transportation, Building, Nature, Village, Animal, Plant, Album, Film, or Book.* *Article:* `[example 1]` *Answer:* `[label 1]` ... *Article:* `[example n]` *Answer:* `[label n]` *Article:* `[query]` *Answer:"*

Table 1: Number of test samples, class priors in the test set, and prompt used for each dataset in this work. The instruction text for each case is taken from (Zhao et al., 2021).

pected. We can also see for both UCPA and SUCPA (i.e., regardless of how the in-domain priors are estimated), the naive and the iterative approaches give similar performance, indicating that the average posterior in Equation (6) is a good approximation for the model's prior. Both proposed approaches show better performance than the original model for three of the four datasets even when very few (as low as 10) training samples are available to do the prior adaptation. In the case of DBPedia, however, we see that the SUCPA methods degrade performance compared to the baseline when the number of training samples is smaller than 80. This is due to the fact that the priors estimated as N_k/N cannot be robustly estimated on so few samples for this 14-class. Since the priors in this dataset are close to uniform (see Table 1), in this case it is better to assume them uniform than to estimate them from a very small dataset. A similar trend can be found for SST-2 and AGNews for which the priors are perfectly uniform so that assuming them is always better than estimating them from data. On the other hand, for the TREC dataset we can see that, given enough training samples, SUCPA works better than UCPA when the test priors are not uniform. Similar trends to those seen in this figure were found for a prompt containing 1, 4 and 8 shots.

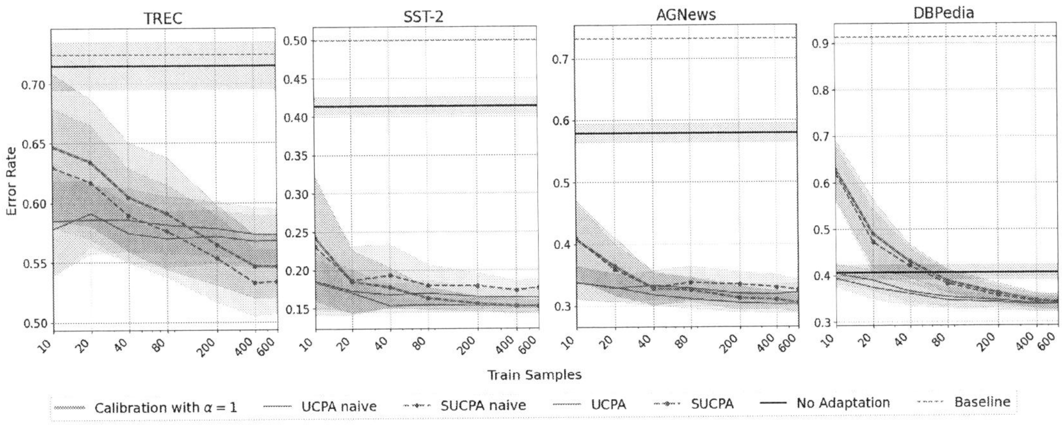

Figure 2: Error rate vs. the number of training samples used in the prior adaptation process in a zero-shot configuration. The red lines show the iterative approach for UCPA and SUCPA, whereas the blue lines show the naive version. The orange curve shows the calibration results for $\alpha = 1$. The black curve shows the results without adaptation and the grey dotted line represents the majority-class classifier (both are constant because they do not use training data).

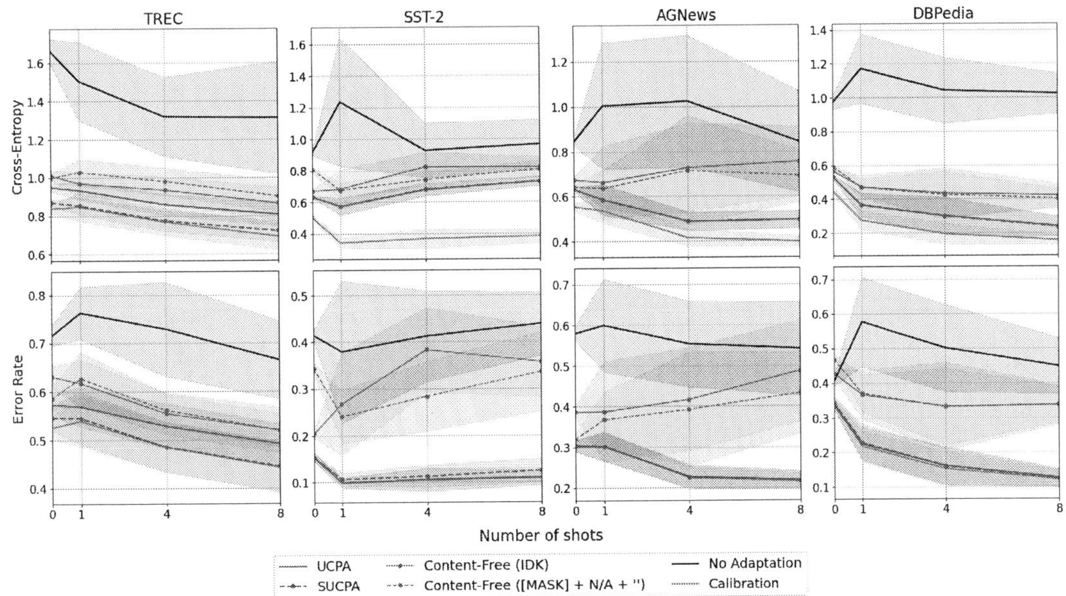

Figure 3: Cross-Entropy and Error Rate (1-Accuracy) vs. the number of examples (shots) contained in the prompt for 600 training samples. The red lines show the iterative approach for UCPA and SUCPA. The lines in purple show the results for content-free adaptation and the green line is the calibration using parameters α and β. As before, the black line shows the case for which no adaptation has been performed.

7 Effect of the Number of Shots

Figure 3 shows the effect of the number of examples (shots) added to the preface for each dataset in terms of error rate and cross-entropy when the number of training samples is 600. We compare our proposed methods with four systems: 1) the non-adapted posteriors (solid black line), 2) the affine calibration method (solid green line) in which parameters α and β are trained using the labelled training data, and 3) and 4) the two content-free calibration methods explained in Section 3.1 with the two sets of content-free inputs that were used in the authors' code (see footnote above), namely, {'IDK'} and {'[MASK]', 'N/A', ''}. We can see that, for 600 training samples, our proposed methods consistently improve upon the content-free baseline, as well as over the non-adapted posteriors. In most cases, the non-adapted model presented a mean cross-entropy close to or higher than 1 for all number of shots, which implies that the model is useless for this task and cannot learn from the prompt shots. They also tend to have small standard deviation and a more stable tendency across the number of shots. Of course, the content-free approaches have the advantage that they do not require training data at all. Yet, these results show that, if unlabelled training data is available, we can obtain significant gains from our proposed UCPA approach. Further, if an estimate of the class priors is available, the SUCPA approach can lead to additional gains in datasets with imbalanced priors, like TREC.

Figure 3 also shows that the affine calibration system performs consistently better than our proposed approaches, particularly in terms of cross-entropy which better highlights issues of miscalibration compared to accuracy. This is expected since the calibrator is taking advantage of the labelled training data. Note that affine calibration is one specific case of a downstream classifier, one with very few parameters which can be trained with a small number of samples. A more complex downstream classifier may give further improvements, but would require larger labelled training datasets.

With some exceptions (like in SST-2), increasing the number of examples added to the preface leads to gains in all methods that do some kind of adaptation. The original posteriors, on the other hand, have erratic behavior as a function of the number of shots with a very large standard deviation resulting from the specific selection of examples.

Additional experiments were performed when the number of training samples is set to 40 showing similar trends to those in Figure 3 with the exception that SUCPA works worse than UCPA in most cases due to a bad estimate of the class priors. In practice, the class priors would be estimated from knowledge of the task rather than from the training dataset, so that the SUCPA performance would in fact depend on how good that estimate is.

Overall, we can see that the proposed method leads to a large gain with respect to the non-adapted posteriors, even in a scenario where a relatively small amount of unlabelled data is available for training. In terms of computational requirements in comparison with the baseline method, the proposed approach requires the computation of the probabilities $P(y|\mathrm{e})$. The time needed to compute these probabilities depends linearly on the number of training samples. During evaluation, the proposed approach has a negligible overhead with respect to the baseline system since the only difference is that it needs to compute Equation (5) using the pre-computed $P(y|\mathrm{e})$ and target priors $\hat{P}(y|\mathrm{e})$.

8 Conclusion and Future Work

In this work we proposed a method for calibrating the posteriors generated by an LLM for a certain text-classification task. We assume that only a relatively small number of unlabelled in-domain samples are available for adaptation. We propose a simple method for calibrating the posteriors generated by the LLM by adapting the prior class distribution to the task of interest in an unsupervised manner. Optionally, the method allows the new priors to be set to the ones we expect to see during deployment, when known. When such priors are unknown, they can be assumed uniform. We show that, as long as the test priors can be estimated reasonably well, or that the uniform assumption is not too far off from the test distribution, the proposed approach works significantly better than the un-adapted posteriors even with a small amount of available adaptation samples. Further, we show that it works better than a previous approach where calibration is performed without using any adaptation data.

In our experiments, the proposed method was shown to work well for classification tasks where the number of classes was relatively small in number compared to the amount of training data. We hypothesize that the requirement on training data would increase linearly with the number of classes. Future work will include a comparison with finetuning techniques, as well as experiments with LLMs larger than GPT-2 XL. Further, we will explore the generalization of the proposed method to other NLP tasks like question-answering and summarization where the required output is not necessarily restricted to just a few tokens and to tasks outside of the NLP domain where prior mismatch may also be a common scenario.

References

Mark Braverman, Xinyi Chen, Sham M. Kakade, Karthik Narasimhan, Cyril Zhang, and Yi Zhang. 2019. Calibration, entropy rates, and memory in language models. *CoRR*, abs/1906.05664.

Tom B. Brown, Benjamin Mann, Nick Ryder, Melanie Subbiah, Jared Kaplan, Prafulla Dhariwal, Arvind Neelakantan, Pranav Shyam, Girish Sastry, Amanda Askell, Sandhini Agarwal, Ariel Herbert-Voss, Gretchen Krueger, Tom Henighan, Rewon Child, Aditya Ramesh, Daniel M. Ziegler, Jeffrey Wu, Clemens Winter, Christopher Hesse, Mark Chen, Eric Sigler, Mateusz Litwin, Scott Gray, Benjamin Chess, Jack Clark, Christopher Berner, Sam McCandlish, Alec Radford, Ilya Sutskever, and Dario Amodei. 2020. Language models are few-shot learners. *CoRR*, abs/2005.14165.

Niko Brummer. 2010. *Measuring, refining and calibrating speaker and language information extracted from speech*. Ph.D. thesis, Stellenbosch: University of Stellenbosch.

Niko Brummer and David A. Van Leeuwen. 2006. On calibration of language recognition scores. In *2006 IEEE Odyssey - The Speaker and Language Recognition Workshop*, pages 1–8.

Hyung Won Chung, Le Hou, Shayne Longpre, Barret Zoph, Yi Tay, William Fedus, Yunxuan Li, Xuezhi Wang, Mostafa Dehghani, Siddhartha Brahma, Albert Webson, Shixiang Shane Gu, Zhuyun Dai, Mirac Suzgun, Xinyun Chen, Aakanksha Chowdhery, Alex Castro-Ros, Marie Pellat, Kevin Robinson, Dasha Valter, Sharan Narang, Gaurav Mishra, Adams Yu, Vincent Zhao, Yanping Huang, Andrew Dai, Hongkun Yu, Slav Petrov, Ed H. Chi, Jeff Dean, Jacob Devlin, Adam Roberts, Denny Zhou, Quoc V. Le, and Jason Wei. 2022. Scaling instruction-finetuned language models.

Jacob Devlin, Ming-Wei Chang, Kenton Lee, and Kristina Toutanova. 2018. BERT: pre-training of deep bidirectional transformers for language understanding. *CoRR*, abs/1810.04805.

Luciana Ferrer. 2023. Analysis and comparison of classification metrics.

T. S. Filho, H. Song, M. Perello-Nieto, R. Santos-Rodriguez, M. Kull, and P. Flach. 2021. Classifier calibration: How to assess and improve predicted class probabilities: a survey. *arXiv preprint arXiv:2112.10327*.

Tilmann Gneiting and Adrian E Raftery. 2007. Strictly proper scoring rules, prediction, and estimation. *Journal of the American Statistical Association*, 102(477):359–378.

Chuan Guo, Geoff Pleiss, Yu Sun, and Kilian Q. Weinberger. 2017. On calibration of modern neural networks. *CoRR*, abs/1706.04599.

Abhyuday Jagannatha and Hong Yu. 2020. Calibrating structured output predictors for natural language processing. In *Proceedings of the 58th Annual Meeting of the Association for Computational Linguistics*, pages 2078–2092, Online. Association for Computational Linguistics.

Zhengbao Jiang, Jun Araki, Haibo Ding, and Graham Neubig. 2021. How Can We Know When Language Models Know? On the Calibration of Language Models for Question Answering. *Transactions of the Association for Computational Linguistics*, 9:962–977.

Mikaela Keller, Samy Bengio, and Siew Wong. 2005. Benchmarking non-parametric statistical tests. In *Advances in Neural Information Processing Systems*, volume 18. MIT Press.

Omar Khattab, Keshav Santhanam, Xiang Lisa Li, David Hall, Percy Liang, Christopher Potts, and Matei Zaharia. 2022. Demonstrate-search-predict: Composing retrieval and language models for knowledge-intensive nlp. *arXiv:2212.14024*.

Jens Lehmann, Robert Isele, Max Jakob, Anja Jentzsch, Dimitris Kontokostas, Pablo N. Mendes, Sebastian Hellmann, Mohamed Morsey, Patrick van Kleef, S. Auer, and Christian Bizer. 2015. Dbpedia - a large-scale, multilingual knowledge base extracted from wikipedia. *Semantic Web*, 6:167–195.

Brian Lester, Rami Al-Rfou, and Noah Constant. 2021. The power of scale for parameter-efficient prompt tuning. *CoRR*, abs/2104.08691.

Haokun Liu, Derek Tam, Mohammed Muqeeth, Jay Mohta, Tenghao Huang, Mohit Bansal, and Colin A Raffel. 2022. Few-shot parameter-efficient fine-tuning is better and cheaper than in-context learning. *Advances in Neural Information Processing Systems*, 35:1950–1965.

Shashi Narayan, Shay B. Cohen, and Mirella Lapata. 2018. Don't give me the details, just the summary! topic-aware convolutional neural networks for extreme summarization. *CoRR*, abs/1808.08745.

Reham Omar, Omij Mangukiya, Panos Kalnis, and Essam Mansour. 2023. Chatgpt versus traditional question answering for knowledge graphs: Current status and future directions towards knowledge graph chatbots. *arXiv:2302.06466*.

OpenAI. 2023. Gpt-4 technical report.

Long Ouyang, Jeffrey Wu, Xu Jiang, Diogo Almeida, Carroll Wainwright, Pamela Mishkin, Chong Zhang, Sandhini Agarwal, Katarina Slama, Alex Ray, et al. 2022. Training language models to follow instructions with human feedback. *Advances in Neural Information Processing Systems*, 35.

John Platt et al. 1999. Probabilistic outputs for support vector machines and comparisons to regularized likelihood methods. *Advances in large margin classifiers*, 10(3):61–74.

Alec Radford, Jeffrey Wu, Rewon Child, David Luan, Dario Amodei, Ilya Sutskever, et al. 2019. Language models are unsupervised multitask learners. *OpenAI blog*, 1(8):9.

Colin Raffel, Noam Shazeer, Adam Roberts, Katherine Lee, Sharan Narang, Michael Matena, Yanqi Zhou, Wei Li, and Peter J. Liu. 2019. Exploring the limits of transfer learning with a unified text-to-text transformer. *CoRR*, abs/1910.10683.

Richard Socher, Alex Perelygin, Jean Wu, Jason Chuang, Christopher D. Manning, Andrew Ng, and Christopher Potts. 2013. Recursive deep models for semantic compositionality over a sentiment treebank. In *Proceedings of the 2013 Conference on Empirical Methods in Natural Language Processing*, pages 1631–1642, Seattle, Washington, USA. Association for Computational Linguistics.

Robert J Tibshirani and Bradley Efron. 1993. *An introduction to the bootstrap*, volume 57. Monographs on statistics and applied probability.

Hugo Touvron, Thibaut Lavril, Gautier Izacard, Xavier Martinet, Marie-Anne Lachaux, Timothée Lacroix, Baptiste Rozière, Naman Goyal, Eric Hambro, Faisal Azhar, et al. 2023. Llama: Open and efficient foundation language models. *arXiv preprint arXiv:2302.13971*.

Ashish Vaswani, Noam Shazeer, Niki Parmar, Jakob Uszkoreit, Llion Jones, Aidan N. Gomez, Lukasz Kaiser, and Illia Polosukhin. 2017. Attention is all you need. *CoRR*, abs/1706.03762.

Ellen M. Voorhees and Dawn M. Tice. 2000. Building a question answering test collection. In *Proceedings of the 23rd Annual International ACM SIGIR Conference on Research and Development in Information Retrieval*, SIGIR '00, page 200–207, New York, NY, USA. Association for Computing Machinery.

Jason Wei, Maarten Bosma, Vincent Y. Zhao, Kelvin Guu, Adams Wei Yu, Brian Lester, Nan Du, Andrew M. Dai, and Quoc V. Le. 2021. Finetuned language models are zero-shot learners. *CoRR*, abs/2109.01652.

Zhilin Yang, Zihang Dai, Yiming Yang, Jaime G. Carbonell, Ruslan Salakhutdinov, and Quoc V. Le. 2019. Xlnet: Generalized autoregressive pretraining for language understanding. *CoRR*, abs/1906.08237.

Rowan Zellers, Ari Holtzman, Yonatan Bisk, Ali Farhadi, and Yejin Choi. 2019. Hellaswag: Can a machine really finish your sentence?

Xiang Zhang, Junbo Jake Zhao, and Yann LeCun. 2015. Character-level convolutional networks for text classification. *CoRR*, abs/1509.01626.

Zihao Zhao, Eric Wallace, Shi Feng, Dan Klein, and Sameer Singh. 2021. Calibrate before use: Improving few-shot performance of language models. In *International Conference on Machine Learning*. PMLR.

Controllable Active-Passive Voice Generation using Prefix Tuning

Valentin Knappich[1,2], **Timo Pierre Schrader**[1,2,3]
[1]Bosch Center for Artificial Intelligence, Renningen, Germany
[2]University of Stuttgart, Germany [3]University of Augsburg, Germany
valentin.knappich|timo.schrader@de.bosch.com

Abstract

The prompting paradigm is an uprising trend in the field of Natural Language Processing (NLP) that aims to learn tasks by finding appropriate prompts rather than fine-tuning the model weights. Such prompts can express an intention, e.g., they can instruct a language model to generate a summary of a given event. In this paper, we study how to influence ("control") the language generation process such that the outcome fulfills a requested linguistic property. More specifically, we look at controllable active-passive (AP) voice generation, i.e., we require the model to generate a sentence in the requested voice. We build upon the prefix tuning approach and introduce control tokens that are trained on controllable AP generation. We create an AP subset of the WebNLG dataset to fine-tune these control tokens. Among four different models, the one trained with a contrastive learning approach yields the best results in terms of AP accuracy ($\approx 95\%$) but at the cost of decreased performance on the original WebNLG task.

1 Introduction

Prompt-based learning is an uprising trend in Natural Language Processing. In contrast to the pre-train and fine-tune paradigm, prompt-based methods aim to adapt to new downstream tasks by finding or using new prompts that maximize the task performance. In that way, arbitrary tasks can be wrapped as language modeling tasks (Radford et al., 2019; Brown et al., 2020). This approach has the advantage that the pre-trained model parameters remain intact, and a single model can be used to solve many tasks by using the appropriate prompt without having to readjust all model parameters. However, it poses the challenge of finding a prompt with satisfactory performance. Manually finding such prompts can be tedious, and the results can sometimes be unintuitive (Gao et al., 2020). To that end, many techniques have been proposed to automatically find good discrete (Shin et al., 2020) or continuous prompts (Lester et al., 2021; Qin and Eisner, 2021; Li and Liang, 2021).

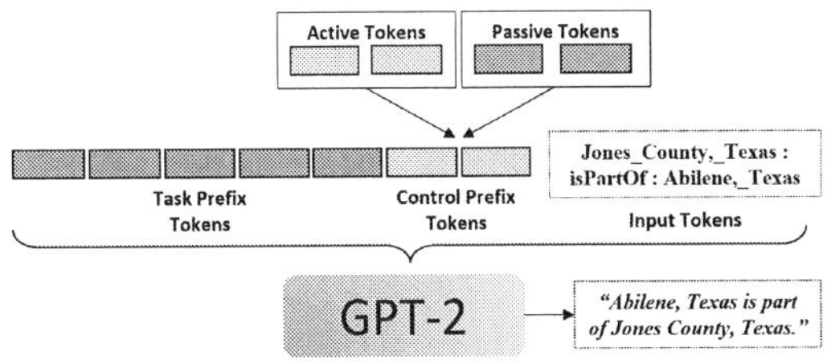

Figure 1: Our proposed method inputs task-specific prefix tokens and control tokens into GPT-2 in order to create a sentence from an input triple in the requested voice (active or passive).

Our work investigates the use of continuous prompts, as proposed by Li and Liang (2021), for controllable generation. More specifically, we attempt to guide a generative model to create sentences that are formulated in either active or passive voice. For instance, the fact that "J.V. Jones" wrote the book "A Fortress of Grey Ice" can be formulated in either active voice (*The author of A Fortress of Grey Ice is J.V. Jones.*) or passive voice (*A Fortress of Grey Ice was written by J. V. Jones.*). We use the data-to-text dataset WebNLG (Gardent et al., 2017) as a benchmark and measure both task performance and the model's ability to generate outputs in the requested voice.

We use *task-specific prefix tokens* and additional *control prefix tokens* (cf. Figure 1), similar to Clive et al. (2021), and propose three different training objectives to train the additional control prefix tokens: implicit training, classifier guidance, and contrastive learning. We compare these three approaches and use the model without control prefix tokens as the baseline. Both implicit training and classifier guidance achieve only minor improvements in terms of control abilities but pre-

Proceedings of the Student Research Workshop associated with RANLP-2023, pages 23–32, Varna, Bulgaria, Sep 4–6, 2023.
https://doi.org/10.26615/issn.2603-2821.2023_003

serve most of the task performance. In contrast, a contrastive learning approach achieves the highest active-passive (AP) voice generation accuracy of $\approx 95\%$. However, the semantic accuracy of the generated sentences is decreased compared to the other approaches, which is reflected in our qualitative and quantitative analyses.

The core contributions of this paper are as follows: first, we propose two new datasets that are derived from the WebNLG dataset called WebNLG-AP and WebNLG-AP-Pairs, which can be used to train on active/passive voice generation. Second, based on GPT-2 (Radford et al., 2019), we compare four training setups and assess their ability to control the voice while accurately performing the data-to-text task. Last, we make our dataset publicly available.[1]

2 Related Work

Controllable text generation is the task of generating natural language text while controlling secondary aspects of the output (Prabhumoye et al., 2020). These aspects can for instance be the sentiment, formality, persona, or content. Leng et al. (2020) control the length of generated sentences, as well as the sentence split, i.e., how many sentences are generated and how many facts each sentence contains. Zhang et al. (2022) propose a categorization of generative tasks involving control, including *Data to Text* and *Format Control*. Therefore, the WebNLG task can be seen as a control task where the control aspect is the information content, while our active-passive control falls into the category of *Format Control*.

Li and Liang (2021) propose *prefix tuning*, a prompt-based method that trains a set of continuous prompts that are prepended to the input. To increase the expressiveness of the method, a set of prefix tokens is not only learned for the input layer, but for every layer. This was later found to be beneficial for natural-language understanding (NLU) as well (Liu et al., 2021). Based on empirical results, the authors decide to reparameterize the prefix tokens using a multi-layer perceptron in order to stabilize training and improve performance. They find that prefix tuning outperforms other lightweight fine-tuning methods like adapters (Houlsby et al., 2019) in few-shot settings and provides competitive performance to regular fine-tuning in full data settings.

[1]https://github.com/ValeKnappich/WebNLG-AP-RANLP

Split	Sample Counts	Active	Passive	Mixed
WebNLG				
Train	18,102	8,849	5,758	3,495
Dev	2,268	1,127	719	422
Test	4,928	2,546	1,485	897
WebNLG-AP				
Train	11,516	5,758	5,758	
Dev	1,438	719	719	
Test	2,970	1,485	1,485	

Table 1: The sample counts of the WebNLG and our newly created WebNLG-AP dataset for train, dev, and test split and their classification into active, passive, and mixed voice.

Clive et al. (2021) extend the prefix tuning method by adding input-dependent control tokens. For each of the domain categories, a set of control tokens is created and dynamically chosen based on the category. Contrary to our work, their main goal is to improve task performance and the control tokens are trained with a regular language modeling loss.

3 Modeling and Dataset Preparation

3.1 Task Description

We use the WebNLG dataset, which provides triples extracted from a knowledge base, e.g., {*Jones_County,_Texas : isPartOf : Abilene,_Texas*}. The task in this dataset is to generate a natural language sentence from a set of input triples. In the example above, the corresponding target sentence (also referred to as *lexicalization*) is "Abilene, Texas is part of Jones County, Texas." Counts for the different splits as well as the initial active/passive distribution are provided in Table 1. These triples are categorized into seven distinct topics. Five of them occur within the train and dev sets, namely "Airport, Astronaut, Building, Food, WrittenWork". The last two topics "Artist" and "Politician" only occur within the test set.

3.2 Active-Passive Dataset

To learn the control over active or passive voice, we construct a dataset, WebNLG-AP, based on WebNLG including voice annotations. We use a heuristic to identify active or passive voice in the samples of the original dataset. To annotate the complete WebNLG dataset, we use the dependency parser provided by spaCy (Honnibal et al., 2020) configured with the "en_core_web_trf" language model. We assume that a sentence is written in passive voice if one of the following dependency tags occurs within this sentence: { NSUBJPASS, AGENT, AUXPASS }[2], where NSUBJPASS refers to a nominal subject in a passive clause, AUXPASS denotes an auxiliary verb in passive and AGENT refers to the cause or initiator of an event. For example, in "The kid was stung by a bee," *kid* is the (passive) nominal subject (NSUBJPASS), *was* the passive auxiliary verb (AUXPASS) and *bee* the agent (AGENT). This implies that passive voice has precedence over active voice, i.e., if a sentence contains multiple verbs and one of them is tagged as passive, the entire sentence is treated as passive voice. Furthermore, if a sample consists of multiple sentences, we only conclude that a sample is in active or passive voice if all sentences that are part of the same lexicalization are classified into the same voice in our WebNLG-AP dataset. Mixed samples are not treated as active or passive and are thus filtered out. Moreover, we require that the dataset includes the same number of active and passive examples and thus truncate the set of samples for the predominant voice. The distribution across all splits in WebNLG-AP is provided in Table 1.

This active/passive detection pipeline is based on a heuristic and potentially creates noise in the dataset. Since this heuristic is used to create our dataset as well as to evaluate the results in Section 4, we verify that it works robustly. To that end, we randomly sample 100 sentences that have been tagged as either active, passive, or mixed and manually inspect the results. Out of these 100 random samples, all 25 mixed samples were classified correctly and only two out of 41 active samples were misclassified; one of these two because of a typographical error in the WebNLG dataset. Edge cases arise in the 34 passive samples. As already mentioned above, a sentence with multiple verbs is considered to be in passive voice if at least one passive voice signal occurs in it. Under this assumption, there are no misclassifications. Moreover, 12 out of 34 passive voice samples do not fall under this case and have been correctly tagged as well. This leads to a total tagging accuracy of 98%. Based on these observations, we conclude that the heuristic creates very little noise while allowing us to automate both dataset creation and model evaluation.

There are also verb phrases for which there is no analogue in the opposite voice. For instance, there is no passive voice for statements about someone dying, since "is died" is not a valid grammatical form. Furthermore, some passive voice samples are instances of the so-called *stative passive*. This term refers to verbs that are formulated in passive voice and that describe a potentially static condition, e.g., *Stuttgart is located in Germany* is a fact that is formulated in stative passive and does not change over time. We treat these cases as instances of passive voice.

We additionally introduce WebNLG-AP-Pairs, which, unlike WebNLG-AP, contains only triples for which WebNLG contains both active and passive lexicalizations. This is required for the contrastive learning approach described in Section 3.3.3. There are 1,858 samples in the train split, 225 samples in the dev split, and 459 samples in the test split.

3.3 Computational Modeling

We use the OpenPrompt framework (Ding et al., 2021) for our modeling tasks, which provides an implementation of prefix tuning. We extend this implementation to additionally use control prefix tokens, as proposed by Clive et al. (2021).

In all training setups, we first train the task-specific prefix tokens for a GPT-2 model (Radford et al., 2019) on the WebNLG dataset and verify that the results are consistent with state-of-the-art publications. In a second fine-tuning stage, we add a set of *control prefix tokens* for every control label, i.e., one set of active tokens $\{c_{a_1}, c_{a_2}\}$ and one set of passive tokens $\{c_{p_1}, c_{p_2}\}$ that are abstract numerical vectors and therefore not human-interpretable. Depending on the desired voice of the output sentence, either the active or the passive tokens are added after the prefix tokens. For a sentence that is supposed to be in active voice, the input looks as follows:

$$input = [\underbrace{p_1, p_2, p_3, p_4, p_5}_{\text{Prefix Tokens}}, \overbrace{c_{a_1}, c_{a_2}}^{\text{AP Control Tokens}}, \mathbf{X}; \mathbf{Y}]$$

where **X** is the sequence of input triples formatted as strings and **Y** is the ground truth sentence (as for example presented in Section 3.1). Since the prefix tokens are vectors and **X** and **Y** are lists of tokens, the actual concatenation happens after computing

[2]Explanation can be found here: https://github.com/explosion/spaCy/blob/master/spacy/glossary.py

the key and value hidden states of the attention block for **X** and **Y**. This representation of the input is simplified in the way that trainable parameters are not only injected at the embedding layer but at every layer, as proposed by Li and Liang (2021). Following preliminary empirical results, we keep the task-specific prefix tokens frozen during the second fine-tuning stage. The LM weights remain frozen during the entire training.

To train the control prefix tokens, we propose three different training objectives: implicit training, classifier guidance, and contrastive learning.

3.3.1 Baseline: Implicit Training

In the baseline training procedure, we do not modify the training objective, i.e., we use cross entropy as the loss function:

$$l_{CE}(y, \hat{y}) = -\sum_i y_i \cdot \log(\hat{y}_i)$$

where y is the set of ground truth tokens and $\hat{y}$ is the set of logits. The ground truth labels are the indices of tokens in the vocabulary that are expected to be generated by the model.

The control prefix tokens are selected for each sample individually, depending on whether this sample is marked as active or passive. This approach is comparable to jointly training the model backbone with both voices and separately training two language modeling heads for the respective voices. Esentially, parts of the parameters are shared between voices to learn the task (model backbone or task-specific prefix tokens), while others are specific to the voice (separate language modeling heads or control prefix tokens). Therefore, we want the model to learn that the active control tokens are only trained on active samples and vice versa.

We find that this is not sufficient to accurately control the voice of the output sentence. Intuitively, the representations of semantically equivalent active and passive sentences are very similar. Therefore, the signal from this implicit training objective is too weak to properly guide the model. Details on the experiment results will be discussed in Section 4.2. Motivated by this finding, we propose two methods to provide a stronger, more explicit signal between the active and passive sentences.

3.3.2 Classifier Guidance

To provide a stronger signal about the voice, we first propose to use a frozen classifier on top of our model which is used to backpropagate whether the model generated the correct voice. This approach is comparable to Prabhumoye et al. (2018), who use a similar setup for style transfer. Unlike Dathathri et al. (2019), we use the classifier loss to train the tokens, rather than directly optimizing the hidden representations.

Features	Accuracy
last-token	87%
mean-3	99.18%
concat-3	99.86%
mean-5	99.86%
concat-5	100%

Table 2: Experimental results for different aggregation strategies of token embeddings for the classifier guidance approach. The *concat-5* strategy performs best.

The first step is to train the classifier. The main challenge is that we cannot train a classifier on the output text directly because beam search is not differentiable and would hence break the backpropagation. Therefore, we train it on the hidden representations of the GPT-2 model including the task-specific prefix tokens. Since GPT-2 is an autoregressive model, the hidden representation of the last token is dependent on all previous tokens and can thus be used as a sentence representation. However, we find that an aggregation of the last n token embeddings significantly improves performance. We experiment with $n \in \{1, 3, 5\}$. On top of that, we test mean and concatenation as aggregation methods and find that using the concatenation of the last 5 tokens works best. Table 2 shows how accurately the different approaches can classify active and passive voice given the respective hidden states of the model.

The classifier is an MLP with 2 linear layers, GELU activation function (Hendrycks and Gimpel, 2016), and sigmoid output. We proceed with the best classifier, attach it to GPT-2 as a second classification head and backpropagate an additional loss term:

$$L(y, \hat{y}, l, \hat{l}) = \frac{1}{w+1}(\overbrace{-\sum_i (y_i \log(\hat{y}_i))}^{\text{LM CE}} + w \cdot \underbrace{(l \cdot \log(\hat{l}) + (1-l) \cdot \log(1-\hat{l}))}_{\text{Classifier BCE}})$$

where l is the flag indicating whether the sentence is active or passive, $\hat{l}$ is the classifier output, and w

is a hyperparameter to balance the tradeoff between language modeling and classification. The total loss is normalized by $\frac{1}{w+1}$ such that high values for w don't change the magnitude of the gradients too much.

3.3.3 Contrastive Learning

We furthermore implement *Contrastive Learning* as a means to provide a direct gradient signal between active and passive voice. To that end, we use *Contrastive Cross Entropy (CCE)* as loss function:

$$CCE(y^+, y^-, \hat{y}) = \overbrace{\sum_{t \in y^+} - \log(\hat{y_t})}^{\text{Cross Entropy}} + \underbrace{\sum_{\substack{t' \in y^- \\ t' \notin y^+}} -w_c \cdot \log(1 - \hat{y_{t'}})}_{\text{Contrastive Term}}$$

where y^+ denotes the target sentence corresponding to the currently prompted voice and y^- to the respective contrastive sample. The contrastive term iterates over all tokens only occurring in the contrastive counterpart but not in the actual target sentence. The aim is to reduce the probability of these exclusive counterpart tokens for the currently requested voice by taking the respective logit values into account. For instance, consider an example where y^+ = [Apollo, 8, is, operated, by, NASA] and y^- = [The, Apollo, 8, operator, is, NASA]. In this case, the loss function would reduce the likelihood of the tokens "The" and "operator".

The weight w_c is a hyperparameter that influences the importance of the contrastive term. In our experiments, $w_c = 3$ has yielded the best results. Since this approach requires both alternatives in terms of active and passive voice, we use our WebNLG-AP-Pairs dataset that contains at least one active and one passive sample for each input triple.

3.4 Evaluation

To evaluate the performance of our models on the WebNLG task, we use the evaluation scripts provided by Nan et al. (2021) in their Github repository.[3] We use them to calculate BLEU scores (Papineni et al., 2002) on the three categories "seen, unseen," and "all", which refer to the different categories in the dataset and indicate whether the topic occurred during training or not (hence, "seen" or "unseen" by the model during training). We also evaluate with respect to the BLEURT score (Sellam et al., 2020) since we believe that NLG tasks are much more complex than scores such as BLEU are able to reflect.

We evaluate the voice control ability using the accuracy of the AP generation process:

$$acc(\mathbf{L}, \hat{\mathbf{L}}) = \frac{\sum_i \mathbb{1}_{l_i, \hat{l}_i}}{|\mathbf{L}|}, l_i \in \hat{\mathbf{L}}$$

where $\mathbf{L}$ denotes the set of ground truth AP labels, $\hat{\mathbf{L}}$ the AP labels of generated sentences (again determined by using our heuristics as described in Section 3.2) and $\mathbb{1}_{l_i, \hat{l}_i}$ is an indicator function evaluating to 1 if both labels are equal to each other for sample i.

Hyperparameter	Value
Training	
`epochs`	5
`lr`	5e−5
`eps` (AdamW)	1e−8
`n_prefix_tokens`	5
`n_control_tokens`	2×2
Decoding	
`num_beams`	5
`top_p`	0.9
`top_k`	0
`temperature`	1

Table 3: The hyperparameters used for training the GPT-2 model.

4 Experiments

4.1 Setup

As described in Section 3.3, we train our models in two stages. We first train 5 task-specific prefix tokens on the WebNLG dataset and afterward train 2×2 control tokens using one of the approaches introduced above. In each stage, the model is trained for 5 epochs with the hyperparameters listed in Table 3. Training a model in this setup takes approximately two hours on an Nvidia V100 GPU.

4.2 Results

Table 4 shows the results of our four models. The first row shows the scores of the model, which only uses the five WebNLG task-specific prefix tokens on top of the GPT-2 LM. It has therefore never

[3] https://github.com/Yale-LILY/dart

Configuration	WebNLG						WebNLG-AP	
	BLEU			BLEURT			BLEU	AP-Acc
	S	U	A	S	U	A		
WebNLG	**61.13**	43.29	**54.25**	**0.40**	0.25	**0.33**	42.12	75.69
WebNLG $\rightarrow$ implicit	59.22	45.79	53.16	0.38	**0.26**	0.32	41.78	76.36
WebNLG $\rightarrow$ classifier	59.16	**46.20**	53.32	0.39	**0.26**	0.32	**42.13**	78.08
WebNLG $\rightarrow$ contrastive	52.22	34.76	44.67	0.31	0.19	0.25	35.77	**95.22**

Table 4: Experimental results in terms of BLEU, BLEURT, and AP accuracy. S, U, and A correspond to the "seen, unseen," and "all" categories, respectively.

been specialized in the AP control task. The second model uses the two additional control tokens implicitly learned by exchanging them based on the sample that is currently presented. The third model uses classifier guidance, and the last one has been trained using the contrastive dataset and loss function.

The baseline model without AP control tokens achieves the best results on the original WebNLG task. The BLEU score is 54.25 and therefore almost consistent with the results reported by Li and Liang (2021) (55.1). When it comes to active-passive generation, the baseline model already yields an accuracy of 75.69%. That is, the model already scores above random without target voice information. We conclude that there are biases in the input that hint at the target voice in some cases. Some samples only sound natural in one of the voices. For instance, in the sentence "Juan Peron belongs to the Labour Party in Argentina.", *belongs* is an intransitive verb and hence does not have a passive counterpart.

The second row in the table shows the model with additional control tokens that have been trained implicitly. It almost fully preserves the performance on the original WebNLG task, with both scores decreasing by approximately 1% in absolute terms. The AP accuracy has increased by approximately 0.8% which means that the two implicitly trained AP control tokens provide the model with some guidance in terms of active and passive generation. However, the absolute gain is rather small compared to the additional training time. As a result, we draw the conclusion that the approach of just implicitly learning these AP control tokens is not sufficient to achieve meaningful results.

Consequently, the last two rows in the table show the results of our approaches that provide an explicit signal regarding the voice. The first is the one trained with classifier guidance. As with the implicitly trained one, original task performance is almost preserved. Moreover, there is an absolute gain in AP accuracy of around 2.5%, which is around three times as high as the gain of the approach before. We experiment with the hyperparameter w that controls the tradeoff between the language modeling loss and the classifier loss and report the results in Table 5.

	BLEU	BLEURT	AP-Acc
$w = 1$	52.93	**0.32**	77.27
$w = 5$	52.95	**0.32**	76.97
$w = 10$	53.12	**0.32**	76.70
$w = 999$	**53.32**	**0.32**	**78.08**

Table 5: Results for experiments on the tradeoff between language modeling and classifier loss. Higher values for w lead to a higher weight on the classifier loss.

The model trained with contrastive learning shows by far the highest increase in AP performance with an absolute gain of almost 20% compared to the baseline. On the other hand, both BLEU and BLEURT scores significantly decrease by around 10% and 8%, respectively. This is a non-negligible performance drop since preserving performance on the WebNLG task is an important aspect when it comes to evaluating the overall quality of the model. Having such a significant decrease indicates that this model either generates unnatural-sounding sentences or it does not fully reconstruct all information provided by the input triples. We provide further insights in the qualitative analysis presented in the next section.

5 Discussion

This section provides detailed insights into the results of our models by analyzing the generated sentences. This helps to understand why the contrastive learning approach decreases original performance scores far more significantly than the other approaches. Our analysis provides guidance for possible improvements for future research.

5.1 Contrastive Learning

As already discussed in Section 4, the model trained using a contrastive loss function loses around 10% in terms of BLEU and 8% in terms of BLEURT on the WebNLG task. Especially the much lower BLEURT score is an indicator of the reduced semantic quality of the generated sentences. Table 6 lists four different comparisons between generated sentence and the corresponding target sentence.

The first example is an instance for which the model generated the <*pad*> token instead of a real token. It could reflect a problem that is introduced by the contrastive loss function as it strictly decreases the likelihood of some tokens being generated. As a result, the model might be confused here as there is no real token likely to be generated. The <*pad*> token is generated 86 times across 12 samples during evaluation on the full WebNLG dataset. Compared to an overall count of 1,862 test samples, we can conclude that this is indeed a smaller issue. Another issue that can be seen in this sample is that there are two distinct parts in the generated sentence that are not semantically connected at all. This is definitely reflected by both BLEU and BLEURT scores since there is not just a large difference to the target sentence, but there is also no real semantic meaning at all.

The second sample shows an instance where the same word is being generated over and over again until the maximum sequence length is reached (e.g., in this case, it is *California*). This of course also lowers the scores on the WebNLG task since there cannot be any matching n-grams for a repeating sequence of a specific word.

The third sample is an example of a generated sentence that sounds unusual and lacks some additional words. This is also an issue that occurs multiple times. The model trained with contrastive cross-entropy sometimes tends to generate unnatural-sounding sentences. A possible explanation for this behavior might be that the model focuses more strictly on generating the correct voice rather than on generating the most naturally sounding sentence. However, this is also a rare sample in which the voice does not match.

The last comparison in Table 6 shows that the contrastive model also has problems with leaving out specific information, which of course is also reflected by the BLEURT score in the end. On the one hand, the first part of the target sentence is indeed generated by the model in a semantically equivalent way. On the other hand, the second part of the target sentence is completely left out by the contrastive model. This, of course, implies a performance drop as the model tends to leave out relevant information that must be considered in evaluating the overall performance of this approach.

However, as the AP accuracy score already indicates, there are many samples on which the contrastive model performs really well. One example is the generated sentence *Antwerp International Airport is located in Antwerp, Belgium, where the German language is spoken.* The target sentence is marked as passive in the WebNLG-AP dataset and it gets clear that the model strictly followed the passive prompt when it generated this sentence. There are two semantic parts in it: One which states where the airport is located and one which describes the language spoken there. Both parts are formulated in the passive voice as requested. This makes clear that the contrastive model indeed has a strong sense of what is active and passive voice and is furthermore able to apply it during generation. Another positive example is the generated sentence *A.C. Chievo Verona is managed by Rolando Maran.* It has been correctly generated using the passive prompt. In contrast, the model with classifier guidance produced the active sentence *A.C. Chievo Verona's manager is Rolando Maran*, although it has been prompted with the passive flag. These are two of many examples in which the contrastive model strictly followed the prompt whereas the other models did not. Furthermore, these are well-formulated instances without any grammatical or other semantic issues. Hence, these are promising results to build upon.

To sum up the findings of the contrastive learning approach, there are a few issues that almost fully explain the decreased performance on the WebNLG task. First of all, the model sometimes seems to have problems with semantically unconnected parts within a generated sentence, i.e., it lacks a proper structure. Secondly, there are samples in which information is clearly missing or put into the wrong context. This is not a syntactic, but rather semantic

Ground Truth Lexicalization	Generated Lexicalization
"Juan Peron belongs to the Labour Party in Argentina."	*"Juan Perón is a member <pad> Juan Perón is the Labour Party."*
"Antioch is part of Contra Costa County in California [...]"	*"Antioch, California is part of Contra Costa County, California, California, California, California, [...]"*
"The novel "Castle" is written in English."	*"Castle is in the English language."*
"Aleksandr Chumakov was born in Moscow, Russia and he died in Russia. The leader of Moscow is Sergey Sobyanin."	*"Aleksandr Chumakov, born in Moscow, died in Russia."*

Table 6: Comparison between sentences generated using the model trained with contrastive loss and ground truth sentences. Four different error cases are shown.

issue since the model should also be able to generate correct facts. Finally, one issue is tokens being generated multiple times in a row. However, this does not happen very often. Still, this approach yields by far the best AP accuracy in our experiments. Section 6 discusses possible improvements for future research work.

5.2 Classifier Guidance

Classifier Guidance resulted in a small but significant improvement of the AP accuracy compared to implicit training. However, the results are in parts unintuitive to us. A larger increase in AP accuracy and a larger decrease in task performance would have been expected from this explicit signal about the voice. Instead, we observe a small improvement in AP accuracy and even slightly better task performance compared to implicit training (see Table 4). Furthermore, the results from experimenting with the loss weights in Table 5 elicit a very counterintuitive trend: increasing the weight of the classifier loss improves task performance and has no apparent correlation with the AP accuracy. Further investigations are necessary to better understand these results and make better use of this technique.

6 Conclusion and Outlook

We studied controllable active-passive generation using continuous prefix prompts on top of a generative language model. Our goal was to explicitly guide a generative model into generating sentences formulated in either active or passive voice. Three different approaches that we tested have shown different strengths and weaknesses. It becomes clear that there is a trade-off between the semantic quality of generated sentences and the strict enforcement of active or passive voice. The model which is trained using contrastive learning achieves the best results in terms of controllable AP generation. However, the quality of the generated sentences decreased, as reflected by BLEU and BLEURT scores, as well as a qualitative analysis of the generated sentences. On the contrary, the model trained using classifier guidance was able to maintain the task performance quite well but only improved voice control very slightly.

Future work should investigate how to maintain more of the task performance while achieving a high AP accuracy. The most apparent technique towards that goal would be to combine the contrastive learning and classifier guidance objective functions, given that their results were complementary: one is good at maintaining task performance while the other is good at controlling the voice. It could also be beneficial to include additional loss functions in the experiments, like less strict contrastive loss functions or directly optimizing the BLEURT score (Sellam et al., 2020; Shu et al., 2021). Furthermore, a promising direction for future research is instance-dependent prompt tuning (Tang et al., 2022; Jin et al., 2022), where the prefix tokens depend on the input rather than being static per task or control class.

In the broader context of applying prompt tuning methods to controllable text generation, future research should investigate whether our insights from studying active-passive voice control generalize to other control tasks such as sentiment or formality control. In particular, it would be interesting to see if control prefix tokens are composable (flexibly controlling multiple aspects at the same time) and transferable between domains and datasets (Su et al., 2021; Gu et al., 2021; Vu et al., 2021).

Limitations and Broader Impact

This work results from a student research project conducted in the summer of 2022 as part of graduate studies. A few months after project completion, new state-of-the-art models like ChatGPT and GPT-4 have been made publicly available. As a result, our work does not consider models that have been released past the summer of 2022. Therefore, this paper does not investigate the AP performance of these new models. This is subject to future research. We believe that our work still provides valuable contributions and insights into prefix and prompt tuning when relying on the more traditional fine-tuning paradigm, which itself is still a very commonly used technique for low-resource and domain-specific settings.

Acknowledgements

We would like to thank Esra Dönmez and Thang Vu from the IMS at the University of Stuttgart for their great supervision and always helpful input during this research project.

References

Tom Brown, Benjamin Mann, Nick Ryder, Melanie Subbiah, Jared D Kaplan, Prafulla Dhariwal, Arvind Neelakantan, Pranav Shyam, Girish Sastry, Amanda Askell, et al. 2020. Language models are few-shot learners. *Advances in neural information processing systems*, 33:1877–1901.

Jordan Clive, Kris Cao, and Marek Rei. 2021. Control prefixes for text generation. *arXiv preprint arXiv:2110.08329*.

Sumanth Dathathri, Andrea Madotto, Janice Lan, Jane Hung, Eric Frank, Piero Molino, Jason Yosinski, and Rosanne Liu. 2019. Plug and play language models: A simple approach to controlled text generation. *arXiv preprint arXiv:1912.02164*.

Ning Ding, Shengding Hu, Weilin Zhao, Yulin Chen, Zhiyuan Liu, Hai-Tao Zheng, and Maosong Sun. 2021. Openprompt: An open-source framework for prompt-learning. *arXiv preprint arXiv:2111.01998*.

Tianyu Gao, Adam Fisch, and Danqi Chen. 2020. Making pre-trained language models better few-shot learners. *arXiv preprint arXiv:2012.15723*.

Claire Gardent, Anastasia Shimorina, Shashi Narayan, and Laura Perez-Beltrachini. 2017. Creating training corpora for NLG micro-planners. In *Proceedings of the 55th Annual Meeting of the Association for Computational Linguistics, ACL 2017, Vancouver, Canada, July 30 - August 4, Volume 1: Long Papers*, pages 179–188. Association for Computational Linguistics.

Yuxian Gu, Xu Han, Zhiyuan Liu, and Minlie Huang. 2021. Ppt: Pre-trained prompt tuning for few-shot learning. *arXiv preprint arXiv:2109.04332*.

Dan Hendrycks and Kevin Gimpel. 2016. Gaussian error linear units (gelus). *arXiv preprint arXiv:1606.08415*.

Matthew Honnibal, Ines Montani, Sofie Van Ladeghem, and Adrian Boyd. 2020. spacy: Industrial-strength natural language processing in python.

Neil Houlsby, Andrei Giurgiu, Stanislaw Jastrzebski, Bruna Morrone, Quentin De Laroussilhe, Andrea Gesmundo, Mona Attariyan, and Sylvain Gelly. 2019. Parameter-efficient transfer learning for nlp. In *International Conference on Machine Learning*, pages 2790–2799. PMLR.

Feihu Jin, Jinliang Lu, Jiajun Zhang, and Chengqing Zong. 2022. Instance-aware prompt learning for language understanding and generation. *arXiv preprint arXiv:2201.07126*.

Yuanmin Leng, François Portet, Cyril Labbé, and Raheel Qader. 2020. Controllable neural natural language generation: comparison of state-of-the-art control strategies. In *Proceedings of the 3rd International Workshop on Natural Language Generation from the Semantic Web (WebNLG+)*, pages 34–39, Dublin, Ireland (Virtual). Association for Computational Linguistics.

Brian Lester, Rami Al-Rfou, and Noah Constant. 2021. The power of scale for parameter-efficient prompt tuning. *arXiv preprint arXiv:2104.08691*.

Xiang Lisa Li and Percy Liang. 2021. Prefix-tuning: Optimizing continuous prompts for generation. In *Proceedings of the 59th Annual Meeting of the Association for Computational Linguistics and the 11th International Joint Conference on Natural Language Processing (Volume 1: Long Papers)*, pages 4582–4597, Online. Association for Computational Linguistics.

Xiao Liu, Kaixuan Ji, Yicheng Fu, Zhengxiao Du, Zhilin Yang, and Jie Tang. 2021. P-tuning v2: Prompt tuning can be comparable to fine-tuning universally across scales and tasks. *arXiv preprint arXiv:2110.07602*.

Linyong Nan, Dragomir Radev, Rui Zhang, Amrit Rau, Abhinand Sivaprasad, Chiachun Hsieh, Xiangru Tang, Aadit Vyas, Neha Verma, Pranav Krishna, Yangxiaokang Liu, Nadia Irwanto, Jessica Pan, Faiaz Rahman, Ahmad Zaidi, Murori Mutuma, Yasin Tarabar, Ankit Gupta, Tao Yu, Yi Chern Tan, Xi Victoria Lin, Caiming Xiong, Richard Socher, and Nazneen Fatema Rajani. 2021. Dart: Open-domain structured data record to text generation. *arXiv preprint arXiv:2007.02871*.

Kishore Papineni, Salim Roukos, Todd Ward, and Wei-Jing Zhu. 2002. Bleu: a method for automatic evaluation of machine translation. In *Proceedings of the*

40th annual meeting of the Association for Computational Linguistics, pages 311–318.

Shrimai Prabhumoye, Alan W Black, and Ruslan Salakhutdinov. 2020. Exploring controllable text generation techniques. *arXiv preprint arXiv:2005.01822*.

Shrimai Prabhumoye, Yulia Tsvetkov, Ruslan Salakhutdinov, and Alan W Black. 2018. Style transfer through back-translation. *arXiv preprint arXiv:1804.09000*.

Guanghui Qin and Jason Eisner. 2021. Learning how to ask: Querying lms with mixtures of soft prompts. *arXiv preprint arXiv:2104.06599*.

Alec Radford, Jeff Wu, Rewon Child, David Luan, Dario Amodei, and Ilya Sutskever. 2019. Language models are unsupervised multitask learners.

Thibault Sellam, Dipanjan Das, and Ankur P Parikh. 2020. Bleurt: Learning robust metrics for text generation. In *Proceedings of ACL*.

Taylor Shin, Yasaman Razeghi, Robert L Logan IV, Eric Wallace, and Sameer Singh. 2020. Autoprompt: Eliciting knowledge from language models with automatically generated prompts. *arXiv preprint arXiv:2010.15980*.

Raphael Shu, Kang Min Yoo, and Jung-Woo Ha. 2021. Reward optimization for neural machine translation with learned metrics. *arXiv preprint arXiv:2104.07541*.

Yusheng Su, Xiaozhi Wang, Yujia Qin, Chi-Min Chan, Yankai Lin, Zhiyuan Liu, Peng Li, Juanzi Li, Lei Hou, Maosong Sun, et al. 2021. On transferability of prompt tuning for natural language understanding. *arXiv preprint arXiv:2111.06719*.

Tianyi Tang, Junyi Li, and Wayne Xin Zhao. 2022. Context-tuning: Learning contextualized prompts for natural language generation. *arXiv preprint arXiv:2201.08670*.

Tu Vu, Brian Lester, Noah Constant, Rami Al-Rfou, and Daniel Cer. 2021. Spot: Better frozen model adaptation through soft prompt transfer. *arXiv preprint arXiv:2110.07904*.

Hanqing Zhang, Haolin Song, Shaoyu Li, Ming Zhou, and Dawei Song. 2022. A survey of controllable text generation using transformer-based pre-trained language models. *arXiv preprint arXiv:2201.05337*.

Age-Specific Linguistic Features of Depression via Social Media

Charlotte Rosario
The Nueva School
San Mateo, United States
charlottearosario@gmail.com

Abstract

Social media data has become a crucial resource for understanding and detecting mental health challenges. However, there is a significant gap in our understanding of age-specific linguistic markers associated with classifying depression. This study bridges the gap by analyzing 25,241 text samples from 15,156 Reddit users with self-reported depression across two age groups: adolescents (13-20 year olds) and adults (21+). Through a quantitative exploratory analysis using LIWC, topic modeling, and data visualization, distinct patterns and topical differences emerged in the language of depression for adolescents and adults, including social concerns, temporal focuses, emotions, and cognition. These findings enhance our understanding of how depression is expressed on social media, bearing implications for accurate classification and tailored interventions across different age groups.

1 Introduction

Depression, a prevalent mental health condition that impacts over 300 million individuals worldwide (World Health Organization, 2017), has historically been approached with a generalization that it impacts all individuals in the same way. However, in recent years, there has been a growing recognition of depression's impact on specific subgroups, including teens and young children (Ahrens, 2002). Recent research has found that depression manifests differently for individuals at different stages of life (Rice et al., 2019; Kaufman et al., 2001). This shift in perspective underscores the importance of exploring the causes and correlates of emotional distress specific to different age groups.

It is crucial to observe and understand the unique linguistic markers of depression in different age groups, as indicators of depression for adults may not hold true when applied to adolescent populations, and vice versa. This "one-size-fits-all" approach can lead to misdiagnosis, inappropriate interventions, and limited access to suitable support services, thus jeopardizing the well-being of individuals (Spector, 1991; Taylor and Brown, 1988). Given the absence of a comprehensive global surveillance system and the rapid evolution of global health trends, there is an imperative need to gather up-to-date insights on the impact of mental health disorders of different subpopulations (Ormel et al., 1994; Patel et al., 1999).

Recently, there has been a surge of interest in leveraging social media data to gain valuable psychological insights (Karim et al., 2020; Homan et al., 2014). Analyzing social media data has been proven to complement traditional mental health assessments, including the Patient Health Questionnaire-9 (Liu et al., 2022) and the Behavioral Risk Factor Surveillance System (BFRSS) survey (Eichstaedt et al., 2015; Culotta, 2014). Due to the growing popularity of social media platforms for receiving online peer support among those facing mental health challenges, social media data has demonstrated potential for reflecting greater sociological trends.

Most social media investigations of mental health have either overlooked age as a feature or focused solely on the platforms' predominant young adult populations (Low et al., 2020; Coppersmith et al., 2014). However, it is important to recognize that age-based expression of different subgroups may significantly differ; per the principles of postcolonial computing, analytical insight and intervention strategies cannot be simply transplanted from one subgroup to another without modification (Irani et al., 2010). Each age group has its unique context and characteristics that must be considered to ensure the relevance and effectiveness of intervention strategies.

This study quantitatively examines language use in individuals sharing their experiences with depres-

Proceedings of the Student Research Workshop associated with RANLP-2023, pages 33–43, Varna, Bulgaria, Sep 4–6, 2023.
https://doi.org/10.26615/issn.2603-2821.2023_004

sion on social media, specifically on Reddit. Two age groups—adolescents (below 21) and adults (above 21)—are analyzed to explore two primary questions: (1) How do these groups differ in expressing their depression on social media? and (2) How do they differ compared to neurotypical individuals of the same age group? The contributions of this paper are twofold: first, prior research on the existence of language markers that distinguish depression on social media is affirmed through comparative analyses with control users; second, linguistic insights into age-specific markers of depression are revealed using closed- and open-vocabulary approaches. The findings provide a nuanced understanding of how depression manifests on online social media platforms, laying the foundation for future hypothesis-driven research on mental health diagnosis and treatment strategies tailored to different age groups.

2 Related Works

2.1 Language for Psychological Assessment

Language has been extensively used in previous research to identify linguistic patterns associated with psychological traits, such as emotional stability and personality (Eichstaedt et al., 2015). The profound influence of language, particularly one's native language, on thoughts, actions, and social relationships is widely acknowledged (Maynard and Peräkylä, 2006). Studies, including the work of Boroditsky et al. (2003), have demonstrated the intricate relationship between language perception and its impact on social processes. Linguistic styles encompass various indicators of lexical density, temporal references, social support and connectivity, and environmental awareness. Previous research has emphasized the significance of these linguistic cues in comprehending mental health, both in everyday and social media contexts (Ramírez-Esparza et al., 2008).

2.2 Social Media and Mental Health

Numerous studies have turned to online social media data, particularly in terms of language and conversational patterns, as a valuable source for understanding and detecting global health trends. This line of inquiry encompasses various areas, such as utilizing social media to gain insights into diseases (Paul and Dredze, 2011), substance abuse (MacLean et al., 2015; Murnane and Counts, 2014), postpartum depression (Choudhury et al., 2014), eating disorders (Chancellor et al., 2016), and other mental health conditions (Coppersmith et al., 2014; Liu et al., 2022; Tsugawa et al., 2015).

Social media language has revealed several distinctive ways individuals with depression express themselves. For instance, Coppersmith et al. (2014) discovered that depressed users tend to exhibit higher levels of self-focus, anxiety, and anger in their online writings. Social media users with depression often exhibit various symptoms and behaviors, including anhedonia, social difficulties, health and sleep problems, inactivity, thoughts of death, perceived hopelessness, tentativeness, overall negativity, sadness, interpersonal hostility, and disinterest in self-care and leisure (Schwartz et al., 2014; Preoţiuc-Pietro et al., 2015; Resnik et al., 2015; Chancellor et al., 2016; Choudhury et al., 2013). They also use first-person singular pronouns and swear more frequently than neurotypical users (Chung and Pennebaker, 2007).

These investigations have revealed compelling evidence that individuals with depression display unique linguistic patterns in their online communication that distinguish them from the broader population. However, it is important to recognize that the majority of existing research has generalized these findings across various social groups. This prompts the question of whether linguistic markers of depression remain consistent when examined within specific demographic cohorts.

2.3 Demographic Language Markers of Depression

Previous research has sought to investigate nuances in the language markers of depression specific to different demographic subgroups. Choudhury et al. (2016) identified differences in experiences of depression between users of different genders and countries of origin on Twitter. Loveys et al. (2018) explored cultural differences in online language data regarding depression of users from different racial and ethnic backgrounds. Ramírez-Esparza et al. (2008) found that Spanish-speaking depressed individuals were more likely to mention relational concerns than English-speaking individuals. Mittal et al. (2023) discovered differential mental health language markers around race, politics, violence, employment, and affordability for immigrant populations. While these studies highlight the variation in linguistic features of depression across different gender, cultural, racial, and political subgroups,

<table>
<tr><th>Regex Patterns</th></tr>
<tr><td>(i) I (was | am) born in <four digit year></td></tr>
<tr><td>(ii) I (was | am) born in <two digit year></td></tr>
<tr><td>(iii) I am <age>(years old | yrs old | yo)</td></tr>
<tr><td>(iiii) I am a <age>(year old | yo)</td></tr>
<tr><td>(v) I am <age>(<punctuation>| <conjunction>)</td></tr>
</table>

Table 1: Regular expression patterns for identifying age disclosures in Reddit posts.

there is a gap in research regarding the language features of depression that vary among different age groups.

The present study presents a data-driven exploratory analysis of the social media language of diverse age profiles who express their symptoms of depression online.

3 Data

Reddit, an online discussion-based social media platform, was selected as the data source for this study. The platform encourages self-disclosure by enforcing anonymity of users, which can contribute to obtaining less biased results (Gaur et al., 2018). An initial collection of 512,876 Reddit posts was collected from the r/depression, r/suicidewatch, and r/mentalhealth subreddits. This included the 252,459 posts extracted from the r/depression, r/mentalhealth, and r/SuicideWatch subreddits of the Reddit Mental Health Dataset proposed by Low et al. (2020) and 7,000 r/depression Reddit posts from the dataset of Pirina and Çagri Çöltekin (2018). The rest of the posts were obtained directly from Reddit using the PRAW API.

3.1 Annotating for age

Demographic information of users on Reddit is unavailable due to the platform's policy of anonymity, which introduces the need for inferring the age of users. Prior research in this field has sought to identify the best automated method of annotating age in social media data, with several studies using machine learning or lexicon-based approaches (Yatam and Reddy, 2014; Chen et al., 2015). These methods, however, were not used in the present study to avoid adding additional uncertainty or bias into the dataset. Since Reddit users often explicitly disclose their age in their post, stating "I'm 15 years old" or their age in brackets (e.g., "I [17f] just broke up with bf [18m]"), age was inferred based on natural language patterns. Using a similar approach as Tigunova et al. (2020), user's age was extracted using five variations of regular expressions patterns, as listed in Table 1, with pattern (v) specifically designed to avoid false positives (e.g., "I am 60 miles away" or "I feel like I am 60"). All users younger than 13 were excluded, as this violates Reddit's terms of service.

3.2 Validation of age inference

Following a similar approach as Chew et al. (2021), the age inference methods were validated based on annotations obtained from two independent raters on a sample of 100 users. Agreement was found between the raters' annotations and the one given by our method with a total accuracy of 97%.

3.3 Filtering for genuine mental health disclosure

Posts were filtered for explicit key phrases indicating depression based on the method of Choudhury et al. (2016), which was sourced from consultation with a psychiatrist. This was necessary given that the Reddit corpus is susceptible to significant noise from sarcastic, humorous, or flippant usage (e.g., "i have to do the laundry, kill me now" is not indicative of genuine depression). Additionally, regular expression patterns were used to ensure content and age disclosures were representative of actual individuals with depression (e.g., avoiding "my best friend is depressed right now").

After filtering for genuine age-disclosure and mental health expression, a total of 25,241 posts with 15,156 unique Reddit users were extracted. This dataset will be referred to in the present study as MID (i.e. mental illness disclosure).

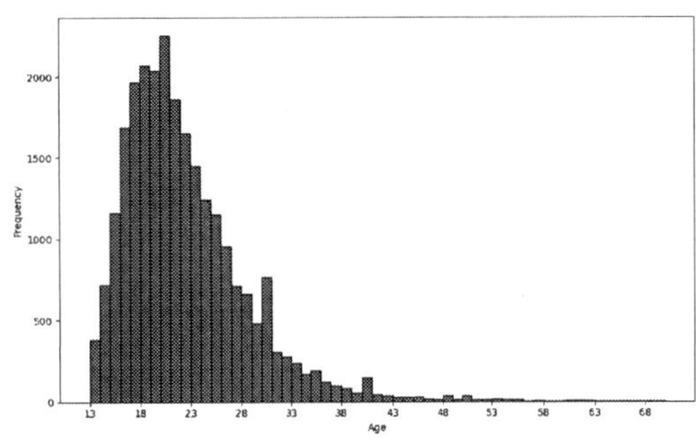

Figure 1: Distribution of ages of Reddit users. (Ages 70+ not shown due to negligible frequencies.)

3.4 Categorizing into age groups

Users were then categorized into age groups. Due to binary age groups (under/over 20 years old) resulting in more distinct results in previous research (Cesare et al., 2017) and the unique distribution of users' ages in the MID dataset, as seen in Figure 1, users were ultimately split into two groups, adolescent (13-20) and adult (21+).

3.5 Gathering a control dataset

To enable robust statistical comparisons between depressed and neurotypical users of different ages, we also obtained a control data sample from non-mental health-related subreddits. This data was taken from the Reddit Mental Health Dataset (Low et al., 2020) and included 11 non-mental health subreddits, resulting in a total of 302,172 posts initially. To ensure data integrity, posts with age-disclosure that were not present in the MID dataset and did not match any key phrases listed in Table 1 were extracted. In total, the control dataset (referred to as CTL) yielded 30,489 posts from 17,092 unique authors, with 10,327 adolescent and 20,162 adult users.

4 Methods

Reddit posts were characterized using two sets of language features: (a) dictionary-based psycholinguistic features, and (b) open-vocabulary topics.

4.1 Closed vocabulary: LIWC Analysis

An established language dictionary known as Linguistic Inquiry and Word Count (LIWC) (Boyd et al., 2022) was employed as a closed-vocabulary approach to analyze the language patterns. This top-down approach has been extensively used in language research to detect emotions and personality (Eichstaedt et al., 2020). Three categories of linguistic measures derived from the LIWC2022 software were analyzed: (1) affective attributes, (2) cognitive attributes, and (3) linguistic style attributes. As seen in Table 2, the **affective measures** include negativity, anger, anxiety, sadness, and swearing; the two **cognitive measures** include Cognition (insight, tentativeness, and differentiation) and Perception (spacial, visual, auditory, time, past-focused, present-focused, and future-oriented); and the three **linguistic measures** include Lexical Density (articles, prepositions, verbs, auxiliary verbs, nouns, and adverbs), Social/Personal Concerns (words belonging to family, friends, death, work, money, substances, health, wellness, and sexual), and Interpersonal Focus (personal or impersonal pronouns). The relative frequency of each LIWC measure was calculated by taking the mean of each measure within each of the two age groups. Since multiple features are examined concurrently (31 LIWC categories), coefficients are deemed statistically significant if their values fall below a Benjamini-Hochberg-corrected two-tailed p-value of 0.05.

	μ (adolescent)	*μ (adult)*	*effect size*	*p*
Affective attributes				
Negativity	2.113	2.005	0.073	***
Anger	0.283	0.248	0.069	***
Anxiety	0.460	0.431	0.042	**
Sadness	0.691	0.646	0.053	***
Swearing	0.476	0.382	0.118	***
Cognitive attributes				
Cognition				
Insight	3.502	3.335	0.095	***
Tentative	3.129	2.957	0.093	***
Differentiation	4.226	4.134	0.054	***
Perception				***
Visual	0.531	0.573	-0.053	***
Auditory	0.180	0.148	0.078	***
Time	5.572	5.765	-0.087	***
Focus Past	5.423	4.802	-0.106	***
Focus Present	7.439	7.144	0.115	***
Focus Future	1.576	1.496	0.059	***
Linguistic style attributes				
Lexical density				
Articles	4.022	4.369	-0.219	***
Prepositions	12.600	12.920	-0.127	***
Auxiliary Verbs	11.705	11.466	0.090	***
Adverbs	7.838	7.488	0.148	***
Negations	3.168	3.054	0.073	***
Verbs	21.893	21.415	0.142	***
Social/Personal Concerns				
Family	0.708	0.659	0.050	***
Friend	0.541	0.478	0.083	***
Work	1.425	1.594	-0.113	***
Money	0.225	0.402	-0.297	***
Health	1.803	1.870	-0.038	**
Wellness	0.037	0.062	-0.117	***
Substances	0.072	0.085	-0.042	***
Sexual	0.117	0.131	-0.032	*
Death	0.632	0.535	0.117	***
Interpersonal Focus				
Personal Pronouns	15.630	14.791	0.271	***
Impersonal Pronouns	5.534	5.292	0.120	***

Table 2: Differences between posts from youth and adult MID users based on linguistic measures. All effect sizes (measured as Cohen's D) between are significant at $p < .05$, two-tailed t-test, Benjamini-Hochberg corrected.

4.2 Open vocabulary: LDA Topic Modeling

The second method employed an open-vocabulary approach utilizing Latent Dirichlet Allocation topic modeling (LDA) (Blei et al., 2003) to generate data-driven linguistic features known as topics. LDA identifies common topics present in text documents by capturing sets of words (e.g., 'september', 'october', 'november') that frequently co-occur, allowing for manual inspection and assessment of recurring themes. Although topic modeling may not capture the same level of detailed insights as human observation due to its unsupervised nature, it offers the potential to discover patterns in users' concerns that may otherwise go unnoticed (Low et al., 2020).

Data was pre-processed by removing high-frequency words (occurring in more than 75% of the documents), words that occur fewer than five times, URLs, @mentions, #hashtags, emoticons, emojis, numbers, punctuation marks, and special characters. Reddit posts were then tokenized using *happierfuntokenizing* from the DLATK Python library (Schwartz et al., 2017). We employed Gensim's multi-core LDA implementation with default hyper-parameter settings and 10 topics, determined through the coherence score and the average corpus likelihood value over ten runs. The words associated with each topic generated by the LDA model were inspected by two researchers familiar with mental health content to extract descriptive topical themes.

5 Results

Adolescent and adult MID users show considerable differences in the linguistic features and topics discussed in their Reddit posts.

5.1 Affective Attributes

As shown in Table 2, adolescent MID users received higher LIWC scores across all affect measures than the adult MID subgroup, including higher negativity (effect size = 0.073; 5.4% higher), anger (effect size = 0.069; 14.0% higher), anxiety (effect size = 0.042; 6.7% higher), and sadness (effect size = 0.053; 7.08% higher). While all four affect measures had small effect sizes, the frequency of swearing (effect size = 0.118) for adolescents was significantly greater than adults by 24.57%. This mean relative difference in the frequency of swearing was also seen within the adolescent age group between MID and CTL users, where adolescents with depression swore 260.2% more than those of the same age without depression.

The extent to which the adolescent and adult CTL users differ along the aggregate of these affective attributes is also reported. Per Figure 2, this mean difference separating the two age groups in the control cohort is only 1.13%, which is lower in comparison to 2.46% in the case of the MID cohort. This indicates that the adolescents and adults in the MID cohort show differences beyond that accounted for in the control sample.

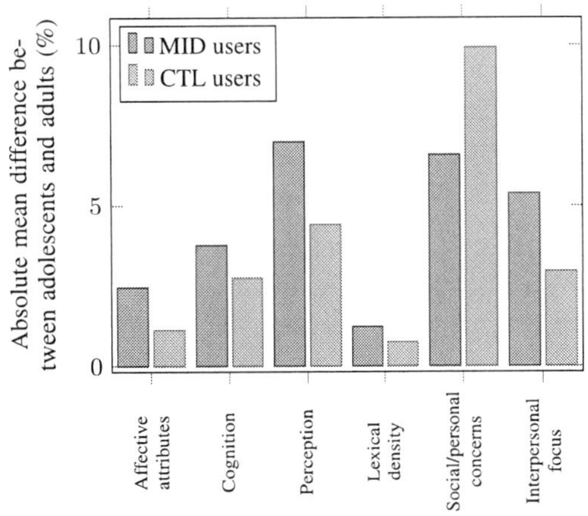

Figure 2: Mean absolute differences between adolescent and adult users with depression (MID) versus control (CTL) users per the various categories of linguistic measures. Difference for a specific measure is calculated as the ratio of the difference between the values of the measure for adolescents and adults, to the value of the measure among adults.

5.2 Cognitive Attributes

Adult MID users showed lower cognition (i.e. greater cognitive impairment) in their Reddit posts compared to adolescent MID users. For instance, insight (effect size = 0.095) is higher in adolescents relative to adults by 5.01%. Similarly, adolescents showed greater tentativeness (effect size = 0.093; 5.81% higher). Overall, the adolescent and adult users differ by 3.77% in the MID cohort, whereas this difference is significantly smaller (2.25%) in the CTL cohort across the various cognitive attributes, per Figure 2, indicating that these results are significant to depression.

5.3 Perception

Adolescent MID users used more words relating to auditory experiences (effect size = 0.078) in their Reddit posts when discussing depression compared to adults by 21.12%. Adult MID users, on the other hand, were more likely to reference language relating to visual attributes (effect size = -0.053; 7.8% higher). Adult MID users also focused more on time (effect size = -0.087; 3.5% higher) and used more past-tense (effect size = -0.106; 6.2% higher) to express their depression, whereas adolescent MID users used more future-oriented language (effect size = 0.059; 5.4% higher) in their posts.

> "I'm afraid of what I might do to myself when I leave for college" (↑ adolescent)

> "What really hurt me [...] was, after all these years, coping with an inner bully" (↑ adult)

The adolescent and adult subgroups in the CTL cohort did not exhibit noticeable differences in their use of temporal language (4.4%) compared to adolescents and adults in the MID cohort (6.99%).

5.4 Lexical Density

Lexical density in the Reddit posts of adult MID users is higher compared to the adolescent subgroup, as observed through the usage of prepositions (effect size = −0.127; 2.5% higher) and articles (effect size = −0.219; 8.6% higher). However, compared to the adolescent MID users, adults had a lower proportion of verbs (effect size = 0.142; 2.3% lower), auxiliary verbs (effect size = 0.090; 2.1% lower), and adverbs (effect size = 0.148; 4.7% lower). Per Figure 2, the aggregrate of the mean differences in lexical density between adolescents and adults for the MID cohort is greater than the difference between the two subgroups in the CTL sample.

5.5 Social and Personal Concerns

In contrast to the previous four categories of LIWC measures, the mean difference for the aggregate of social LIWC measures between adolescents and adults is higher in the control group (9.93%) compared to MID users (6.58%), as depicted in Figure 2. However, when examining specific LIWC measures within the social/personal category, adolescent and adult MID users exhibit distinct linguistic patterns associated with social and personal concerns in their Reddit posts.

To start, adolescent MID users used more words relating to 'friendship' (effect size = 0.083) and 'family' (effect size = 0.050) than adult MID users, by 13.2% and 7.5% respectively, and discussed social relationships 60.5% more than neurotypical adolescents.

> "I found out that my father had been cheating on my mum and now my life is going downhill" (↑ adolescent)

Adult MID users, on the other hand, associated depression with 'work' (effect size = -0.113; 11.8% higher) more than the adolescent subgroup. They also used more words relating to 'money' (effect size = -0.297) by 78.5%.

> "my mind is going haywire. Money, my career, school, should I quit my job, I hate my job" (↑ adult)

The Reddit posts of adult MID users concerning depression exhibited a higher emphasis on wellness (effect size = -0.117; 66.6% higher), substances (effect size = -0.042; 17.7% higher), and sexual matters (effect size = -0.032; 12.5% higher).

5.6 Interpersonal Focus

Adolescent MID users showed a higher use of personal pronouns (z = 0.271; 5.68% higher), an indicator of self-focus. Per Figure 2, for the CTL cohort, the interpersonal focus measures account for a difference of 2.95% between adolescent and adult users, while for MID users, the difference is more considerable at 5.38%, which indicates distinct variations beyond the control sample.

5.7 Topical Differences

Topic modeling revealed significant differences in the topics discussed in relation to depression between adolescents and adults in the MID and CTL cohorts.

Four topics from both the adolescent MID and adult MID subgroups stood out as having apparent clusterings and term overlap. For adolescent MID users, the terms associated with topic #1 relate to friendships, specifically the transience of social relationships (e.g., 'friend', 'year', 'day', 'still', 'long', trying'). The rest of the topics center largely around parents and family, with topic #7 relating to parental pressures (e.g., 'parent', 'dad', 'mom', 'always', 'talk'), topic #3 relating to family responsibilities (e.g., 'help', 'parent', 'work',

Figure 3: Topics significantly associated with depression posts of adolescents (top) and adults (bottom).

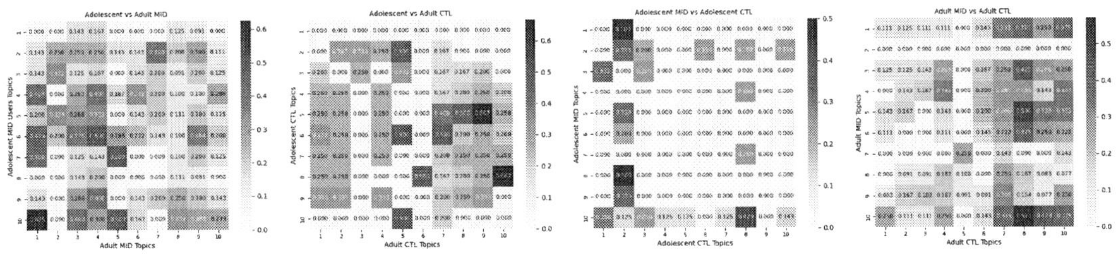

Figure 4: Jaccard similarity coefficients of topics comparing MID adolescent vs adult, CTL adolescent vs adult, adolescent MID vs CTL, and adult MID vs CTL. Darker shades indicate stronger similarities between topics.

problem', 'bad'), and topic #8 relating to emotions (e.g., 'family', 'anymore', 'sad', 'love', 'feeling'), per Figure 3. For adult MID users, the topics center largely around work (e.g., 'work', 'day', 'job', 'help', 'think' in topic #1) and exhaustion (e.g., 'nothing',' tired', 'live', 'depression' in topic #4), as seen in Figure 3. Topic #9 and topic #10 also focus on work, but in the context of family burdens (e.g., 'work', 'family', 'lonely', 'living') and negative emotions (e.g., 'job', 'hate', 'need', 'getting') respectively.

Figure 4 depicts the term overlap of topics discussed within the adolescent and adult groups in the MID and CTL cohorts. Approximately 21 out of 100 topic comparisons between adolescents and adults with depression exhibited a similarity coefficient above 0.3, indicating about a third of shared terms. This implies that 79% of topic comparisons had statistically insignificant term overlap, indicating distinct topics for adolescents relative to adults. In contrast, when comparing adolescents and adults in the control group, only 17 out of 100 topic comparisons had a similarity coefficient of 0.3 or higher. Comparisons between MID and control users within the specific age groups showed even lower term overlap. Specifically, among the topic comparisons of adolescents MID and CTL users, only 7 topics had a similarity coefficient of 0.3 or higher. For the comparison between adult MID and CTL, 15 out of 100 topic comparisons had a similarity coefficient of 0.3 or higher.

6 Discussion

This study has three main findings. First, adolescents and adults with depression share several topic similarities with each other (21% of topics in the MID sample exhibited significant term overlap for the two age groups, while this was only 17% in the control sample). The shared topics revolved predominantly around family matters and negative emotions, aligning with previous research that depressed users tend to exhibit higher levels of sadness, anxiety, and anger in their online writings (Schwartz et al., 2014; Preoţiuc-Pietro et al., 2015). This finding may suggest that depression has language markers that distinguish it from standard social media content, while also highlighting the universality of negative emotion and family challenges as markers of depression that transcend age groups.

Second, adolescents and adults with depression possess several distinct linguistic features of depression specific to their age group. Adolescent social media users with depression were more likely to associate their condition with social relationships, using words relating to friendships more frequently than adults with depression. This finding remained significant when controlling for neurotypical users, indicating that the topic of social relationships may be uniquely correlative with depression for adolescents. In contrast, adults with depression were more likely to associate their condition with job responsibilities, financial status, and health, evident in the higher prevalence of terms related to money and physical health (i.e. exhaustion, sexual matters, and substances). This not only aligns with prior research that depressed adults display more somatic symptoms than younger individuals with depression (Fiske, 2009), but also highlights how adults discuss their depression differently than adolescent users on social media.

Adolescent social media users with depression exhibited a higher usage of future-tense language when discussing their mental health experiences, suggesting a preoccupation with future stressors potentially correlative with the onset of depression. In contrast, adults with depression employed more past-tense language, indicating a focus on past grievances or regrets. This differs from prior research with neurotypical social media users, where as users increased in age, they used more future-tense (Pennebaker and Stone, 2003), indicating that these temporal linguistic features may be unique to depression and can be age-specific language markers.

Third, the linguistic features that distinguish depression were more prominent and effective among adolescent social media users compared to adults. While adults with and without depression had several similarities in the topics they discussed (15% of topics had significant term overlap), the topics discussed by adolescents with and without depression had considerably less overlap (only 7%). This suggests that among older social media users, the correlative topics of depression may become less discernible and intertwined with normal discussion topics. Prior research suggests that the reason for this discrepancy is because adults are less open to expression on social media compared to younger individuals (Pennebaker and Stone, 2003; Barbieri, 2008); other results from the present study also supports this finding, as adults were shown to use more impersonal and less emotional expression when discussing their depression compared to adolescent users. Overall, this finding indicates that identifying depression expression on social media platforms may be more difficult within adult subpopulations compared to adolescent groups.

7 Limitations

The present study had limitations that should be acknowledged. First, the infrequency of age self-disclosure on Reddit made it challenging to obtain samples for a wider range of age categories, such as individuals over the age of 60. This resulted in a dataset predominantly composed of users aged 13-40, as seen in Figure 1, necessitating a focus on binary age groups rather than narrower ranges. The age group of "adults" in the present study may be more advantageously interpreted as "young adults." Further research is thus needed with a larger amount of age-labeled data for analysis of more precise age ranges.

Another limitation was the topic modeling process, where the interpretation of results relied on observation rather than a psychologist's expertise. This introduces potential bias, and the topics should therefore be validated by further research. Future studies should also employ more rigorous linguistic models and methodologies for precise topic categorization.

Moreover, due to Reddit's interactive forum structure, the posts analyzed in the present study may have belonged to larger chains/dialogues that influenced the user's behavior and language use. Future studies should incorporate additional contextual information to avoid hidden confounding variables.

Finally, the sample of Reddit users may not be representative of the global population, limiting the generalizability of our findings. The present study focused solely on Reddit and the English language, while mental health discussions may occur on other platforms or in different languages. Future research should consider incorporating data from multiple platforms and languages for a more comprehensive understanding.

8 Conclusion

This exploratory study contributes to a growing body of literature on mental health expression in online language data by quantitatively examining age-based linguistic differences in expressing depression on Reddit. By investigating social media data through psycholinguistic feature extraction and open-vocabulary topic modeling, adolescents and adults with depression were found to engage in discussions about several common topics; however, they also exhibited distinct age-specific linguistic markers, with adolescents being more prone to associating their depression with friendships, while adults were more likely to focus on work and health concerns. Depression language markers were also found to be more discernible among adolescent social media users compared to adult users. These findings highlight the importance of recognizing language variations across age groups when detecting depression on social media.

Acknowledgements

I would like to express my gratitude to Audrey Acken and Matthew Hesby for their encouragement, help and valuable feedback for my research.

References

Cheryl Ahrens. 2002. Age differences and similarities in the correlates of depressive symptoms. *Psychology and aging*, 17:116–24.

Federica Barbieri. 2008. Patterns of age-based linguistic variation in american english1. *Journal of Sociolinguistics*, 12:58 – 88.

D. M. Blei, A. Y. Ng, and M. I. Jordan. 2003. Latent dirichlet allocation. *The Journal of Machine Learning Research*, 3:993–1022.

Lera Boroditsky, Lauren A. Schmidt, and Webb Phillips. 2003. *Sex, syntax and semantics.*, chapter Sex, syntax and semantics. The MIT Press.

A. Boyd, Ashokkumar, Seraj, and Pennebaker. 2022. The development and psychometric properties of LIWC-22.

Nina L. Cesare, Christan Earl Grant, and Elaine Okanyene Nsoesie. 2017. Detection of user demographics on social media: A review of methods and recommendations for best practices. *ArXiv*, abs/1702.01807.

Stevie Chancellor, Zhiyuan Jerry Lin, Erica L. Goodman, Stephanie Zerwas, and Munmun De Choudhury. 2016. Quantifying and predicting mental illness severity in online pro-eating disorder communities. *Proceedings of the 19th ACM Conference on Computer-Supported Cooperative Work & Social Computing*.

Xin Chen, Yu Wang, Eugene Agichtein, and Fusheng Wang. 2015. A comparative study of demographic attribute inference in twitter. In *International Conference on Web and Social Media*.

Rob Chew, Caroline Kery, Laura Baum, Thomas Bukowski, Annice Kim, and Mario Navarro. 2021. Correction: Predicting age groups of reddit users based on posting behavior and metadata: Classification model development and validation. *JMIR public health and surveillance*, 7:e30017.

Munmun Choudhury, Scott Counts, Eric Horvitz, and Aaron Hoff. 2014. Characterizing and predicting postpartum depression from shared facebook data. pages 626–638.

Munmun De Choudhury, Michael Gamon, Scott Counts, and Eric Horvitz. 2013. Predicting depression via social media. *Proceedings of the International AAAI Conference on Web and Social Media*.

Munmun De Choudhury, Sanket S. Sharma, Tomaz Logar, Wouter Eekhout, René Clausen Nielsen, and Georgia Tech. 2016. Quantifying and understanding gender and cross-cultural differences in mental health expression via social media.

Cindy Chung and James Pennebaker. 2007. The psychological functions of function words. *Social communication*.

Glen A. Coppersmith, Mark Dredze, and Craig Harman. 2014. Quantifying mental health signals in twitter. In *CLPsych@ACL*.

Aron Culotta. 2014. Estimating county health statistics with twitter. *Conference on Human Factors in Computing Systems - Proceedings*.

Johannes Eichstaedt, Margaret Kern, David Yaden, H. Schwartz, Salvatore Giorgi, Gregory Park, Courtney Hagan, Victoria Tobolsky, Laura Smith, Anneke Buffone, Jonathan Iwry, Martin Seligman, and Lyle Ungar. 2020. Closed and open vocabulary approaches to text analysis: A review, quantitative comparison, and recommendations.

Johannes Eichstaedt, H. Schwartz, Margaret Kern, Gregory Park, Darwin Labarthe, Raina Merchant, Sneha Jha, Megha Agrawal, Lukasz Dziurzynski, Maarten Sap, Christopher Weeg, Emily Larson, Lyle Ungar, and Martin Seligman. 2015. Psychological language on twitter predicts county-level heart disease mortality. *Psychological science*, 26.

Gatz Fiske, Wetherell. 2009. Depression in older adults. *Annual Review of Clinical Psychology*, pages 363–389.

Manas Gaur, Ugur Kursuncu, Amanuel Alambo, A. Sheth, Raminta Daniulaityte, Krishnaprasad Thirunarayan, and Jyotishman Pathak. 2018. "let me tell you about your mental health!": Contextualized classification of reddit posts to dsm-5 for web-based intervention. *Proceedings of the 27th ACM International Conference on Information and Knowledge Management.*

Christopher Homan, Naiji Lu, Xin Tu, Megan C. Lytle-Flint, and Vincent Michael Bernard Silenzio. 2014. Social structure and depression in trevorspace. *CSCW : proceedings of the Conference on Computer-Supported Cooperative Work. Conference on Computer-Supported Cooperative Work*, 2014:615 – 625.

Lilly C. Irani, Janet Vertesi, Paul Dourish, Kavita Philip, and Rebecca E. Grinter. 2010. Postcolonial computing: a lens on design and development. *Proceedings of the SIGCHI Conference on Human Factors in Computing Systems.*

Fazida Karim, Azeezat Abimbola Oyewande, Lamis F Abdalla, Reem Chaudhry Ehsanullah, and Safeera Khan. 2020. Social media use and its connection to mental health: A systematic review. *Cureus*, 12.

J. Kaufman, A. Martin, R. A. King, and D. Charney. 2001. Are child-, adolescent-, and adult-onset depression one and the same disorder? *Biological Psychiatry*, 49(12):980–1001.

Tingting Liu, Lyle Ungar, Brenda Curtis, Garrick Sherman, Kenna Yadeta, Louis Tay, Johannes Eichstaedt, and Sharath Chandra Guntuku. 2022. Head versus heart: social media reveals differential language of loneliness from depression. *npj Mental Health Research*, 1:16.

Kate Loveys, Jonathan Torrez, Alex B. Fine, Glendon L. Moriarty, and Glen A. Coppersmith. 2018. Cross-cultural differences in language markers of depression online. In *CLPsych@NAACL-HTL.*

Daniel Mark Low, Laurie Rumker, Tanya Talkar, John B Torous, Guillermo A. Cecchi, and Satrajit S. Ghosh. 2020. Natural language processing reveals vulnerable mental health support groups and heightened health anxiety on reddit during covid-19: Observational study. *Journal of Medical Internet Research*, 22.

Diana L. MacLean, S. Gupta, Anna Lembke, Christopher D. Manning, and Jeffrey Heer. 2015. Forum77: An analysis of an online health forum dedicated to addiction recovery. *Proceedings of the 18th ACM Conference on Computer Supported Cooperative Work & Social Computing.*

Douglas Maynard and Anssi Peräkylä. 2006. *Language and Social Interaction*, pages 233–257.

Juhi Mittal, Abha Belorkar, Venu Pokuri, Vinit Jakhetiya, and Sharath Chandra Guntuku. 2023. Language on reddit reveals differential mental health markers for individuals posting in immigration communities.

Elizabeth Murnane and Scott Counts. 2014. Unraveling abstinence and relapse: Smoking cessation reflected in social media. *Conference on Human Factors in Computing Systems - Proceedings.*

J. Ormel, M. VonKorff, T. B. Ustun, S. Pini, A. Korten, and T. Oldehinkel. 1994. Common mental disorders and disability across cultures. results from the WHO collaborative study on psychological problems in general health care. *JAMA*, 272(22):1741–1748.

V Patel, Ricardo Araya, Marcia Guerino De Lima, Ana Bernarda Ludermir, and Charles Todd. 1999. Women, poverty and common mental disorders in four restructuring societies. *Social science & medicine*, 49 11:1461–71.

Michael Paul and Mark Dredze. 2011. You are what your tweet: Analyzing twitter for public health. *Artificial Intelligence*, 38:265–272.

James W. Pennebaker and Lori D. Stone. 2003. Words of wisdom: language use over the life span. *Journal of personality and social psychology*, 85 2:291–301.

Inna Loginovna Pirina and Çagri Çöltekin. 2018. Identifying depression on reddit: The effect of training data. In *Conference on Empirical Methods in Natural Language Processing.*

Daniel Preoţiuc-Pietro, Johannes Eichstaedt, Gregory Park, Maarten Sap, Laura Smith, Victoria Tobolsky, H. Andrew Schwartz, and Lyle Ungar. 2015. The role of personality, age, and gender in tweeting about mental illness. pages 21–30, Denver, Colorado. Association for Computational Linguistics.

Nairán Ramírez-Esparza, Cindy K. Chung, Ewa Kacewicz, and James W. Pennebaker. 2008. The psychology of word use in depression forums in english and in spanish: Texting two text analytic approaches. *Proceedings of the International AAAI Conference on Web and Social Media.*

Ps Resnik, William Armstrong, Leonardo Claudino, and Thang Nguyen. 2015. The university of maryland clpsych 2015 shared task system. pages 54–60.

Frances Rice, Lucy Riglin, Terri C. Lomax, E. Souter, Robert Potter, DJ Smith, Ajay K Thapar, and Ajay K Thapar. 2019. Adolescent and adult differences in major depression symptom profiles. *Journal of affective disorders*, 243:175–181.

H. Schwartz, Johannes Eichstaedt, Margaret Kern, Gregory Park, Maarten Sap, David Stillwell, Michal Kosinski, and Lyle Ungar. 2014. Towards assessing changes in degree of depression through facebook.

H. Schwartz, Salvatore Giorgi, Maarten Sap, Patrick Crutchley, Lyle Ungar, and Johannes Eichstaedt. 2017. Dlatk: Differential language analysis toolkit. pages 55–60.

Rachel E. Spector. 1991. Cultural diversity in health and illness. *Journal of Transcultural Nursing*, 13:197 – 199.

Shelley E. Taylor and J D Brown. 1988. Illusion and well-being: a social psychological perspective on mental health. *Psychological bulletin*, 103 2:193–210.

Anna Tigunova, Paramita Mirza, Andrew Yates, and Gerhard Weikum. 2020. Reddust: a large reusable dataset of reddit user traits. In *International Conference on Language Resources and Evaluation*.

Sho Tsugawa, Yusuke Kikuchi, Fumio Kishino, Kosuke Nakajima, Yuichi Itoh, and Hiroyuki Ohsaki. 2015. Recognizing depression from twitter activity. *Proceedings of the 33rd Annual ACM Conference on Human Factors in Computing Systems*.

World Health Organization. 2017. *Depression fact sheet*.

Satyanarayana Yatam and T. Raghunadha Reddy. 2014. Author profiling: Predicting gender and age from blogs, reviews & social media. *International journal of engineering research and technology*, 3.

Trigger Warnings: A Computational Approach to Understanding User-Tagged Trigger Warnings

Sarthak Tyagi
Vellore Institute of Technology, Chennai, India
sarthak.tyagi2019@vitstudent.ac.in

Adwita Arora, Krish Chopra and **Manan Suri**
Netaji Subhas University of Technology, New Delhi, India
{adwita.ug20, krish.ug20, manan.suri.ug20}@nsut.ac.in

Abstract

Content and trigger warnings give information about the content of material prior to receiving it and are used by social media users to tag their content when discussing sensitive topics. Trigger warnings are known to yield benefits in terms of an increased individual agency to make an informed decision about engaging with content Charles et al. (2022). At the same time, some studies contest the benefits of trigger warnings suggesting that they can induce anxiety and reinforce the traumatic experience of specific identities Bridgland et al. (2019). Our study involves the analysis of the nature and implications of the usage of trigger warnings by social media users using empirical methods and machine learning. Further, we aim to study the community interactions associated with trigger warnings in online communities, precisely the diversity and content of responses and inter-user interactions. The domains of trigger warnings covered will include self-harm, drug abuse, suicide, and depression. The analysis of the above domains will assist in a better understanding of online behaviour associated with them and help in developing domain-specific datasets for further research.

1 Introduction

Trigger warnings are "a statement at the start of a piece of writing, video, etc. alerting the reader or viewer to the fact that it contains potentially distressing material–often used to introduce a description of such content" Bellet et al. (2018). They are used frequently by users online when discussing sensitive issues which might trigger a detrimental response in certain users. Trigger warnings are used in multiple contexts with respect to sensitive content; common examples include narrating one's own experience, talking about someone else's experience, or discussing content that might be sensitive Bridgland et al. (2019); Bellet et al. (2018). Some domains that are commonly associated with the use of trigger warnings include Self-harm, Violence, Drug Abuse, Suicide, and Depression. Trigger warnings thus can be used as a tool for others to self-moderate the content that they are engaging with on the internet with their level of comfort. However, recent empirical studies have shown that trigger warnings may also lead to the centering of traumatic experiences in communities, thus having the exact opposite effect Jones et al. (2020).

While in the wrong circumstances, anything can act as a trigger for a person under distress, some content has a universally accepted nature of being distressing or troubling for a large group of people[1] Charles et al. (2022); Ballestrini (2022). An overwhelming consensus on the classification and typology of these content warnings does not exist, as some sources like providing a more general description of content and trigger warnings (as an example considering violence as the trigger warning). In contrast, others look at the sub-categories as a more appropriate way of describing the nature of the content (animal cruelty, and sexual violence all describe a sub-category of violence, but give the reader a better idea of the nature the content represents).

Nevertheless, these sources agree upon the fact that none of their lists represents an exhaustive account of content that can distress a reader. Through our research, we want to utilize publicly available data from social media to perform an analysis on the use of trigger warnings, the nature of discourse associated with the selected domains, and community modelling of online communities. The analysis would involve the linguistic study of the expressions demonstrated by users. It would also include

[1] University of Michigan, An Introduction to Content Warnings and Trigger Warnings.https://sites.lsa.umich.edu/inclusive-teaching/an-introduction-to-content-warnings-and-trigger-warni

Proceedings of the Student Research Workshop associated with RANLP-2023, pages 44–54, Varna, Bulgaria, Sep 4–6, 2023.
https://doi.org/10.26615/issn.2603-2821.2023_005

topic modelling and keyword analysis to study the nature of posts. A comparison between different domains would help us understand the differences between the communities involved in the respective domain. An additional area of analysis includes the response received to posts tagged with trigger warnings. In our study, we build up a novel dataset of trigger warning posts from various subreddits on Reddit, with our target trigger warnings being self-harm, suicidal ideation, depression, and drug abuse. We perform a multitude of analyses on this extracted data, which includes sentiment analysis of the gathered posts, an analysis of how the frequency of posts in these different subreddits have evolved, extraction of keyphrases from these texts, a look into how common topic models perform in this analysis and finally we tackle a classification problem by assigning classes to the dataset based on what type of post (post asking questions, a post asking advice, rant posts, etc.). We plan to release our dataset after paper acceptance.

2 Related Work

While we are not aware of prior work on computational trigger warning analysis using social media data or specifically warning assignments, We have divided our related work into sections highlighting the advantages of BERTopic over traditional topic modelling techniques, Relevant tasks to our objective, and other relevant papers.

2.1 Employing BERTopic for analysis

In Ogunleye et al. (2023), the authors provide an evaluation of how different topic models measure up to the task of topic extraction from a corpus of tweets about Nigerian Banks. It evaluates how traditional topic modelling techniques like Latent Dirichlet Allocation (LDA), Hierarchical Dirichlet Process (HDP), and Latent Semantic Indexing (LSI) perform in comparison to BERTopic Grootendorst (2022) utilizing a Kernel PCA for dimensionality reduction and K-means for clustering, achieving a maximum coherence score of 0.8463, well above the other techniques studied. LDA with a more well-processed corpus performs well but not better than BERTopic, and it suffers from the different subtleties present in tweets that use Pidgin English. This study highlights the incredible performance of BERTopic as a way to model the key topics present in a corpus in a completely unsupervised way. de Groot et al. (2022) analyzes how the BERTopic performs on the multi-domain short text and tests its generalizability in this context in comparison to LDA in terms of topic coherence and diversity. It uses open-text documents of university students from various domains such as computer science to law. The data is short in its length, with a median of 14 to 20 words in each. BERTopic outperforms LDA on both short-form and long-form documents, however, the coherence declines similar to the decline in coherence for LDA models when we evaluate performance on short documents using BERTopic with HDBSCAN. The performance of BERTopic using k-means clustering shows that the model is the least susceptible to short documents, due to its ability to generate more interpretable topics and fewer outliers than HDBSCAN.

2.2 Identifying Trigger Warning from fictional text corpus

Wolska et al. (2022) presents a very similar task of looking at trigger warning assignments in a corpus built from fanfiction works present on Archive of Our Own (AO3), focusing on trigger warnings related to violence. They provide a binary classification system for assigning trigger warnings and assess their effectiveness on a similar unlabelled dataset of fanfiction documents. They evaluate an SVM classifier and a state-of-the-art BERT model and find out that the simpler SVM model outperforms the BERT classifier, which they reason is due to the limited context present in the BERT model compared to the SVM model which works over the entire set of tokens using a bag-of-words approach. Their study concludes that the task of trigger warning assignment is non-trivial and requires further refinement. We build up on this study to utilize the social media data highlighting the presence of trigger warnings and present an in-depth analysis of our dataset and how computational modelling would improve identifying and flagging such social media posts using keyword detection and intent classification.

2.3 Related Datasets

The establishment of a user-level database of users on Twitter who have self-disclosed their experiences with various mental health problems is described in Suhavi et al. (2022). More than 10,000 Twitter users who have tweeted about their experiences with mental health illnesses, such as anxiety, depression, bipolar disorder, and eating disorders,(all being a type of trigger warning) are included in the database known as Twitter-STMHD. The authors extracted user-level data, including demographic statistics and information about the particular disorder, from tweets relating to mental health issues using a combination of machine learning algorithms and manual annotation. It provides users with a large-scale and well-labelled dataset grouped into 8 disorder categories and may have practical applications for mental health professionals seeking to identify and reach out to individuals who may need support. Gautam et al. (2020) describes the creation of a dataset of Twitter messages related to the #MeToo movement. The authors used manual and automated methods to annotate the dataset on five linguistic aspects: relevance, sarcasm, hate speech, stance, and dialogue acts. It also contains geographical information in the form of the country of origin of the tweet. This dataset labelled #MeTooMA is of particular interest to study in both computational and social linguistics and model how different linguistic components like stance, hate, and sarcasm interact in a social media context. While these papers have made the effort to analyze social media text, They have not explored the presence of trigger warnings in text, Its analysis and classification of various intents present in such content. We use techniques like keyword and keyphrase extraction to understand frequently used words in with maximum similarity with such content and topic modelling to generalize the topic assignment ability of BERTopic over our corpora. We also propose machine learning models to identify the intent of the social media posts using the post content and other user metadata.

3 Methodology

In this section we will briefly explain our data collection and Pre-Processing techniques, Exploratory Data analysis to emphasize the increasing trend of trigger warning posts online, Keyword and KeyPhrase analysis of the collected data, and evaluate various topic generation metrics to generalize the topic modelling quality and benchmark classification performance to predict the intent of posts mentioning trigger warnings. The entire framework is described in Fig 1.

3.1 Dataset

The dataset created is extracted and compiled from Reddit by using the PRAW Tool [2]. for extracting posts on the topics of self-harm, suicide, depression, and drug abuse. For the given topics we extracted data from the following subreddits:

- Self-harm: r/selfharm, r/SelfHarmScars
- Suicide: r/SuicideWatch
- Depression: r/Depression, r/MentalHealth
- Drug Abuse: r/RedditorsInRecovery

We extracted the following fields for our analysis including, A unique identifier for the Reddit Post (id), The username of the author of the post (author), The Title of the post (title), The number of upvotes minus the number of downvotes given to the post give us a measure of how much other users sympathize or agree with the post (score), The subreddit that the data is extracted from (subreddit), The text content of the post (text), The time that the post went up (utc_time), The number of comments, which gives us an idea of the popularity of the posts (num_comments), The comments on the post (comments), Whether the post only contains text, or it has a link to another resource (image, video, etc.) (is_self), A link_flair_text that describes the type of post (a question, asking for advice, etc.), Whether the post is restricted for viewers under the age of 18 (over_18) and the url of the post.

For EDA, Keyphrase mining, Topic modelling, and Classification we remove HTML tags, URLs, emoticons (cases of using emojis where it semantically differs from text is prevalent on social media), and special characters, while punctuation is retained. We extract certain content warning keywords for each category and construct our search phrase to find posts that contain these terms either in the post's title or in its body. We create a search phrase using keywords from a pool of words that are most commonly present in posts from a particular topic from all the posts from the subreddit from 2013 to 2022. Here, *x = ["trigger warning", "tw", "TW", "Trigger Warning"]* is the list of mentions we search in a post, and *y = [keywords_list]* is a curated list of words used by users from different communities, The search phrase created is

$$z = x_i + y_i : x_i \in x \text{ and } y_i \in y$$

[2]PRAW `https://praw.readthedocs.io/en/stable/`

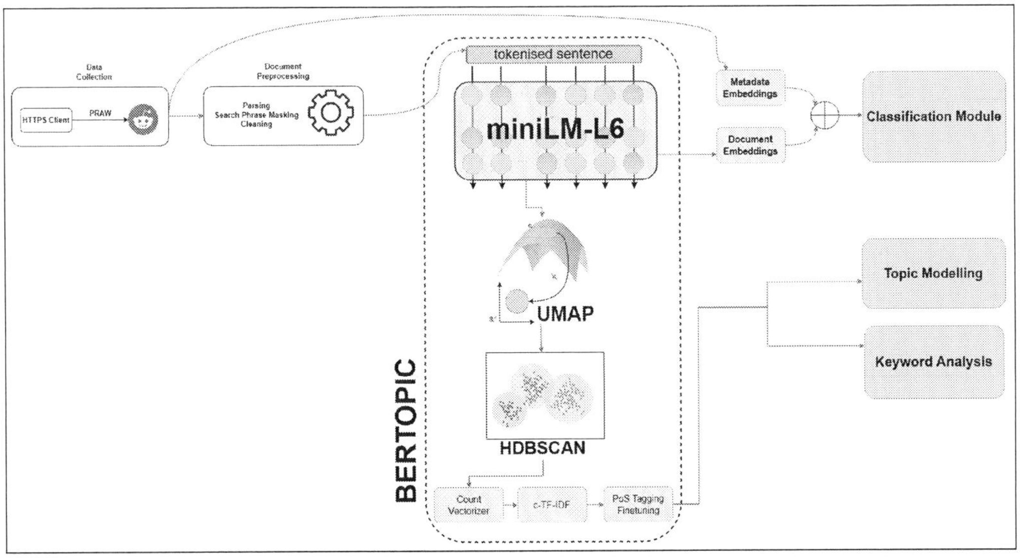

Figure 1: Overall Framework

	DATASET			
Measure	selfharm	suicide	depress	drugabuse
# Num of posts	4322	7090	11606	2437
Avg num of sentences	4.70	6.55	7.54	8.09
Mean Proportion of unique tokens	0.653	0.651	0.509	0.562

Table 1: Statistics of the dataset

3.2 Exploratory Data Analysis

3.2.1 Sentiment Analysis

In order to understand the sentiment, lexical and semantic depth of the user's post across different categories, we employ various techniques to extract such insights. We utilize a valence-aware dictionary and sentiment reasoner (VADER) tool. It is a lexicon and rule-based sentiment analyzer sensitive to the polarity and intensity of sentiments expressed in social media content due to its gold-standard lexicon attuned to a microblog-like context. Fig 2. depicts the Proportions of the documents with negative, neutral, or positive sentiments, These sentiments were calculated using the compound score, which is obtained by summing the valence score which is a value between -4 (negative) and 4 (positive) of each word in the lexicon/sentence which is added and is normalized between -1 and 1. Typical thresholds for a compound score for a positive sentiment are > 0.05, neutral sentiment for > -0.05 and < 0.05, and negative for < -0.05. A striking detail that we can notice is the prevalence of a high percentage of documents with positive sentiment from the drugabuse class. This highlights the point that the consumption of drugs and substance abuse is regarded as an activity that induces a feeling of euphoria and is not regarded as a negative belief within the community. The highest percentage of negative sentiment belongs to the depress class as people tend to convey their feelings and emotions on such social websites in an anonymous manner. The suicide class has the highest percentage of neutral sentiment as users often discuss narratives from films, tv shows, etc, or discuss laws pertaining to suicide in general.

3.2.2 Trend Analysis

We visualize the sudden surge in the frequency of posting on the platform with trigger warnings mentioned in subreddits as shown in Fig 3. corresponding to depress, drugabuse, selfharm, and suicide communities from the year 2019 when COVID-19 was declared and everyone was forced to be isolated and quarantined to ensure public safety. This explains the increase in user posting as people suffer from different mental issues during the surge of COVID-19. It is also evident that during this period

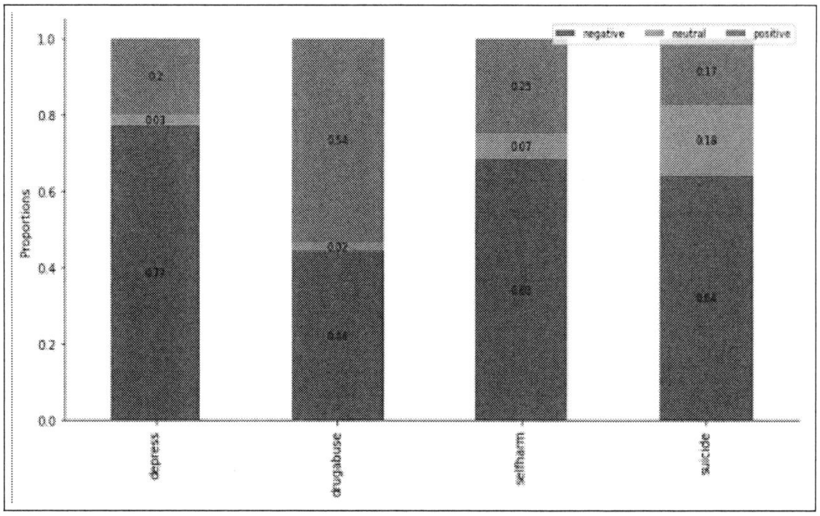

Figure 2: Percentage of posts in each sentiment category using the VADER tool

there was a rise in anxiety-related issues, domestic violence, and drug abuse as people had to stay at home against their choices with little to no physical interaction with the outer world. Many people who were dependent on alcohol and other substances experienced withdrawal symptoms, such as delirium and seizures, as a result of the abrupt closure of all liquor stores during the COVID-19 surge. Several alcohol "addicts," troubled by their urges, had turned to harmful drugs like hand sanitisers as replacements, These people also took to social media about their withdrawal symptoms and the distress they were going through [3].

3.2.3 Keyword/ Keyphrase Analysis

We present a thorough keyphrase analysis to inspect the different keywords and keyphrases used by the users from the collected corpora to understand the utilization of words when describing an incident, experience, or scene mentioning trigger warnings on social media websites. Keyword analysis provides us with a deep insight into the knowledge contained within the text and builds up an idea of the nature of the document. With the vast size of the text resources available on social media websites, manual extraction of keyphrases has become infeasible. Automatic keyword extraction [10] not only streamlines this process but also allows the reader to get an idea about the post's content in a very short period of time without going through the details and disregarding posts containing various sensitive/disturbing keywords or keyphrases. we utilize for KeyBert algorithm for our analysis. KeyBERT Grootendorst (2020) is a technique for extracting keywords and keyphrases from a document that utilizes BERT embeddings. It is simple and straightforward to use and generates keywords and key phrases that closely match the content of the document. The method employed by KeyBERT involves utilizing BERT embeddings and a basic cosine similarity technique to identify the sub-phrases within a document that is most closely related to the document as a whole. Initially, BERT is utilized to extract document embeddings, which results in a representation of the document at a high level. Following this, embeddings for N-gram words or phrases are obtained. Ultimately, cosine similarity is used to identify the words or phrases that are most similar to the document. We sample 5 keywords for each corpus with the highest similarity as it captures the semantics of the entire post's content.

The results from KeyBERT are as follows:

- Self Harm: 'fun': 0.8011, 'anxiety': 0.7559, 'normal': 0.7373, 'relapse': 0.731, 'blades': 0.69
- Depression: 'ptsd': 0.8209, 'desperate': 0.8132, 'hey': 0.8014, 'relapsed': 0.797, 'stories': 0.7636
- Drug abuse: 'relapse': 0.658, 'craving': 0.609, 'ptsd': 0.6087, 'caffeine': 0.6067, 'withdrawal': 0.5809

[3]https://encorerecovery.com/understanding-hand-sanitizer-addiction/

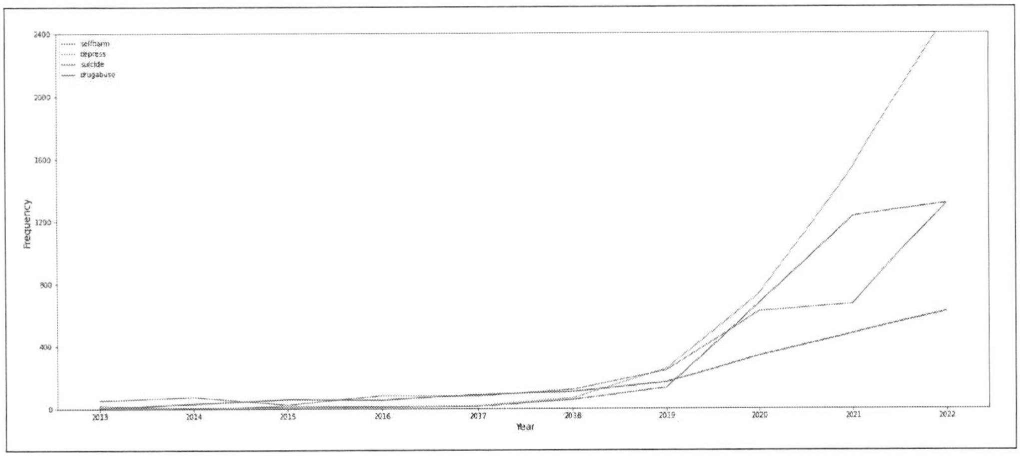

Figure 3: Trend Analysis of posting across different communities

- Suicide: 'game': 0.8591, 'hurts': 0.8366, 'cut': 0.8302, 'urgent': 0.7709, 'relapse': 0.7248, 'help': 0.7217

Selfharm: The keyword "fun" suggests that there may be discussions or mentions of self-harm being perceived as pleasurable or enjoyable. It is important to approach this keyword with sensitivity, as it may indicate dark humour or the complexity of self-harm experiences. The presence of the keyword "anxiety" is likely to be mentioned when discussing anxiety triggers related to self-harm. Discussions involving trigger warnings revolve around understanding and normalizing self-harm experiences and that mention the keyword "normal" and direct a focus on reducing stigma and creating a safe space for individuals and promoting openness. Mentions of "relapse" indicate that individuals within the self-harm subreddit may share experiences or seek support related to relapses in self-harm behaviours. "blades" suggests that discussions or mentions of specific self-harm tools cause self-affliction.

Depression: "ptsd" suggests community discussion to address potential triggers related to post-traumatic stress disorder within the context of depression. This indicates that individuals may share experiences or seek support for co-occurring PTSD and substance abuse issues."desperate" indicates the use of the term in discussions involving desperate situations related to depression and individuals expressing feelings of desperation. The keyword "relapsed" and "stories" are likely to be used when discussing experiences, stories, or offering support, This signifies a likely presence of personal connections in the community.

Drugabuse: "relapse" indicates discussions involving experiences of relapse in drug abuse. It hints towards a discourse about preventing and recovering from relapse and its presence highlights the challenges and complexities individuals face in maintaining their recovery journey. "craving" might insinuate that discussions within the community revolve around the intense desire or urge to use drugs. "ptsd" suggests dialogue which addresses the intersection of drug abuse and post-traumatic stress disorder (PTSD) and draws the need to concurrently deal both at the same. "caffeine" can be used to compare the withdrawal symptoms from lack of caffeine to the withdrawal symptoms of drug addiction, "withdrawal" might imply the various challenges one would face during the recovery process.

Suicide: The presence of the word "game" suggests that discussions within the subreddit may involve references to video games or the gaming culture. This also highlights gaming as a source of comfort or a getaway, A user can also be simply sharing a gaming plot over a discussion thread. The use of the word "hurts" in community discourse focuses on emotional pain, distress, or hopelessness. "cut" implies discussions revolving around self-harm behaviours especially cutting where a user might share their own story or reference other texts emphasizing the use of force to wound themselves. The use of words "urgent" and "help" and their interplay might be used to draw the community's attention toward situations requiring immediate intervention and assistance.

4 Computational Modeling

4.1 Topic Modeling Evaluation

Topic models can automatically extract groups of related words from large collections of text without human guidance. By analyzing the words used in a particular document, these models can identify the key topics discussed within it. The need for coherence metrics Röder et al. (2015); Terragni et al. (2021b) has emerged in the field of text mining, where unsupervised learning methods such as topic models do not provide assurances about the interpretability of their results. We present a thorough evaluation of our trained topic models on both topic coherence and topic diversity to measure their interpretability of identifying appropriate topics from our trigger warnings corpora. In turn, This also helps us to understand the quality of topics discovered by our topic model and its importance in real-world applications to summarize documents with topics comprising potential trigger warnings to avert users from such content. Topic Coherence measures evaluate a particular topic by quantifying the level of semantic similarity between the most highly rated words within that topic Stevens et al. (2012). Such evaluations help distinguish between topics that can be semantically interpreted and those that are merely statistical artifacts of the inference process. We utilize the following topic coherence measures for evaluating the results produced by the BERTopic model: UMass Röder et al. (2015); Stevens et al. (2012) calculates how often two words, w_i and w_j appear together in the corpus and it's defined as

$$C_{UMass} = \frac{2}{N \cdot (N-1)} \sum_{i=2}^{N} \sum_{j=1}^{i-1} \log \frac{P(w_i, w_j) + \epsilon}{P(w_j)} \tag{1}$$

where $D(w_i, w_j)$ indicate how many times words w_i and w_j appear together in documents, and $D(w_i)$ is how many time word w_i appeared alone. To determine the overall coherence of a topic, we take the mean coherence score for each pair of the top N words that best represent the topic. The UMass metric is unique in that it calculates these statistics based on the same corpus that was used to train the topic models, rather than an external corpus. This makes it an intrinsic metric that seeks to validate that the models have indeed learned the data present in all the corpora. C_V Röder et al. (2015)is a widely used method for measuring coherence which involves constructing content vectors based on the co-occurrences of words within a topic. This metric then uses normalized pointwise mutual information (NPMI) and cosine similarity to compute the coherence score. C_{UCI} Röder et al. (2015); Stevens et al. (2012) computes the coherence score by measuring the frequency of two words appearing in a document. Instead, We employ a sliding window method and calculate the pointwise mutual information between all pairs of the top N words by occurrence and examine their co-occurrence within the sliding window. If both words, w_i and w_j are present in a document but not within the same sliding window, we do not consider them as co-occurring.

$$C_{UCI} = \frac{2}{N \cdot (N-1)} \sum_{i=1}^{N-1} \sum_{j=i+1}^{N} PMI(w_i, w_j) \tag{2}$$

where

$$PMI(w_i, w_j) = \log \frac{P(w_i, w_j) + \epsilon}{P(w_i) \cdot P(w_j)} \tag{3}$$

The results are presented in Table 2. We see that the Drug abuse corpus achieves a considerably high coherence score of -0.693,0.701 and 0.701 followed by the suicide corpus with a score of -0.631, 0.642, 0.621 exhibiting that the topic model performs better on the aforementioned datasets in producing highly coherent topics, while the Selharm and Depression dataset shows an intermediate score suggesting some degree of semantic similarity with reasonably interpretable generated topics.

In addition to coherence, we also consider topic diversity as a measure. The greater the diversity among the resulting topics, the broader the coverage of various aspects of the analyzed corpus will be. It's crucial to generate topics that differ from one another as it ensures the topic model produces non-redundant themes and learns a diverse topic distribution. Topic diversity Dieng et al. (2020) refers to the proportion of distinct words among the top n words in all topics. A diversity score of nearly 0 suggests that the topics are redundant, while a score close to 1 implies more diverse topics. Inverted Rank Biased Overlap (IRBO): It measures the overlap between two lists A and B over various depths by taking the number of elements intersecting between the two lists and then normalizing it by the depth (number of topics considered). Averaging over all the depth sizes gives us the RBO score for the two lists. The inversion of this RBO score gives us a measure of how distinct the two lists are Tan and Clarke (2014); Webber et al. (2010). The diversity results are presented in Table 3. We use the OCTIS framework Terragni et al. (2021a) to evaluate the topic diversity metrics. The results indicate that the BERTopic model gives us a diverse set of topics across all four datasets that are used. Suicide and Self Harm show comparatively higher diversity scores across both the used methods. Topic diversity scores for all the datasets are above 0.8 suggesting topics within each dataset are unique, non-repetitive, and cover a wide range of themes.

4.2 Classification

We use the extracted data from various different subreddits which are a part of self-harm, suicide & depression and drug abuse subreddits to determine user intent by using the link flair text as the exogenous variable. The posts with link flair texts were divided into training and test set respectively, Posts with no tags were manually labelled which included text with no trigger warning as well. Labelling was performed as follows:

- Created a lexicon-based dictionary of different link flair text categories.
- Assigned different tags with mentions of the same category into a singular category, Thus reducing the size of unique classes by binning data into semantically similar categories.

We evaluate the problem of user intent prediction as a multi-class classification problem to determine the nature of the post. This is crucial for the automatic intent detection of a user's post which includes several trigger warnings and helps users to view content of their interests by understanding the intention of the post. Our classification problem exhibits a significant imbalance in the distribution of the target classes: for instance, there are several times more posts asking questions, advice, etc. than actually mentioning any distressing event. We use stratified sampling for 10 folds to ensure that relative class frequencies are approximately preserved in each train and validation fold with a division of 70:30 for the training and validation set for each stratified sample comprising 1296, 2127, 3481, and 730 testing samples. We construct a strong baseline by first concatenating the BERTopic embedding of a subreddit's post text with other numerical features like num of comments, the num of likes, the score of the post, and the upvote ratio of the post represented using a singular prompt. This prompt is used to generate embeddings using MiniLM-L6, The same model used to train our Topic model and we then concatenate these embeddings to generate a singular feature vector. The MiniLM-L6 model Wang et al. (2020) is fine-tuned for topic classification and maps the text data to a 384-dimensional vector state, This model is trained on a set of 1B pairs of text using a contrastive learning objective. The model is compressed using a self-attention distillation process to reduce parameter size and make model serving easier. We train xgboost and lightgbm models as our baseline to predict the intent of the post due to their performance on highly sparse input data and make these models our first choice for training on combined embeddings of post content and user metadata. The evaluation metrics utilized are Accuracy, Precision, Recall, and F1 score. We report our scores in Table 4 where the best scores are highlighted in bold for each corpus and model. The xgboost and lightgbm perform well over classifying the posts for our classification task with both models performing quite evenly over the datasets, Only the drugabuse dataset-trained models report the lowest performance metrics due to the comparatively smaller dataset size with the lowest F1 score of 0.858 whereas for other datasets its 0.90 or above. Classification over such trigger warning datasets is the first one to be done which can benefit social media companies to label such posts and enhance user experience.

5 Conclusions

In this paper, we present an initial study of evaluating and inspecting data containing trigger warnings in social network groups dealing with different clinical disorders. We present a unique dataset that contains user-level mentions of trigger warnings present in their content, exploratory data analysis measuring the sentiment across posts using statistical and lexical techniques, trends of such posts

	DATASET			
Measure	**Depression**	**Drug Abuse**	**Self Harm**	**Suicide**
u_mass	-0.562	-0.693	-0.532	-0.631
c_v	0.563	0.701	0.567	0.642
c_uci	0.547	0.701	0.511	0.621

Table 2: Results of U_{Mass}, C_V, and C_{UCI} Topic Similarity measures on the datasets.

	DATASET			
Measure	**Depression**	**Drug Abuse**	**Self Harm**	**Suicide**
Topic Diversity	0.8	0.844	0.878	0.881
IRBO	0.821	0.854	0.882	0.884

Table 3: Results of Topic Diversity and Inverse Rank Based Overlap (IRBO) measures on the datasets.

Corpus	Model	ACC	P	R	F1
selharm	BERTopic+xgboost	0.895 ± 0.0052	0.946	0.835	0.887
	BERTopic+lightgbm	**0.899 ± 0.0051**	**0.948**	**0.857**	**0.900**
suicide	BERTopic+xgboost	**0.920 ± 0.0047**	0.944	**0.890**	**0.916**
	BERTopic+lightgbm	0.910 ± 0.0045	**0.948**	0.883	0.914
depress	BERTopic+xgboost	**0.930 ± 0.0475**	**0.947**	**0.887**	**0.912**
	BERTopic+lightgbm	0.920 ± 0.0048	0.945	0.879	0.910
drugabuse	BERTopic+xgboost	0.890 ± 0.0043	**0.930**	0.796	0.857
	BERTopic+lightgbm	**0.900±0.0042**	0.928	**0.798**	**0.858**

Table 4: Classification performance on the test set for all four datasets reported in accuracy (ACC), precision (P), recall (R), and F1 score.

online, and keyword/keyphrase analysis to discover words used in relation to events accentuating the presence of trigger warnings. We further evaluate topic modelling metrics to generalize the BERTopic model's topic generation ability over the different datasets and measure their quality. In the end, we evaluate the four labelled corpora in a text classification setting using the document's content and other metadata information and build classification models to detect trigger warnings at the document level.

6 Future Work

Our next goals are to study the same phenomenon on other social networking sites such as Twitter and the expansion of this initial study into a wider domain by covering multiple languages by employing multilingual transformer models. We plan to incorporate additional modalities including audio-visual data to be used because different modalities convey relevant psychological and social aspects of a social media user. We aim to include a demographic-based analysis using choropleth maps to represent a fine-grained analysis of trigger warning tags across the world and finally use manual labelling and other prompt-based techniques to create pseudo labels based on a list of seed words of posts and comments into a specific type of trigger warnings context and its stance.

7 Acknowledgements

We would like to convey our gratitude to Dr Divya Dabas Chaudhary, Dr Ian Gorton and Dr Bijender Kumar for their advice and feedback. We would also like to thank the anonymous reviewers for their constructive reflections on the paper.

References

Christine Ballestrini. 2022. University of Connecticut Office of the Provost | Trigger and Content Warning Guidance.

Benjamin W. Bellet, Payton J. Jones, and Richard J. McNally. 2018. Trigger warning: Empirical evidence ahead. *Journal of Behavior Therapy and Experimental Psychiatry*, 61:134–141.

Victoria M. E. Bridgland, Deanne M. Green, Jacinta M. Oulton, and Melanie K. T. Takarangi. 2019. Expecting the worst: Investigating the effects of trigger warnings on reactions to ambiguously themed photos. *Journal of Experimental Psychology: Applied*, 25(4):602–617.

Ashleigh Charles, Laurie Hare-Duke, Hannah Nudds, Donna Franklin, Joy Llewellyn-Beardsley, Stefan Rennick-Egglestone, Onni Gust, Fiona Ng, Elizabeth Evans, Emily Knox, Ellen Townsend, Caroline Yeo, and Mike Slade. 2022. Typology of content warnings and trigger warnings: Systematic review. *PLOS ONE*, 17(5):e0266722.

Adji B. Dieng, Francisco J. R. Ruiz, and David M. Blei. 2020. Topic modeling in embedding spaces. *Transactions of the Association for Computational Linguistics*, 8:439–453.

Akash Gautam, Puneet Mathur, Rakesh Gosangi, Debanjan Mahata, Ramit Sawhney, and Rajiv Ratn Shah. 2020. #MeTooMA: Multi-Aspect Annotations of Tweets Related to the MeToo Movement. *Proceedings of the International AAAI Conference on Web and Social Media*, 14:209–216.

Muriël de Groot, Mohammad Aliannejadi, and Marcel R. Haas. 2022. Experiments on Generalizability of BERTopic on Multi-Domain Short Text.

Maarten Grootendorst. 2020. Keybert: Minimal keyword extraction with bert.

Maarten Grootendorst. 2022. BERTopic: Neural topic modeling with a class-based TF-IDF procedure. ArXiv:2203.05794 [cs].

Payton J. Jones, Benjamin W. Bellet, and Richard J. McNally. 2020. Helping or Harming? The Effect of Trigger Warnings on Individuals With Trauma Histories. *Clinical Psychological Science*, 8(5):905–917.

Bayode Ogunleye, Tonderai Maswera, Laurence Hirsch, Jotham Gaudoin, and Teresa Brunsdon. 2023. Comparison of Topic Modelling Approaches in the Banking Context. *Applied Sciences*, 13(2):797.

Michael Röder, Andreas Both, and Alexander Hinneburg. 2015. Exploring the Space of Topic Coherence Measures. In *Proceedings of the Eighth ACM International Conference on Web Search and Data Mining*, pages 399–408, Shanghai China. ACM.

Keith Stevens, Philip Kegelmeyer, David Andrzejewski, and David Buttler. 2012. Exploring Topic Coherence over Many Models and Many Topics. In *Proceedings of the 2012 Joint Conference on Empirical Methods in Natural Language Processing and Computational Natural Language Learning*, pages 952–961, Jeju Island, Korea. Association for Computational Linguistics.

Suhavi, Asmit Kumar Singh, Udit Arora, Somyadeep Shrivastava, Aryaveer Singh, Rajiv Ratn Shah, and Ponnurangam Kumaraguru. 2022. Twitter-STMHD: An Extensive User-Level Database of Multiple Mental Health Disorders. *Proceedings of the International AAAI Conference on Web and Social Media*, 16:1182–1191.

Luchen Tan and Clarke L. A. Clarke. 2014. A Family of Rank Similarity Measures based on Maximized Effectiveness Difference.

Silvia Terragni, Elisabetta Fersini, Bruno Giovanni Galuzzi, Pietro Tropeano, and Antonio Candelieri. 2021a. OCTIS: Comparing and Optimizing Topic models is Simple! In *Proceedings of the 16th Conference of the European Chapter of the Association for Computational Linguistics: System Demonstrations*, pages 263–270, Online. Association for Computational Linguistics.

Silvia Terragni, Elisabetta Fersini, and Enza Messina. 2021b. Word embedding-based topic similarity measures. In *Natural Language Processing and Information Systems: 26th International Conference on Applications of Natural Language to Information Systems, NLDB 2021, Saarbrücken, Germany, June 23–25, 2021, Proceedings*, page 33–45, Berlin, Heidelberg. Springer-Verlag.

Wenhui Wang, Hangbo Bao, Shaohan Huang, Li Dong, and Furu Wei. 2020. MiniLMv2: Multi-Head Self-Attention Relation Distillation for Compressing Pretrained Transformers.

William Webber, Alistair Moffat, and Justin Zobel. 2010. A similarity measure for indefinite rankings. *ACM Transactions on Information Systems*, 28(4):1–38.

Magdalena Wolska, Christopher Schröder, Ole Borchardt, Benno Stein, and Martin Potthast. 2022. Trigger Warnings: Bootstrapping a Violence Detector for FanFiction.

8 Appendix

This section includes examples of the highest similarity from our collected datasets for the keyphrases detected which supports our speculations about the top 5 detected words for each keyword.

Selfharm: example of the keyword "fun" is "tw child abuse cutting I self-harm for two reasons the first is to help regulate emotions and to cope with things when I'm panicking very stressed and need to calm down quickly I often resort to self-harm I generally do a good job coping with this aspect of self-harm because I have years of healthy coping methods behind me resources like subreddits and friends who can help support me the only time I really slip up with it is if I'm restricted by time in some way the second reason enjoying the scarring it creates is a lot harder to deal with when I used to cut so far I've been able to resist going back to it mostly the scarring was something I liked about it I found the scars I had deeply important to me they were representative of an internal struggle".

Suicide: example of the keyword "game" is "trigger warning for mentions of suicide and sexual assault possible spoilers for cyberpunk number however im going to keep details vague im posting this here instead of on the cyberpunk subreddit because this has less to do with the game and more to do with my reaction to it this is really messy and cobbled together."

Depression: example of the keyword "ptsd" is "I am tired of fighting. My depression, anxiety, PTSD, and being jobless are destroying me."

Drugabuse: example of the keyword "relapse" is "I struggle deeply with anxiety and depression, and the need to relieve my pent-up anger and emotions led me to self-harm several times because I didn't want to relapse on smoking. But I can't decide what's better or worse for me at this point. Would it be so bad if I were to smoke again? I know I previously had issues of self-control, but I really don't know what else to do as I'm doing my very best to make all the positive changes in my life and I still feel horrid."

Evaluating Hallucinations in Large Language Models for Bulgarian Language

Melania Berbatova
Sofia University 'St. Kliment Ohridski'
msberbatova@fmi.uni-sofia.bg

Yoan Salambashev
Sofia University 'St. Kliment Ohridski'
jsalambash@uni-sofia.bg

Abstract

In this short paper, we introduce the task of evaluating the hallucination of large language models for the Bulgarian language. We first give definitions of what is a hallucination in large language models and what evaluation methods for measuring hallucinations exist. Next, we give an overview of the multilingual evaluation of the latest large language models, focusing on the evaluation of the performance in Bulgarian on tasks, related to hallucination. We then present a method to evaluate the level of hallucination in a given language with no reference data, and provide some initial experiments with this method in Bulgarian. Finally, we provide directions for future research on the topic.

1 Introduction

Hallucination in large language models (LLMs) refers to the generation of non-factual statements or information that cannot be verified from the source. The latest generative language models, such as Llama, GPT-4 and other GPT-based models, are known to suffer from hallucination problems. The lack of trustworthiness of the generated outputs of LLMs is one of the main factors that stop their employment in sectors like education and healthcare, where there are high standards for factual accuracy. While numerous annotated evaluation datasets and benchmarks for evaluating the level of hallucinations exist for the English language, it is not the same for most human languages. Evaluation of hallucination in lower-resource languages[1], such as Bulgarian, is still an open research problem.

Due to the lack of annotated data on hallucinations in Bulgarian, we chose to work with a Zero-resource evaluation method called *SelfCheckGPT* (Hardalov et al., 2020), which offers an approximate estimation of the amount of hallucinations in the text. We experimented with data from Bulgarian matriculation exams, part of the EXAMS dataset (Hardalov et al., 2020), which we processed to derive prompts for text generation on different school subjects.

[1]We use the term "lower-resource language" instead of "low-resource", as Bulgarian is sometimes referred as "low-resource" and other times as "medium-resource", depending on the definitions different authors use.

2 Definitions

2.0.1 What is a Hallucination?

Hallucination in LLMs is still an open research problem and there is not a universal definition of the term. According to Ji et al. (2023), there exist two categories of hallucination: intrinsic and extrinsic. *Intrinsic hallucinations* refer to the model's generated text that contradicts the source or input. Cases where intrinsic hallucinations occur are summarization, machine translation and other tasks in which and input text is given. *Extrinsic hallucinations* refer to the model's generations that cannot be verified from the source/input content (or in other words, output that can neither be supported nor contradicted by the source). Extrinsic hallucinations can occur in all text generation tasks. (Bang et al., 2023)

Other authors, such as Preetham, add other types of hallucinations, like *nonsensical statements*, where the model generates a response that doesn't make sense or is unrelated to the context, and *improbable scenarios*, where the model generates a response that describes an implausible or highly unlikely event. Hallucination in large language models can also be related to the model's inability to produce factual and commonsense knowledge (F. Petroni and Riedel, 2019) or low degree of truthfulness, the measure of whether a language model is truthful in generating answers to questions (Lin et al., 2022).

2.1 Evaluation Methods

We group the observed hallucination methods into three main groups: fact-checking evaluation, hu-

Proceedings of the Student Research Workshop associated with RANLP-2023, pages 55–63, Varna, Bulgaria, Sep 4–6, 2023.
https://doi.org/10.26615/issn.2603-2821.2023_006

man evaluation, and counterfactual evaluation, proposed by (Preetham, 2023).

1. *Fact-checking evaluation* (F. Petroni and Riedel, 2019; Kassner et al., 2021; Jifan Yu, 2023) involves comparing the generated outputs of a model with a knowledge base or trusted sources to ensure that the facts presented in the generated text are accurate and supported by evidence.

2. *Human evaluation* (Lin et al., 2022; Li et al., 2023; Manakul et al., 2023) involves employing human evaluators to assess the relevance and truthfulness of the generated outputs. This evaluation metric leverages human judgment to provide insights into the subjective aspects of generated outputs.

3. *Contrastive Evaluation* (Manakul et al., 2023) involves presenting the model with a set of alternative completions or responses, where some options may include hallucinated information. This metric evaluates the model's ability to select the correct or most plausible output among the alternatives.

3 Related Work

3.1 Multilingual Evaluation

There are numerous publications on the performance of large language models in multilingual settings, both provided by the researchers developing large multilingual language models, or independent research groups. In this section, we would focus on the multilingual evaluation of the latest large generative language models, relevant to the Bulgarian language. Previous multilingual large language models, such as mBERT (Devlin et al., 2018), mBART (Liu et al., 2020) and mT5 (Xue et al., 2020) would stay outside the scope of the current research.

One of the first attempts towards a multilingual GPT-based model is XGLM (Lin et al., 2021), based on the GPT-3 architecture but trained on more than 100 languages, including Bulgarian. Lin et al. evaluated XGLM on the XNLI dataset (Conneau et al., 2018) for natural language inference and found that for the Bulgarian language, multilingual training significantly improves the results compared to monolingual training in GPT-3, but still lags behind the results of the combination of monolingual training and machine translation. Another interesting finding shared by XGLM's authors is that while most cross-lingual few-shot settings significantly improve over the 0-shot setting for the target language, Bulgarian is an exception, as it does not benefit from Russian, despite being in the same language family.

mGPT (Shliazhko et al., 2022) is another multilingual model, based on the GPT architecture. mGPT is trained on 61 languages from 25 language families and aimed at improving language understanding for the official and minor languages in Russia and former USSR countries. Authors also provide an interactive API of the model via the Hugging Face platform[2]. The model is evaluated on two tasks – language perplexity and knowledge probing. For the tasks of knowledge probing, which is a form of fact-checking evaluation of the ability of the language models to produce factual knowledge, they use the mLAMA probe (Kassner et al., 2021), which extends the original LAMA probe (F. Petroni and Riedel, 2019) to the multilingual setting. On this task, the performance of Bulgarian is lower than the average, meaning that the model fails at generating factual text in Bulgarian. This result aligns with our observations that the model often hallucinates, producing extrinsic hallucinations and nonsensical statements, when prompted in Bulgarian language, as shown in Table 1.

Recently, Ahuja et al. (2023) and Bang et al. (2023) perform multilingual analysis on the latest large language models, and while both works conduct a massive study on different languages, evaluation for the Bulgarian language is not present in either of them. However, they provide some valuable insights for lower-resource and non-Latin languages. Bang et al. state that despite ChatGPT's strong performance in many high-resource and medium-resource languages, the model still has problems in translating and generating text in languages that do not use the Latin script, even though these languages are considered high-resource. Moreover, Ahuja et al. suggests that one of the factors that lead to a decrease in performance in non-Latin languages is the fact that LLMs by default use a tokenizer build for the English language, which leads to incorrect tokenization of words in other languages. We found evidence of both claims in our experiments with ChatGPT, as the model sometimes responds in Russian, while prompted

[2] `https://huggingface.co/ai-forever/mGPT`

Extrinsic Hallucination	Nonsensical Statement
Столицата на България е най-големият град в Европа, а в него живеят над 1.5 милиона души.	Българите са най-бедни в Европа, но са най-бедни в света.

Table 1: Examples of mGPT text generation for Bulgarian language. Text in black is the prompt, and text in blue – the model generated text. English translations are shown in Table 6.

in Bulgarian, and sometimes generates text with words that are non-existent in Bulgarian, but resemble a truncated version of existing words. Finally, the authors of MEGA (Ahuja et al., 2023) also state that comprehensive assessment of LLMs for non-English languages is very challenging due to the scarcity of datasets available, which also motivated us to search for alternative approaches for the evaluation of hallucinations.

3.2 Zero-Resource Evaluation

When no reference data is present, the level of hallucination of generative models can be estimated in a zero-resource manner. This method is especially useful for lower-resource languages, for which annotated datasets and other publically available language resources are scarce. Manakul et al. (2023) propose the SelfCheckGPT method, which is a simple sampling-based approach that can predict whether responses generated by large language models are hallucinated or factual.

The underlying idea behind SelfCheckGPT is that when a large language model has a deep understanding of a specific concept, the responses it generates will tend to be similar and consistently contain factual information. Conversely, when the model generates hallucinated facts, the sampled responses are likely to diverge and may even contradict one another. By obtaining multiple responses through stochastic sampling from the LLM, it becomes possible to assess the level of information consistency among these responses. This approach enables the identification of factual statements versus those that are likely to be hallucinated, without relying on an external knowledge base.

4 Experiments

4.1 Experimental Setup

We decided to test the models in a black-box, zero-resource manner with the *SelfCheckGPT* framework, proposed by Manakul et al. (2023). The method proposes several evaluation scores, of which we chose Unigram and BERTScore, as they were most suitable for our experimental setup.

In order to create model-generated passages, suitable for black-box, zero-resource evaluation of hallucination, we use the EXAMS dataset (Hardalov et al., 2020), part of the bgGLUE (Hardalov et al., 2023) benchmark. It contains multiple choice questions from the Bulgarian marticulation exam in 6 subjects: Biology, Philosophy, Geography, History, Physics, and Chemistry.

In order to prepare the LLM prompts, we performed the following 3 steps:

1. Filter the dataset to preserve only the Bulgarian data.

2. Remove the irrelevant and non-informative items with no context/value in the actual question like 'Which statement is true for endocytosis?'. This way, our prompts are the open-ended questions (not having '?' in last/penultimate position).

3. Add a navigating prefix to the prompt for each question, "Напиши абзац, започващ с 'Q' translated as "Write a paragraph, starting with 'Q'", where Q is the question.

Input (question): Кондензатор със заряд q = 0,2 C и напрежение U = 4 V, има капацитет C равен на:

Output (prompt): Напиши абзац, започващ с 'Кондензатор със заряд q = 0,2 C и напрежение U = 4 V, има капацитет C равен на:'

As a result, we ended up with a total of 566 prompt questions. They are nearly equally distributed subject-wise: 130 in Biology, 136 in Philosophy, 75 in Geography, 87 in History, 70 in Physics and 68 in Chemistry. We ran 5 iterations of each prompt – the first one was used to generate the main passage for the evaluation, and the rest for the sampled passages.

4.2 Models

We chose to use the following LLMs:

- *text-davinci-003* by OpenAI
- *gpt-3.5-turbo-0613* (the model behind ChatGPT) by OpenAI (Brown et al., 2020)

Our decision to choose these models was based on the fact that they are two of the biggest (in terms of parameters) state-of-the-art large language models which are trained on Bulgarian language.

All experiments were run on both the OpenAI DaVinci and GPT-3.5 Turbo models. We generated the prompt responses using the OpenAI Completions API (model: text-davinci-003) and the Chat Completions API (model: gpt-3.5-turbo-0613) with a token limit of 300.

4.3 Evaluation

We evaluated for the factuality of the generated passages using (i) the BERTScore, (ii) average unigram, and (iii) maximum unigram scores, described in Manakul et al. (2023).

SelfCheckGPT with BERTScore finds the averages BERTScore of a sentence with the most similar sentence of each drawn sample. This method lies on the assumption that if the information in a sentence appears in many drawn samples, it is very likely that the information is factual, whereas if the statement appears in no other sample, it is more likely to be a hallucination. At the other hand, the unigram-based scores aim at approximating the original LLM's. The assumption of this method is that given the sample responses, one could train a new language model, which token probabilities would approximate the ones from the original LLM. [3]

BERTScore scores are in the interval [0.0, 1.0], and higher value estimates a higher chance of hallucination. Unigram scores are in the interval [0.0, +inf) and again a high value means a higher chance of hallucination.

We compute the BERTScore for each subject individually by calculating the average value of the relevant scores for each passage and then calculating the average of all those passage scores. Unigram scores are calculated by taking the average of all document-level scores per subject.

As the unigram scores diverge to infinity for some passages, we were forced to replace those values before the computation of the overall average score per subject. We decided that the most reasonable value substitute would be the maximum among the remaining values for each log probability score, respectively. The final evaluation results are shown in Table 2.

4.4 Results

In our evaluation of hallucination tendencies in LLMs in Bulgarian language, we examined two models: *text-davinci-003* and *gpt-3.5-turbo-0613*. Considering all the metrics we evaluated, the second model tends to hallucinate more. Philosophy has the highest evaluation score for most of the metrics, as the Philosophy questions were relatively broad (such as "Философията е..."(*"Philosophy is... "*)) and therefore resulted in more varying responses, compared to the ones for the rest of the subjects. We still lack a similar assessment of hallucinations in other languages, but the listed unigram scores are significantly higher than the ones shown in the SelfCheckGPT repository[4]. The referred BERTScores, however, are higher, as the authors decided to demonstrate the method with sentences that were quite different from each other. The average scores are summarized in Table 3.

We observe one specific type of hallucination that often occurs in the responses that we can conditionally call *"foreign language hallucination"*, which cover different kinds of language-specific errors, such as spelling errors, wrong word order, and misused words and phrases. What separate them from other nonsensical statements is that they make sense once the text is translated via a machine translation tool, such as Google Translate. An example of such case is the word "резониране" (rezonirane, "resonance"), used in the meaning of "reasoning" in the second example in Table 4. Even though "резониране" sounds similar to the English "reasoning", but does not exist in Bulgarian language with this meaning. Explanations of different kinds of *"foreign language hallucinations"* can be seen in Table 5.

One additional observation we made while conducting our experiments is that the sentence splitting function used in the SelfCheckGPT code does not perform well in Bulgarian language and therefore degrades the reliability of the assessment. In the future, we plan to change it to a sentence splitter

[3]Formulas and more detailed explanations can be found in the original paper.

[4]`https://github.com/potsawee/selfcheckgpt`

	text-davinci-003			gpt-3.5-turbo-0613		
Subject	**Avg-uni**	**Max-uni**	**BERTScore**	**Avg-uni**	**Max-uni**	**BERTScore**
Biology	4.2436	5.1093	0.0831	4.6059	5.9698	0.4496
Philosophy	**4.2849**	**5.1740**	0.0850	**4.6151**	**6.0434**	**0.5040**
Geography	4.1471	5.0612	**0.0906**	4.6097	5.9266	0.4635
History	4.2592	5.0796	0.0864	4.6096	5.8535	0.4780
Physics	4.0798	5.0322	0.0776	4.5365	5.8853	0.4765
Chemistry	4.1946	5.0716	0.0778	4.5009	5.8124	0.4598
Average	4.2170	5.0999	0.0837	4.5988	5.9431	0.4734

Table 2: Average evaluation scores for each subject with *text-davinci-003* and *gpt-3.5-turbo-0613*. Avg-uni means the Average unigram score and Max-uni – Maximum unigram score.

Avg-uni	Max-uni	BERTScore
3.2186	4.0254	0.2627

Table 3: Average evaluation scores from the experiments, provided in the SelfCheckGPT repository.

developed specifically for the Bulgarian language, proposed by Berbatova and Ivanov (2023).

5 Conclusion

In this short paper, we demonstrate our work in progress on the task of evaluating the level of hallucination of large language models in Bulgarian language. We give definitions of different types of hallucinations and methods for evaluation, make an overview of the related work, and provide some initial experiments.

Our research is aimed towards more equally spread employment of the latest technology across different languages. Researchers working on other lower-resource languages can use our work as a source of ideas generation and inspiration.

6 Future Work

In the future, we would like to extend our research in the following directions:

1. Further research on methods and datasets for hallucination evaluation. We would like to do a comprehensive overview of the latest benchmarks for hallucination evaluation, such as TruthfulQA (Lin et al., 2022), HaluEval (Li et al., 2023), Kola (Jifan Yu, 2023) others, and analyze if a similar benchmark can be developed for Bulgarian.

2. Extend our experiments, so we have a more objective estimation on the level of hallucination of different LLMs in Bulgarian language. One of the first experiments that we want to conduct is to evaluate the latest LLMs, such as GPT-3.5 and Llama, on the knowledge probing task with the Bulgarian subset of the mLAMA dataset. We also plan to make use of the available answers in the EXAMS dataset for fact-checking evaluation. Additionally, we would like to further research if we can use other datasets from the bgGLUE benchmark (Hardalov et al., 2023) for our task.

3. Research and employ methods for prompt engineering that improve the multilingual performance of generative models, such as *cross-lingual-thought prompting*, proposed by Huang et al. (2023).

4. Finally, we would like to make our work more comprehensive by providing examples for different kinds of hallucination that occur in LLM-generated responses in Bulgarian.

Acknowledgments

This study is financed by the European Union-NextGenerationEU, through the National Recovery and Resilience Plan of the Republic of Bulgaria, project № BG-RRP-2.004-0008-C01

We would like also to thank our supervisor Dr. Trifon Trifonov for his kind support and suggestions regarding the paper topic.

References

Kabir Ahuja, Rishav Hada, Millicent Ochieng, Prachi Jain, Harshita Diddee, Samuel Maina, Tanuja Ganu, Sameer Segal, Maxamed Axmed, Kalika Bali, et al. 2023. Mega: Multilingual evaluation of generative ai. *arXiv preprint arXiv:2303.12528*.

Model	Response
text-davinci-003	Логиката изучава животните и начините по които се придвижват и решават проблеми. Тя извлича дразнителни и аналитични науки, за да помогне хората да се интелектуално подобрят.Тя може да бъде приложена в различни дисциплини и сфери, като право, економика , наука, философия и много
gpt-3.5-turbo-0613	Логиката изучава законите на рационалното мислене и следва стриктни правила, които уреждат процеса на извод и аргументация. Тя се занимава с анализа на размислите и тяхната структура, разкривайки начините, по които принципите на правилното резониране водят до верни изводи от зададени предпоставки.

Table 4: Example of responses different models give when prompted "Напиши абзац, започващ с 'Логиката изучава':" *("Write a paragraph beginning with 'Logic studies:'")*. Non-factual and nonsensical statements are marked in red. Misused words and phrases, specific for the Bulgarian language, are marked in blue. Translations are provided in Table 7.

Example	Correct form	Automatic translation	Literal translation	Error type
економика	икономика	economics	-	spelling
да се интелектуално подобрят	да се развият интелектуално	to improve intellectually	-	word order and terminology
анализ на размислите	анализ на сълденията	analysis of thoughts	analysis of reflections	terminology
правилно резониране	правилно разсъждение	correct reasoning	correct resonance	terminology

Table 5: Examples of *"foreign language hallucinations"*.Automatic translations were done via Goodle Translate and DeepL translate

Yejin Bang, Samuel Cahyawijaya, Nayeon Lee, Wenliang Dai, Dan Su, Bryan Wilie, Holy Lovenia, Ziwei Ji, Tiezheng Yu, Willy Chung, et al. 2023. A multitask, multilingual, multimodal evaluation of chatgpt on reasoning, hallucination, and interactivity. *arXiv preprint arXiv:2302.04023*.

Melania Berbatova and Filip Ivanov. 2023. An improved bulgarian natural language processing pipeline.

Tom B. Brown, Benjamin Mann, Nick Ryder, Melanie Subbiah, Jared Kaplan, Prafulla Dhariwal, Arvind Neelakantan, Pranav Shyam, Girish Sastry, Amanda Askell, Sandhini Agarwal, Ariel Herbert-Voss, Gretchen Krueger, Tom Henighan, Rewon Child, Aditya Ramesh, Daniel M. Ziegler, Jeffrey Wu, Clemens Winter, Christopher Hesse, Mark Chen, Eric Sigler, Mateusz Litwin, Scott Gray, Benjamin Chess, Jack Clark, Christopher Berner, Sam McCandlish, Alec Radford, Ilya Sutskever, and Dario Amodei. 2020. Language models are few-shot learners.

Alexis Conneau, Ruty Rinott, Guillaume Lample, Adina Williams, Samuel R. Bowman, Holger Schwenk, and Veselin Stoyanov. 2018. Xnli: Evaluating cross-lingual sentence representations. In *Proceedings of the 2018 Conference on Empirical Methods in Natural Language Processing*. Association for Computational Linguistics.

Jacob Devlin, Ming-Wei Chang, Kenton Lee, and Kristina Toutanova. 2018. Bert: Pre-training of deep bidirectional transformers for language understanding. *arXiv preprint arXiv:1810.04805*.

A. H. Miller P. Lewis A. Bakhtin Y. Wu F. Petroni, T. Rocktäschel and S. Riedel. 2019. Language models as knowledge bases? In *In: Proceedings of the 2019 Conference on Empirical Methods in Natural Language Processing (EMNLP), 2019*.

Momchil Hardalov, Pepa Atanasova, Todor Mihaylov, Galia Angelova, Kiril Simov, Petya Osenova, Ves Stoyanov, Ivan Koychev, Preslav Nakov, and Dragomir Radev. 2023. bgglue: A bulgarian general language understanding evaluation benchmark. *arXiv preprint arXiv:2306.02349*.

Momchil Hardalov, Todor Mihaylov, Dimitrina Zlatkova, Yoan Dinkov, Ivan Koychev, and Preslav Nakov. 2020. EXAMS: A multi-subject high school examinations dataset for cross-lingual and multilingual question answering. In *Proceedings of the 2020 Conference on Empirical Methods in Natural Language Processing*, EMNLP '20, pages 5427–5444, Online. Association for Computational Linguistics.

Haoyang Huang, Tianyi Tang, Dongdong Zhang, Wayne Xin Zhao, Ting Song, Yan Xia, and Furu Wei. 2023. Not all languages are created equal in llms: Improving multilingual capability by cross-lingual-thought prompting. *arXiv preprint arXiv:2305.07004*.

Ziwei Ji, Nayeon Lee, Rita Frieske, Tiezheng Yu, Dan Su, Yan Xu, Etsuko Ishii, Ye Jin Bang, Andrea Madotto, and Pascale Fung. 2023. Survey of hallucination in natural language generation. *ACM Computing Surveys*, 55(12):1–38.

Shangqing Tu Shulin Cao Daniel Zhang-Li Xin Lv Hao Peng Zijun Yao Xiaohan Zhang Hanming Li Chunyang Li Zheyuan Zhang Yushi Bai Yantao Liu Amy Xin Nianyi Lin Kaifeng Yun Linlu Gong Jianhui Chen Zhili Wu Yunjia Qi Weikai Li Yong Guan Kaisheng Zeng Ji Qi Hailong Jin Jinxin Liu Yu Gu Yuan Yao Ning Ding Lei Hou Zhiyuan Liu Bin Xu Jie Tang Juanzi Li Jifan Yu, Xiaozhi Wang. 2023. Kola: Carefully benchmarking world knowledge of large language models.

Nora Kassner, Philipp Dufter, and Hinrich Schütze. 2021. Multilingual LAMA: Investigating knowledge in multilingual pretrained language models. In *to appear in Proceedings of the 16th Conference of the European Chapter of the Association for Computational Linguistics*, Online. Association for Computational Linguistics.

Junyi Li, Xiaoxue Cheng, Wayne Xin Zhao, Jian-Yun Nie, and Ji-Rong Wen. 2023. Halueval: A large-scale hallucination evaluation benchmark for large language models.

Stephanie Lin, Jacob Hilton, and Owain Evans. 2022. TruthfulQA: Measuring how models mimic human falsehoods. In *Proceedings of the 60th Annual Meeting of the Association for Computational Linguistics (Volume 1: Long Papers)*, pages 3214–3252, Dublin, Ireland. Association for Computational Linguistics.

Xi Victoria Lin, Todor Mihaylov, Mikel Artetxe, Tianlu Wang, Shuohui Chen, Daniel Simig, Myle Ott, Naman Goyal, Shruti Bhosale, Jingfei Du, et al. 2021. Few-shot learning with multilingual language models. *arXiv preprint arXiv:2112.10668*.

Yinhan Liu, Jiatao Gu, Naman Goyal, Xian Li, Sergey Edunov, Marjan Ghazvininejad, Mike Lewis, and Luke Zettlemoyer. 2020. Multilingual denoising pre-training for neural machine translation. *Transactions of the Association for Computational Linguistics*, 8:726–742.

Potsawee Manakul, Adian Liusie, and Mark J. F. Gales. 2023. Selfcheckgpt: Zero-resource black-box hallucination detection for generative large language models.

Freedom Preetham. 2023. Mathematically evaluating hallucinations in llms like gpt4.

Oleh Shliazhko, Alena Fenogenova, Maria Tikhonova, Vladislav Mikhailov, Anastasia Kozlova, and Tatiana Shavrina. 2022. mgpt: Few-shot learners go multilingual. *arXiv preprint arXiv:2204.07580*.

Hugo Touvron, Thibaut Lavril, Gautier Izacard, Xavier Martinet, Marie-Anne Lachaux, Timothée Lacroix, Baptiste Rozière, Naman Goyal, Eric Hambro, Faisal Azhar, et al. 2023a. Llama: Open and efficient foundation language models. *arXiv preprint arXiv:2302.13971*.

Hugo Touvron, Louis Martin, Kevin Stone, Peter Albert, Amjad Almahairi, Yasmine Babaei, Nikolay Bashlykov, Soumya Batra, Prajjwal Bhargava, Shruti Bhosale, Dan Bikel, Lukas Blecher, Cristian Canton Ferrer, Moya Chen, Guillem Cucurull, David Esiobu, Jude Fernandes, Jeremy Fu, Wenyin Fu, Brian Fuller, Cynthia Gao, Vedanuj Goswami, Naman Goyal, Anthony Hartshorn, Saghar Hosseini, Rui Hou, Hakan Inan, Marcin Kardas, Viktor Kerkez, Madian Khabsa, Isabel Kloumann, Artem Korenev, Punit Singh Koura, Marie-Anne Lachaux, Thibaut Lavril, Jenya Lee, Diana Liskovich, Yinghai Lu, Yuning Mao, Xavier Martinet, Todor Mihaylov, Pushkar Mishra, Igor Molybog, Yixin Nie, Andrew Poulton, Jeremy Reizenstein, Rashi Rungta, Kalyan Saladi, Alan Schelten, Ruan Silva, Eric Michael Smith, Ranjan Subramanian, Xiaoqing Ellen Tan, Binh Tang, Ross Taylor, Adina Williams, Jian Xiang Kuan, Puxin Xu, Zheng Yan, Iliyan Zarov, Yuchen Zhang, Angela Fan, Melanie Kambadur, Sharan Narang, Aurelien Rodriguez, Robert Stojnic, Sergey Edunov, and Thomas Scialom. 2023b. Llama 2: Open foundation and fine-tuned chat models.

Linting Xue, Noah Constant, Adam Roberts, Mihir Kale, Rami Al-Rfou, Aditya Siddhant, Aditya Barua, and Colin Raffel. 2020. mt5: A massively multilingual pre-trained text-to-text transformer. *arXiv preprint arXiv:2010.11934*.

Appendix A Additional experiments

We aimed to run our experiments also with the large language models LLama (Touvron et al., 2023a) and LLama 2 (Touvron et al., 2023b), developed by Facebook. The company has not yet made a public application programming interface (API) available for these models, leading us to employ their minimal open-source software (OSS) version, LLaMa-7B, and its successor LLaMa-2-7B, on our local system. Our attempts to replicate the experiments encountered notable time constraints arising from hardware limitations, as the computations were performed on our local machine. Therefore, we decided to leave these experiments for our future work.

Appendix B Translations of Examples

Tranlsations of examples of model-generated text in Bulgarian are given in Table 6 and Table 7.

Extrinsic Hallucination	**Nonsensical Statement**
The capital of Bulgaria is the largest city in Europe, and over 1.5 million people live in it.	Bulgarians are the poorest in Europe, but they are the poorest in the world.

Table 6: English translations of the examples shown in Table 1.

Model	**Response**
text-davinci-003	Logic studies animals and how they move and solve problems. It derives provocative and analytical sciences to help people improve intellectually. It can be applied in various disciplines and fields, such as law, economics, science, philosophy and many
gpt-3.5-turbo-0613	Logic studies the laws of rational thinking and follows strict rules that govern the process of inference and argumentation. It deals with the analysis of thoughts and their structure, revealing the ways in which the principles of correct resonance lead to correct conclusions from given premises.

Table 7: Translated examples of Table 4.

Leveraging Probabilistic Graph Models in Nested Named Entity Recognition for Polish

Jędrzej Jamnicki
Wrocław University of Science and Technology Wrocław, Poland
jedrzej.jamnicki@pwr.edu.pl

Abstract

This paper presents ongoing work on leveraging probabilistic graph models, specifically conditional random fields and hidden Markov models, in nested named entity recognition for the Polish language. NER is a crucial task in natural language processing that involves identifying and classifying named entities in text documents. Nested NER deals with recognizing hierarchical structures of entities that overlap with one another, presenting additional challenges. The paper discusses the methodologies and approaches used in nested NER, focusing on CRF and HMM. Related works and their contributions are reviewed, and experiments using the KPWr dataset are conducted, particularly with the BiLSTM-CRF model and Word2Vec and HerBERT embeddings. The results show promise in addressing nested NER for Polish, but further research is needed to develop robust and accurate models for this complex task.

1 Introduction

Named Entity Recognition (NER) is a fundamental task in natural language processing (NLP) that involves identifying and classifying named entities, such as names of people, organizations, locations, and more, within text documents. The ability to accurately extract and categorize these entities plays a crucial role in various NLP applications, including information retrieval, question answering, text summarization, and machine translation. NER serves as the foundation for understanding the semantics and context of textual data, enabling more advanced language understanding systems.

In the realm of NER, there exists a more intricate and challenging variant known as Nested NER. While traditional NER focuses on identifying individual named entities within a sentence, Nested NER deals with the recognition of nested or hierarchical structures of entities that overlap with one another. This added complexity arises when named entities, such as organizations or locations, encompass other entities within them, such as person names or specific addresses. Nested entities refer to entities that are embedded within other entities. For instance, consider the entity „John Smith" Here entity can include two additional entities inside of it – „John" and „Smith" which can be labeled as first and last names. The goal of Nested NER is to accurately extract these overlapping entities while preserving their hierarchical relationships, allowing for a more nuanced understanding of the information contained within the text.

I will examine the methodologies and approaches employed in this task, focusing on probabilistic graph models, such as conditional random fields (Lafferty et al., 2001) and hidden Markov models (Eddy, 1996), which have proven effective in capturing the contextual dependencies and relationships between entities. These methods are further described in the sections 2 and 3.

2 Conditional Random Fields

Conditional Random Fields (CRF) are probabilistic models used for structured prediction tasks, particularly in the field of natural language processing. They are often employed in tasks such as sequence labeling, named entity recognition, part-of-speech tagging, and speech recognition.

In the context of nested entity recognition, CRF play a significant role in identifying and labeling hierarchical or nested entities within a text. Nested entity recognition involves identifying and labeling both the outer and inner entities correctly. This task is challenging because the boundaries of nested entities can overlap, making it difficult to determine the correct labeling. CRF address this challenge by considering the dependencies and correlations among neighboring words and labels in a sequence.

Proceedings of the Student Research Workshop associated with RANLP-2023, pages 64–67, Varna, Bulgaria, Sep 4–6, 2023.
https://doi.org/10.26615/issn.2603-2821.2023_007

3 Hidden Markov Models

Hidden Markov Models (HMM) are statistical models widely used in various fields, including natural language processing. They are particularly useful in sequence labeling tasks, such as nested entity recognition, where the goal is to identify and classify named entities within a text.

In the context of NER, HMM are often employed for the task of Nested Named Entity Recognition, which involves identifying named entities that are hierarchically structured and nested within each other.

The basic idea behind HMM is to model the underlying structure of a sequence of observations and their corresponding labels. In the case of NER, the observations are the words or tokens in a text, and the labels represent different named entity categories. HMM assume that the underlying labels (states) generating the observations (emissions) form a Markov chain, where the current state depends only on the previous state. One common approach is to use a layered HMM, where each layer corresponds to a level of nesting. The innermost layer represents the most specific entities, and as we move outward, the layers represent progressively broader entities.

During the training phase, the model learns the transition probabilities between different states (labels) based on the training data. It also learns the emission probabilities, which represent the likelihood of observing a particular word given a certain state. These probabilities are estimated using techniques such as the maximum likelihood estimation or the Viterbi algorithm. The Viterbi algorithm is often employed to efficiently compute the most probable label sequence.

4 Related Works

(Shen et al., 2003) leveraged the HMM and integrated various features, including simple deterministic features, morphological features, part-of-speech (POS) features, and semantic trigger features, to recognize flat entities. They presented a simple algorithm to solve the abbreviation problem and a rule-based method to deal with the cascaded phenomena.

(Alex et al., 2007) introduced three models based on CRF which can reduce the nested NER problem into one or more sequence tagging problems. They separately built inside-out and outside-in layered CRF for addressing nested NER, both of which can use the current guesses as to the input to the next layer. They also cascaded separate CRF of each entity category by using output from the previous CRF as features of the subsequent CRF, yielding the best performance in their work.

(Ju et al., 2018) proposed a novel neural model to identify nested entities by dynamically stacking flat NER layers. Each flat NER layer is based on a state-of-the-art (SoTA) flat NER model that captures sequential context representation – BiLSTM, that feeds the output further to the cascaded CRF layer.

(Shibuya and Hovy, 2020) proposed a method where each named entity type output from BiLSTM is being handled by multiple CRF independently. As a result, contributed to handling situations where the same mention span in assigned multiple entity types. Their method allowed them to recognize not only outermost named entities but also inner nested ones. Used decoding method iteratively recognizes entities from outermost ones to inner ones in an outside-to-inside way.

For Polish, there is a system for the NER task called PolDeepNer2 (Marcinczuk and Radom, 2021). It is based on a pre-trained language model of the Transformer type. It has the ability to detect nested NER by extending the set of possible label classes to include classes representing overlapping annotation types. The solution was trained and tested on a dataset available as part of the PolEval 2018 (Wawer and Malek, 2018) competition. A noticeable problem of such a solution is that with numerous label classes (and this is the collection we are dealing with in this work), the number of class combinations that can overlap grows very quickly. For example, in the case of the set we are analyzing, assuming that we are only analyzing one degree nesting we will get 13,285 classes, and assuming that we are analyzing possible double nesting it will already be 1,062,721.

5 Experiments

The purpose of the experiments is to identify the best model in terms of prediction accuracy for the Polish language, which is challenging due to its rich inflectional system, compound words, ambiguity, and context sensitivity. The methods will be tested on a larger set for the nested NER task, which is several times bigger than the current best-known corpora in terms of class size.

The solution presented in (Shibuya and Hovy, 2020) scored the highest F1-score in nested NER task benchmark corpora such as ACE2005 (Walker and Consortium, 2005) and GENIA (Kim et al., 2003). Therefore, it will be adopted as the first to the Polish corpus.

5.1 Corpus

Well known corpus in the domain of the Polish language is The National Corpus of Polish (Tomaszczyk et al., 2012) which was not used during the experiments due to the insufficient number of classes (14) that makes it impossible to test methods on a multi-class, fine-grained collection.

The experiment's dataset, named KPWr (Broda et al., 2012), has been divided into three sets: train, dev, and test, as displayed in table 1. This particular dataset comprises only Polish text and has been sourced from platforms such as *Wikipedia*, *Wikinews*, and information portals under a Creative Commons license. Contrary to ACE2005 (7) or GENIA (36), KPWr includes as many as 120 fine-grained classes, for example, first and last names, cities, countries, districts, postal codes, and many others. It is essential to note that the dataset's class frequency is imbalanced, making it even more challenging.

5.2 BiLSTM-CRF

The algorithm discussed in (Shibuya and Hovy, 2020) underwent testing using two embedding sources: Word2Vec (Piasecki et al., 2017) and HerBERT (Mroczkowski et al., 2021). The vector lengths of the HerBERT and Word2Vec models were 768 and 100 respectively. Moreover, the HerBERT model considers context, while Word2Vec does not.

In figure 1, you can see the curves of F1 values that have been tracked throughout the training epochs. Surprisingly, a smaller and non-contextual embedding model does perform better in this comparison with a value of F1 at *67.94%* on the test set and recall, precision at values of 77.91%, 60.23% respectively. HerBERT, on the other hand, performed as follows: F1 - *61.11%*, recall - 48.56%, and precision - 82.42%. Nonetheless, results should be repeated a few times and confirmed with statistical tests.

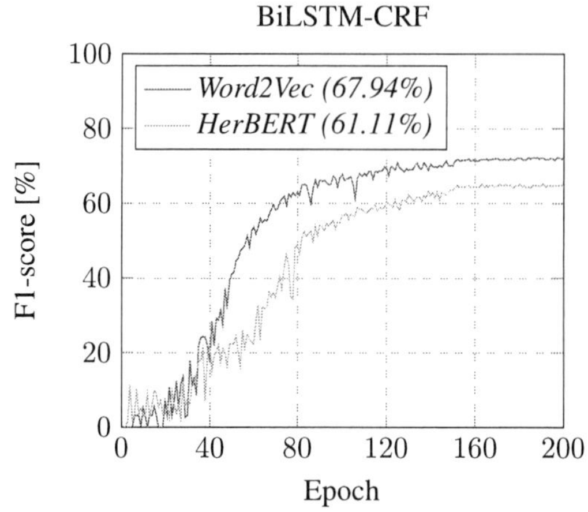

Figure 1: Comparison of *embedding methods (best on test set)* – F1-score over epochs during the training of BiLSTM-CRF

6 Future Work

Future work will involve training and evaluation of other methodologies for nested NER from the literature. The analysis of the experimental results will focus on the prediction accuracy of nested entities given the degree of nesting. Core benchmark corpora do not include as many classes as KPWr, therefore, analyzing the algorithms used on the NNE (Ringland et al., 2019) set, which is closer to the KPWr set given the number of classes (112) and nesting entities, may prove valuable results.

Due to the number of classes in the set for the Polish language, it would also be necessary to take into account the computational complexity of the solutions, which affects the processing time of the data, which should be taken into account in the case of mass text processing services.

The interesting direction will be the validation of prediction accuracy on samples strongly dependent on the given context. To achieve this, it would be necessary to collect such partly by rules based on the number of assigned classes for a particular token in the collection but it would also be worthwhile to select such samples manually by a linguist.

7 Conclusions

In this paper, I have focused on exploring the task of nested named entity recognition (NER) for the Polish language and investigated the use of probabilistic graph models, specifically conditional random fields (CRF) and hidden Markov models (HMM), to address this challenging problem.

I reviewed a few related works that have employed CRF and HMM for nested NER. These studies proposed various models and techniques, such as incorporating semantic features, cascading CRF layers, and leveraging neural models, to improve nested NER performance.

	Train	(%)	Dev	(%)	Test	(%)
# documents	1,424	(87)	100	(6)	113	(7)
# sentences	24,815	(86)	2,001	(7)	2,000	(7)
# tokens	392,351	(87)	27,318	(6)	30,316	(7)
# entities	28,882	(86)	2,498	(7)	2,219	(7)
- nested	8,049	(28)	772	(31)	526	(24)

Table 1: Statistics of the dataset used in the experiments – *KPWr*

To evaluate the effectiveness of these approaches for the Polish language, I conducted experiments using the KPWr dataset focusing on the BiLSTM-CRF model and comparing the performance of Word2Vec and HerBERT embeddings.

Overall, leveraging probabilistic graph models, such as CRF and HMM, shows promise for addressing nested NER in the Polish language. Further research and experimentation are needed to develop robust and accurate models for this complex task, which has important implications for various NLP applications.

References

Beatrice Alex, Barry Haddow, and Claire Grover. 2007. Recognising nested named entities in biomedical text. In *Biological, translational, and clinical language processing*, pages 65–72.

Bartosz Broda, Michał Marcińczuk, Marek Maziarz, Adam Radziszewski, and Adam Wardyński. 2012. KPWr: Towards a free corpus of Polish. In *Proceedings of the Eighth International Conference on Language Resources and Evaluation (LREC'12)*, pages 3218–3222, Istanbul, Turkey. European Language Resources Association (ELRA).

Sean R Eddy. 1996. Hidden markov models. *Current opinion in structural biology*, 6(3):361–365.

Meizhi Ju, Makoto Miwa, and Sophia Ananiadou. 2018. A neural layered model for nested named entity recognition. In *Proceedings of the 2018 Conference of the North American Chapter of the Association for Computational Linguistics: Human Language Technologies, Volume 1 (Long Papers)*, pages 1446–1459.

J.-D. Kim, T. Ohta, Y. Tateisi, and J. Tsujii. 2003. GENIA corpus—a semantically annotated corpus for bio-textmining. *Bioinformatics*, 19(suppl$_1$) : $i180 - -i182$.

John Lafferty, Andrew McCallum, and Fernando CN Pereira. 2001. Conditional random fields: Probabilistic models for segmenting and labeling sequence data.

Michal Marcinczuk and Jarema Radom. 2021. A single-run recognition of nested named entities with transformers. In *International Conference on Knowledge-Based Intelligent Information & Engineering Systems*.

Robert Mroczkowski, Piotr Rybak, Alina Wr 'oblewska, and Ireneusz Gawlik. 2021. HerBERT: Efficiently pretrained transformer-based language model for Polish. In *Proceedings of the 8th Workshop on Balto-Slavic Natural Language Processing*, pages 1–10, Kiyv, Ukraine. Association for Computational Linguistics.

Maciej Piasecki, Arkadiusz Janz, Dominik Kaszewski, and Gabriela Czachor. 2017. Word embeddings for polish. CLARIN-PL digital repository.

Nicky Ringland, Xiang Dai, Ben Hachey, Sarvnaz Karimi, Cecile Paris, and James R Curran. 2019. Nne: A dataset for nested named entity recognition in english newswire. *arXiv preprint arXiv:1906.01359*.

Dan Shen, Jie Zhang, Guodong Zhou, Jian Su, and Chew Lim Tan. 2003. Effective adaptation of hidden markov model-based named entity recognizer for biomedical domain. In *Proceedings of the ACL 2003 workshop on Natural language processing in biomedicine*, pages 49–56.

Takashi Shibuya and Eduard Hovy. 2020. Nested named entity recognition via second-best sequence learning and decoding. *Transactions of the Association for Computational Linguistics*, 8:605–620.

Barbara Lewandowska Tomaszczyk, Mirosław Bańko, Rafał Górski, Piotr Pęzik, and Adam Przepiórkowski. 2012. Narodowy korpus języka polskiego.

C. Walker and Linguistic Data Consortium. 2005. *ACE 2005 Multilingual Training Corpus*. LDC corpora. Linguistic Data Consortium.

Aleksander Wawer and E Malek. 2018. Results of the poleval 2018 shared task 2: Named entity recognition. In *Proceedings of the PolEval 2018 Workshop*, pages 53–62.

Crowdsourcing Veridicality Annotations in Spanish: Can Speakers Actually Agree?

Teresa Martín Soeder
Saarland University / Saarbrücken, Germany
temart@lst.uni-saarland.de

Abstract

In veridicality studies, an area of research of Natural Language Inference (NLI), the factuality of different contexts is evaluated. This task, known to be a difficult one since often it is not clear what the interpretation should be Uma et al. (2021), is key for building any Natural Language Understanding (NLU) system that aims at making the right inferences. Here the results of a study that analyzes the veridicality of mood alternation and specificity in Spanish, and whose labels are based on those of Saurí and Pustejovsky (2009) are presented. It has an inter-annotator agreement of $AC_2 = 0.114$, considerably lower than that of de Marneffe et al. (2012) ($\kappa = 0.53$), a main reference to this work; and a couple of mood-related significant effects. Due to this strong lack of agreement, an analysis of what factors cause disagreement is presented together with a discussion based on the work of de Marneffe et al. (2012) and Pavlick and Kwiatkowski (2019) about the quality of the annotations gathered and whether other types of analysis like entropy distribution could better represent this corpus. The annotations collected are available at https://github.com/narhim/veridicality_spanish.

1 Introduction

Often when hearing an utterance we try to assess whether the information conveyed is likely to be truthful or not, that is, if it corresponds to actual situations in the real world (Saurí and Pustejovsky, 2009). Furthermore, as speakers or authors, we normally seek to convey what we know about the **truthfulness** or **factuality** of the events conveyed. For simplicity, here events are just considered as *anything that happens or is* like "being tall" or "having read a book".

In the realm of linguistics, several features lead us to make the correct inferences about the factuality of an event, and comprehending them is key for building any system that aims at understanding human language. For example, the presence of the negation adverb "not" in "Pedro has not done the laundry", leads us to infer that the event "Pedro has done the laundry" did not happen, unless we know something about the speaker or Pedro that makes us think otherwise. Furthermore, in "Pedro could have done the laundry" the modal verb "can" makes the event a possibility. This kind of analysis is what is called a veridicality study, more specifically, **veridicality** is an area of research within natural language inference (NLI) and theoretical linguistics that studies the truth value of a proposition or event in a specific context (Giannakidou, 2014; Giannakidou and Mari, 2015).

As to NLI, it is a branch of natural language understanding (NLU) with its main task being entailment classification, that is, as it has been done above, to classify the relationship between two sentences, a premise, and a hypothesis, by picking a label from a usually small set of labels like {*entailment, neutral, contradiction*} (Williams et al., 2017) or {*yes, unknown, not*}, depending on how the task is defined. So for example, we can classify the relationship between the premise "Pedro has not done the laundry" and the hypothesis "Pedro has done the laundry" as a contradiction or not.

Here a study of veridicality judgments in Spanish is presented. Specifically, the goal is to analyze how mood alternation, in other words, the possibility of using a verb either in indicative or subjunctive mood; and the specificity of the syntactic subject, that is, the identifiability of the referent in the discourse universe (Caudet, 1999), affect factuality judgments about an event. This goal is realized in the following research questions:

Proceedings of the Student Research Workshop associated with RANLP-2023, pages 68–77, Varna, Bulgaria, Sep 4–6, 2023.
https://doi.org/10.26615/issn.2603-2821.2023_008

RQ1.- In a complex sentence, how does the mood alternation of the embedded verb that occurs due to the negation of the main or matrix verb affect the factuality value of the embedded event?

RQ2.- How does an individual subject affect the factuality judgment of the event?

RQ3.- How does a subject that refers to a collective entity like an institution, affect the factuality judgment of the event?

To answer these questions a crowdsourcing experiment was run on Toloka (Pavlichenko et al., 2021) in which annotations from linguistically naive native Spanish speakers were gathered for a corpus specifically designed. The corpus and the annotations are publicly available and their analysis is shown here.

Next, Section 2 introduces the main concepts used here and presents the most important references to this work. Then, Section 3 explains how the corpus was designed and how the annotations were gathered. After that, Section 4 presents the statistical and linguistic analysis of the annotations gathered, Section 5 discusses the main issues seen throughout the study, and, finally, Section 6 answers the research questions and proposes some lines of future work.

2 Background

2.1 Veridicality and Factuality

Let us consider examples (1a) to (1d), where we have events that are intrinsically related. If we were to do an NLI study with these examples, we could directly study the *thruthfulness* of each of them as a single event, i.e., we could study the **factual nature** of each example towards the real world or the events in the discourse (Saurí and Pustejovsky, 2009). Another option would be to study the factual nature of the event *Anna's father has arrived* in the different contexts in which is presented: standing completely on its own (1a), or as part of a complex event (1b) to (1d). In this case, the goal would be not to understand the factuality of *Anna's father has arrived*, but rather to understand how its factuality changes when the event is embedded under an epistemic verb (1b), a verb of believe (1c), and a verb of speech (1d). The former case is a factuality study and examples of it are the XNLI corpus (Conneau et al., 2018) and the work of Pavlick and Kwiatkowski (2019). The latter is a **veridicality study**, as the study of Ross and Pavlick (2019) and the experiment presented here.

(1) a. Anna's father has arrived.

b. John knows that Anna's father has arrived.

c. John believes that Anna's father has arrived.

d. John says that Anna's father has arrived.

2.2 Lexical and Pragmatic Approach

When designing an NLI study there are two main possible approaches: lexical and pragmatic. In the first case, the aim is to model the aspects of a sentence semantics (Ross and Pavlick, 2019), and thus, its representation can be derived from the lexicon and is independent of context, which mean the omission of world knowledge. To follow this approach, annotations must be gathered from linguistic experts. Examples of corpora with this approach are the FactBank corpus Saurí and Pustejovsky (2009) in English, and the SenSem (Fernández-Montraveta and Vázquez, 2014) and TAGFACT (Fernández Montraveta et al., 2020) corpora in Spanish.

As to the pragmatic approach, which is used here, it aims at modeling a representation of the sentence that considers the communication intent for that sentence in a specific context, that is, a goal-directed representation of a sentence within the context it was created (Ross and Pavlick, 2019). To obtain such a representation one needs to consider world knowledge and embrace uncertainty (de Marneffe et al., 2012). Furthermore, to follow this approach, annotations must be gathered from linguistically naive workers. Examples of studies that follow this approach are de Marneffe et al. (2012); Conneau et al. (2018); Ross and Pavlick (2019) and Pavlick and Kwiatkowski (2019).

2.3 Mood Alternation in Spanish

In its most basic definition mood is said to be the grammaticalization of modality (Lyons, 1995; Sánchez-Jiménez, 2011), and thus it has been traditionally related to the speaker's attitude towards an utterance (Lyons, 1995; Real Academia Española, 2011). Furthermore, since the commitment of the speaker usually takes form in different degrees (Lyons, 1995), in most languages, mood takes form in different subcategories. For Spanish, nowadays most of grammarians agree on the existence of three subcategories of mood: indicative, subjunctive, and imperative. Only indicative and subjunctive are relevant for our purposes here.

One of the ways in which the different mood categories are distinguished is based on their syntactic behavior. Specifically, authors often talk about a dependent and an independent mood (Real Academia Española, 2011), the first one being the one that requires a grammatical inductor to appear, and the second being the one that does not need any grammatical elements to appear in the sentences. This distinction mostly correlates with the subjunctive and the indicative moods, that is, normally, for a verb to be in the subjunctive mood there must be a grammatical element that induces it.

Usually, the induced mood is *mandatory*, that is, using the verb in a different mood category is not accepted. But there are cases in which a different mood category, in most cases the indicative, is accepted and this is what is called **mood alternation**, one of the veridicality contexts analyzed here.

Specifically, the focus here lays on the mood alternation that occurs in the embedded predicate of a complex sentence due to the negation of the main or matrix verb, as in example (2), where due to the presence of the negation adverb *no* (not), the embedded verb *tener* is allowed to appear both in the subjunctive (example (2b)) and in the indicative (example (2a)). Since there is no direct way of translating the mood differences into English, here, as in Faulkner (2021), the translations are identical.

In this case, the difference in the interpretation between indicative and subjunctive is interpreted in terms of old and new information. That is, when the speaker chooses to use the subjunctive mood it is understood that the embedded event is already part of the common ground. Contrary to this, when using the indicative, the embedded event is presented as new information (Mejías-Bikandi, 1998; Real Academia Española, 2011; Faulkner, 2021). Consequently, the event *el país tenía problemas económicos* (the country had economic problems) is presented as part of the common ground in (2b), and as new knowledge in (2a). Because it was assumed that speakers associate different factuality values with old and new information, it was expected that mood alternation would alter the factuality of the embedded event.

(2) a. El presidente no
the.M.SG president.M.SG not
dijo que el
say.PST.PFV.IND.3SG that the.M.SG
país **tenía**
country.M.SG **have.PST.IPFV.IND.3SG**
problemas económicos.
problem.M.PL economic.M.PL
"The president didn't say that the country **had** economic problems."

b. El presidente no
the.M.SG president.M.SG not
dijo que el
say.PST.PFV.IND.3SG that the.M.SG
país **tuviera**
country.M.SG **have.PST.IPFV.SBJV.3SG**
problemas económicos.
problem.M.PL economic.M.PL
"The president didn't say that the country had economic problems."

2.4 Specificity

Following Caudet (1999), here specificity is considered as the identifiability of the referent in the discourse universe and is shown, for example, in the amount and type of information used in the referral expression. So when referring to Olaf Scholz, the current German chancellor, we could use the expression "the German chancellor" or "the chancellor". Assuming the reference is successful in both cases, in the first case the speaker uses more information because she assumes that in the mind speaker, there is more than one chancellor with equal prominence, and thus more information is needed to ensure the right one is chosen. In the second case, no additional information is needed because the speaker assumes only Olaf Scholz is prominent in the mind of the speaker.

Here, the specificity of the subject is manipulated by changing the type of information by having individual vs. collective nouns as subjects. With this, we are manipulating the number of individual entities the subject refers to in singular. In the first case, with an individual noun like *el presidente* (the president) we are referring to one single entity, whereas in the second case with a collective noun like *el gobierno* (the government) we are referring to a set of entities. Because I assumed that there is a different factuality associated with individual and collective nouns, it was expected that there could be a veridicality effect, but not a strong one.

2.5 Previous Work

An important reference is that of de Marneffe et al. (2012), which aimed at identifying some of the linguistics and contextual factors that shape readers' veridicality judgments. To fulfill this goal they crowdsourced annotations on a part of the FactBank corpus and built a system for veridicality assessment. For our purposes, the most important part of their work is the consideration of the possible occurrence of **label split**, that is, that for some premise-hypothesis pairs, there is not just one ground truth and therefore label, associated with them, but at least two, which they concluded from the analysis of the **agreement patterns**, that is, of how the votes for each label are distributed in each pair.

Another relevant work is Pavlick and Kwiatkowski (2019), whose goal was to determine whether the disagreement often seen in NLI datasets is noise or an important reproducible signal. To do so they gathered factuality judgments on 500 pairs, with 50 annotators per pair, of these, 496 pairs with a mean of 39 workers were left to analyze. The results showed that for 20% of the pairs a second ground truth or label can be associated with them, which they blame on **inherent disagreement**.

In Spanish, the main related works are the following corpora: XNLI Conneau et al. (2018), SenSem (Fernández-Montraveta and Vázquez, 2014) and TAGFACT (Fernández Montraveta et al., 2020). XNLI is a multilingual corpus that follows the premise-hypothesis design, but the other two do not. Thus the corpus presented here covers the lack of Spanish corpora in the form of premise-hypothesis pairs and, as far as I know, is the only dataset that focuses on specific phenomena. This, together with the fact that as far as I know the inter-annotator agreement score used here has not been used in any previous NLI corpora, forces us to take any comparisons with previous work skeptically.

3 Corpus and Annotation Process

The first step for creating the corpus was defining the experimental design. To do so, each of the research questions was set as one experimental condition: negation, individual, and collective. Then the negation condition was divided into three categories: baseline, indicative, and subjunctive. The first refers to the case where there is no mood inductor, as in *El presidente dijo que el país tenía problemas económicos* (The president said that the country had economic problems). For both the indicative and the subjunctive categories we have the mood inductor *no* (not), but on the former the embedded verb is in the indicative mood, as in (2a), and on the latter, the verb is in the subjunctive mood, as in (2b). Finally, these three negation categories were crossed with the specificity conditions, that is, with the individual and collective conditions.

Once the design was defined, the pairs were created. 30% of them were written manually and the rest were based on different corpora. Specifically, possible premises in the indicative category were extracted with the help of Linguakit (Gamallo et al., 2018) from the following corpora: a section of the Davie's Corpus del Español (Davies, 2016), the Old News Corpus for Spanish (Kaggle, 2018), *El Quijote* by Miguel de Cervantes (as found in Dario (2017)), the XNLI corpus, and the United Nations corpus in Spanish for the years 2000, 2001, 2002, and 2003 (Eisele and Chen, 2010). After that, some small modifications like reference resolution and reducing the number of words were done, hypotheses were extracted and pairs were modified according to the experimental design. Finally, each pair was automatically annotated with additional information that could be used to later model the results.

To annotate the corpus the labels displayed in Figure 1 were used. These labels correspond to the set from Saurí and Pustejovsky (2009) minus *certain but unknown output* (CTu), as in de Marneffe et al. (2012), and although they mapped them to the traditional square of opposition, here the labels are presented in an ordered linear scale of factuality. Furthermore, given that the acceptability of mood alternation is not always certain, the label "not a sentence" (NaS) was added. Since does not fit within the scale, it is presented outside of it. Consequently, the final set of labels is: certainly yes (CT+), probably yes (PR+), possibly yes (PS+), unknown or uncommitted (Uu), possibly not (PS-), probably not (PR-), certainly not (CT-), not a sentence (NaS).

The experiment was run on the platform Toloka (Pavlichenko et al., 2021). To select the workers two main criteria were used: language and country. They were required to have set up Spanish as a language and their IP address from a country where Spanish is an official language or an important minority one. In the beginning, all annotators under these criteria were eligible, but then this was reduced to the top 30% of annotators. They were paid \$0.433 per set of pairs, which consisted of no more than 10 pairs. Once all the annotations were gathered, pairs for which one worker or more used the label NaS were removed, and if an annotator had labeled more than 1 pair within a single combination of experimental conditions, all his annotations in that combination were removed. This left a total of 477 pairs and 7 annotators per pair.

The task was designed as in de Marneffe et al. (2012): Given a context (the premise), workers had to label the factuality of the event (hypothesis) by choosing one of the labels in Figure 1 from a drop list.

4 Analysis of Annotations

Overall Distribution. As we can see in Figure 2, the distribution of label counts is negatively skewed, that is, there is a clear preference for the positive labels, even if more than half of the corpus sentences are negated. Furthermore, the frequencies for probability and possibility, with their respective + and - signs, are almost identical. This points to a likely confusion for the annotators between probability and possibility. Lastly, we have that for 42.348% of the pairs annotators could not agree upon one label, which suggests a considerable lack of agreement.

Inter-Annotator Agreement Score for Different Subsets	
Subset	AC_2
ALL	0.114
Baseline	0.194
Indicative	0.070
Subjunctive	0.085
saber (to know)	0.170
olvidar (to forget)	0.181
creer (to believe)	0.131

Table 1: Inter-annotator-agreements scores for the whole corpus and different subsets.

Inter-Annotator Agreement Scores. Given that the labels used are not nominal, but ordinal; and the highly skewed distribution seen in Figure 2, here I follow Vanacore and Pellegrino (2022) and computed the inter-annotator agreement score as measured by Gwet's AC_2 (Gwet, 2014). This yielded a value of 0.114, which is barely within the range of slight agreement (Shrout, 1998). Given this, I decided to explore the value of this score in different subsets of the data and the most informative values are in Table 1. There we see that there is a considerable difference between the baseline and two mood alternation categories, but barely between the latter. In addition, we have the scores for the subset of pairs where *saber* (to know) is the matrix verb, and where we have *olvidar* (to forget) as the matrix verb. The agreement in the subsets is quite close, despite being very different in its size (120 pairs for the first one, 24 for the latter), which suggests that agreement depends not on the frequency of the matrix, but on the matrix itself. Further proof of this is the fact that agreement for the subset of *creer* (to believe) is quite lower than the other two, despite having double the pairs than the *olvidar* (to forget) subset.

Model Fitting. A cumulative link mixed model (CLMM) with a logit link was fitted to the whole dataset by using the R software, specifically the ordinal package (Christensen, 2018). This

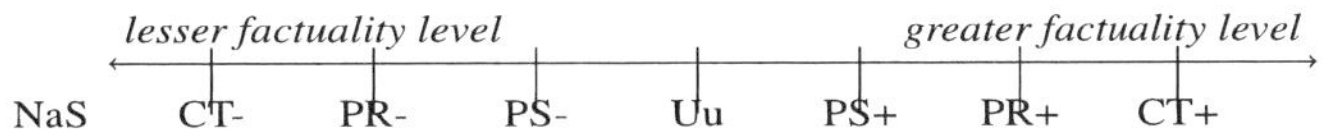

Figure 1: Ordered representation of the labels used for annotating the corpus. Each label stands for: certainly yes (CT+), probably yes (PR+), possibly yes (PS+), unknown or uncommitted (Uu), possibly not (PS-), probably not (PR-), certainly not (CT-), not a sentence (NaS). The latter doesn't fit in the scale, thus it's presented outside of it.

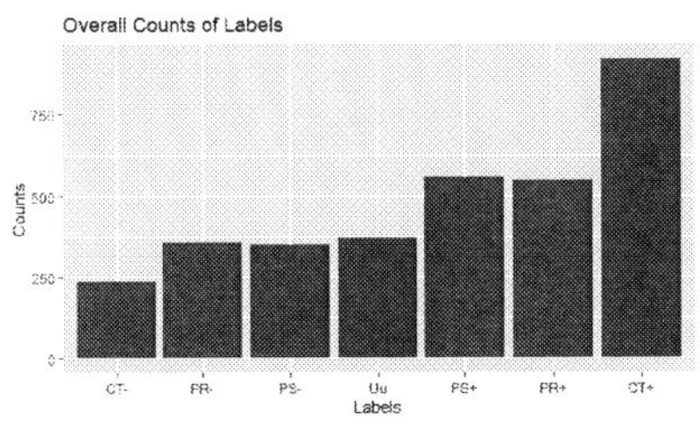

Figure 2: Overall distribution of the proportion of labels used by annotators.

type of model was chosen to reflect the ordered nature of the labels. Mood categories were set as predictors, labels as outcome, and annotator and pair as random variables. Results showed that both the indicative and subjunctive categories are significantly different from the baseline, which is consistent with the agreement scores. The coefficients for these two categories are both negative, rather small in value (< 0.5), and barely different from each other (< 0.1). To assess whether this difference is significant or not, a CLMM was fitted to just these two categories and the results show that in general there is no significant difference between the verb being in the indicative or in the subjunctive mood. Furthermore, the possibility of adding two other predictors, specificity conditions and matrix, to the overall model was considered. In the first case, it was proved that the specificity conditions are not informative. On the second one, the value of the conditional Hessian increased so much (from 1.4×10^2 to 3.3×10^5), that the model was disregarded. Since it was suspected that this increase could be due to the uneven distribution of matrices, the same two models were fitted to the subset corresponding to the 5 most frequent matrices (frequencies ranging from 36 to 102) and it was observed that the conditional Hessian values are much closer (1.4×10^2 to 2.6×10^3) and there are more significant effects for the model with matrix as a predictor, than for the exact same model for the whole dataset. In addition, for the model fitted with both predictors fitted to this subset, the difference between the coefficients for the indicative and subjunctive increased to 0.61. Lastly, when fitting the model with both predictors to the indicative and subjunctive pairs of this small subset, a small ($p = 0.0347$) significant effect for the subjunctive category was found, although not for the specific matrices.

Agreement Patterns. As in de Marneffe et al. (2012), the distribution of the votes for each label in each pair, which can be seen in Figure 3, was analyzed. Although several patterns occur less than 25 times, there are a few that have a non-neglectable frequency. Particularly, $[3, 2, 1, 1]$ and $[2, 2, 1, 1, 1]$ have a frequency of 112 and 134 (23.480% and 28.092%) respectively, which suggests that there are pairs for which disagreement is not an error but rather their underlying truth, even if they cannot be matched to an exact label split. In other words, Figure 3 shows that there is inherent disagreement for $\sim 50\%$ of the corpus.

Manual Analysis. An exploratory manual analysis of the annotations showed that there are other veridicality contexts and other factors that can at least partially explain the lack of agreement found. The two most salient factors are world knowledge and the presence of modal verbs in either the main or the embedded predicate. In support of the former, we have example (3), which was annotated as CT+ by 4 workers, even its variants in the indicative and the subjunctive conditions had the same label with 6 votes for each of them. This is because the factuality of the hypothesis, shown in (3b), cannot be easily negated, even in the presence of more than one veridicality context, since its often considered a *universal truth*. In support of the latter, we have the fact that for 15 out of 30 pairs that have the modal verb *deber + infinitive* (to must + infinitive)[1] in the embedded predicate, there is no agreement

[1] In Spanish there are two constructions with *deber*: deber + infinitive and deber + de + infinitive.

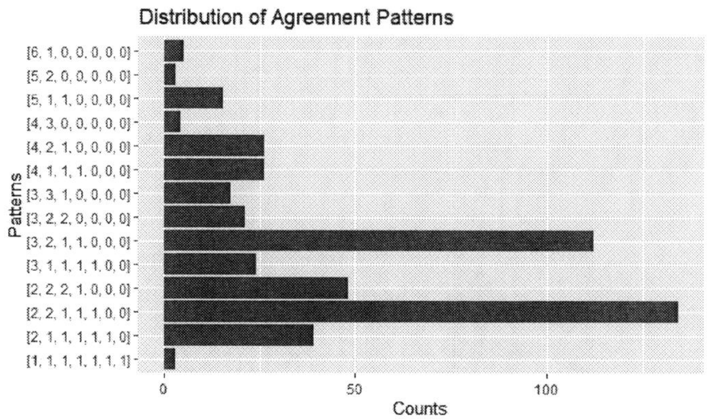

Figure 3: Distribution of agreement patterns, that is of how the annotators' votes are distributed for each pair. Therefore each number in the pattern represents the number of votes for a label (which one depends on the pair) and the counts stand for the number of pairs that have such agreement pattern.

upon one label, proportion $\sim 8\%$ higher than for the whole corpus.

(3) a. Algunos delegados
some.M.PL representative.M.PL
gubernamentales saben
governmental.M.PL know.PRS.IND.3SG
que también las mujeres
that also the.F.PL woman.F.PL
son seres humanos.
be.PRS.IND.3PL being.M.PL human.M.PL

Some governmental representatives know that women are also human beings.

b. Las mujeres son
the.F.PL woman.F.PL be.PRS.IND.3PL
seres humanos.
being.M.PL human.M.PL

Women are human beings.

5 Discussion

The results of this study have shown that there is a tendency for annotators to use positive labels, even when most of the pairs of the corpora are negated. Furthermore, the inter-annotator agreement score, $AC_2 = 0.114$, is rather low since it is barely within the range of slight agreement. Therefore, it is important to discuss what could have caused such a lack of agreement.

Uma et al. (2021) defines five sources of disagreement: errors and interface problems, annotation scheme, ambiguity, item difficulty, and subjectivity. Although the first factor cannot be completely disregarded, given the persistence of some quite divided agreement patterns seen in Figure 3 and that the interface was a simple drop list, the higher level of disagreement cannot entirely be blamed on this first factor.

As to the annotation scheme, some improvements could most certainly be implemented. Specifically, implementing training and testing. This was not done in fear of leading annotators towards concrete labels, but after encountering the work of Nie et al. (2020), where they used carefully crafted training and testing that did not fully prevent disagreement, I understood it could be possible, even if not easy. Also, given that the specific criteria for quality control, like what exactly annotations done too fast look like, more carefully defined criteria would clear out results. In addition, since the model fittings for subsets with more even distributions concerning the matrices showed better results, a more balanced corpus could yield more informative CLMMs, but there is no reason to believe that it would improve agreement. Lastly, given the negatively skewed distribution for the label counts, the assumptions made about the veridicality of negation need to be revised.

Regarding the ambiguity of the relation between the different premises and their hypothesis, the two factors mentioned in the manual analysis (world knowledge and modal verbs) and the highly frequent divided agreement patterns shown in Figure 3, suggest that there is not always one clear label for a pair. This supports the existence of *inherent* disagreement between annotators, although more data is needed to confirm it. Furthermore, the fact that these annotations are done from a pragmatic perspective and that mood alternation is a pragmatic phenomenon, also increases the uncertainty, and therefore ambiguity, of the annotations.

Concerning the fourth possible cause of disagreement, item difficulty is here a certain cause of disagreement. Firstly, in the manual analysis, it was demonstrated that there are different factors to be considered when given a factuality judgment, mainly world knowledge. Secondly, previous work has shown NLI annotations to be difficult (Pavlick and Kwiatkowski, 2019; Uma et al., 2021).

As to the last factor for disagreement, subjectivity, it also influences the results presented here. Although, to my knowledge, there is no previous work that supports this as cause for disagreement in NLI annotations, the analysis of example 3 shows that world knowledge influences speakers' judgments, consequently making annotations dependent upon annotators' knowledge and point of view.

Now that it has been explained what caused disagreement in these studies, the question is if an inter-annotator agreement score, let it be AC_2 or any other, can reflect the nature and quality of the annotations gathered. The simple answer is no, at least not entirely. As stated in Gwet (2014), inter-annotator agreement scores reflect how much the annotations change when small adjustments in the annotators like replacing a number of them are made, that is, it is a measure of data reproducibility based on the individual annotators. However given that it has been proven that these annotations are highly dependent on the speaker, measuring the reproducibility of the data based on such small variations is misguided and different evaluation scores are needed.

6 Conclusions

Based on the results presented here we can conclude that the specificity of the subject, defined in terms of the identifiability of the referent in the discourse universe and manipulated by having individual and collective nouns does not have a significant effect on the factuality of the embedded predicate in complex sentences, or in other words, individual vs. collective subjects are non-veridical contexts concerning the embedded predicate.

As to the effect of mood alternation due to the negation of the matrix verb, that is, when due to negative adverb *no* (not) modifying the main verb of a complex sentence the subjunctive mood is induced in the embedded predicate but the indicative is also accepted; there is overall a significant difference on the factuality of the embedded predicate between having or not the negative adverb, but not between having the embedded verb in the subjunctive or in the indicative mood. However, the results from fitting different models to specific subsets of the corpus suggest that there is a small significant difference between the indicative and the subjunctive categories in specific cases.

The analysis presented here has focused more on what the data looks like and it has scrapped the surface of why it looks like that. Therefore, an important line of future work is a thorough analysis of the annotations in terms of what causes the results found. A second line of work is a different statistical analysis. The methods chosen here assume that there is one single underlying truth for each premise-hypothesis pair, but as the analysis of the disagreement patterns has shown, there is a non-neglectable number of pairs for which this is not the case. Consequently, methods that expect disagreement, like the entropy distribution seen in Nie et al. (2020), might be insightful. The third and last line of work proposed is the inclusion of out-of-sentence context in the corpus, especially since it was recommended in Manning (2006). The question about its inclusion was already raised while designing the corpus, but it was disregarded due to its cumbersome implementation and the increased difficulty in the analysis. But given the results obtained and the influence of context in mood alternation (Faulkner, 2021), adding context to the pairs could yield more informative results.

Acknowledgments

First I want to thank my Master Thesis supervisors Lucia Donatelli and Vera Demberg, thanks to their guidance I run this study. Secondly, I want to acknowledge and express my gratitude to Toloka (Pavlichenko et al., 2021), who provided the funds to collect the annotations.

References

María Amparo Alcina Caudet. 1999. *Las expresiones referenciales. Estudio semántico del sintagma nominal.* Ph.D. thesis, Universitat de València.

Rune Haubo B Christensen. 2018. Cumulative link models for ordinal regression with the r package ordinal. *Submitted in J. Stat. Software*, 35.

Alexis Conneau, Guillaume Lample, Ruty Rinott, Adina Williams, Samuel R Bowman, Holger Schwenk, and Veselin Stoyanov. 2018. Xnli: Evaluating cross-lingual sentence representations. *arXiv preprint arXiv:1809.05053.*

JS. Dario. 2017. El quijote.

M. Davies. 2016. El corpus del español.

Andreas Eisele and Yu Chen. 2010. Multiun: A multilingual corpus from united nation documents. In *LREC.*

Tris J Faulkner. 2021. *A Systematic Investigation of the Spanish Subjunctive: Mood Variation in Subjunctive Clauses.* Georgetown University.

Ana Fernández-Montraveta and Gloria Vázquez. 2014. The sensem corpus: An annotated corpus for spanish and catalan with information about aspectuality, modality, polarity and factuality. *Corpus Linguistics and Linguistic Theory*, 10(2):273–288.

Ana María Fernández Montraveta, Hortènsia Curell i Gotor, Glòria Vázquez García, and Irene Castellón Masalles. 2020. The tagfact annotator and editor: A versatile tool. *Reproducció del document publicat a: Research in Corpus Linguistics, 2020, vol. 8, núm. 1, p. 131-146.*

P. Gamallo, M. García, R. Martíez-Castaño C. Piñeiro, and J.C. Pichel. 2018. Linguakit: a big data-based multilingual tool for linguistic analysis and information extraction. In *In Proceedings of The Second International Workshop on Advances in Natural Language Processing (ANLP 2018) co-located at SNAMS-2018*, pages 239–244.

Anastasia Giannakidou. 2014. (non) veridicality, evaluation, and event actualization: evidence from the subjunctive in relative clauses. In *Nonveridicality and Evaluation*, pages 17–49. Brill.

Anastasia Giannakidou and Alda Mari. 2015. Mixed (non) veridicality and mood choice with emotive verbs. In *CLS 51.*

Kilem L Gwet. 2014. *Handbook of inter-rater reliability: The definitive guide to measuring the extent of agreement among raters*, volume 1. Advanced Analytics, LLC.

Kaggle. 2018. Old newspapers.

John Lyons. 1995. *Linguistic semantics: An introduction.* Cambridge University Press.

Christopher D Manning. 2006. Local textual inference: it's hard to circumscribe, but you know it when you see it–and nlp needs it.

Marie-Catherine de Marneffe, Christopher D Manning, and Christopher Potts. 2012. Did it happen? the pragmatic complexity of veridicality assessment. *Computational linguistics*, 38(2):301–333.

Errapel Mejías-Bikandi. 1998. Pragmatic presupposition and old information in the use of the subjunctive mood in spanish. *Hispania*, pages 941–948.

Yixin Nie, Xiang Zhou, and Mohit Bansal. 2020. What can we learn from collective human opinions on natural language inference data? *arXiv preprint arXiv:2010.03532.*

N. Pavlichenko, I. Stelmakh, and D. Ustalov. 2021. Crowdspeech and voxdiy: Benchmark datasets for crowdsourced audio transcription. *arXiv preprint arXiv:2107.01091.*

Ellie Pavlick and Tom Kwiatkowski. 2019. Inherent disagreements in human textual inferences. *Transactions of the Association for Computational Linguistics*, 7:677–694.

RAE Real Academia Española. 2011. *Nueva gramática de la lengua española: Manual.* Espasa.

Alexis Ross and Ellie Pavlick. 2019. How well do nli models capture verb veridicality? In *Proceedings of the 2019 Conference on Empirical Methods in Natural Language Processing and the 9th International Joint Conference on Natural Language Processing (EMNLP-IJCNLP)*, pages 2230–2240.

David Sánchez-Jiménez. 2011. Una aproximación teórica a la definición del modo verbal español.

Roser Saurí and James Pustejovsky. 2009. Factbank: a corpus annotated with event factuality. *Language resources and evaluation*, 43(3):227–268.

Patrick E Shrout. 1998. Measurement reliability and agreement in psychiatry. *Statistical methods in medical research*, 7(3):301–317.

Alexandra N Uma, Tommaso Fornaciari, Dirk Hovy, Silviu Paun, Barbara Plank, and Massimo Poesio. 2021. Learning from disagreement: A survey. *Journal of Artificial Intelligence Research*, 72:1385–1470.

Amalia Vanacore and Maria Sole Pellegrino. 2022. Robustness of κ-type coefficients for clinical agreement. *Statistics in Medicine*, 41(11):1986–2004.

Adina Williams, Nikita Nangia, and Samuel R Bowman. 2017. A broad-coverage challenge corpus for sentence understanding through inference. *arXiv preprint arXiv:1704.05426*.

Weakly-Supervised Learning for Aspect-Based Sentiment Analysis of Urdu Tweets

Zoya
Department of Computing
School of Electrical Engineering & Computer Science
National University of Sciences & Technology
H-12, Islamabad, Pakistan
zmaqsood.phdcs17seecs@seecs.edu.pk

Abstract

Aspect-based sentiment analysis (ABSA) is vital for text comprehension which benefits applications across various domains. This field involves the two main sub-tasks including aspect extraction and sentiment classification. Existing methods to tackle this problem normally address only one sub-task or utilize topic models that may result in overlapping concepts. Moreover, such algorithms often rely on extensive labeled data and external language resources, making their application costly and time-consuming in new domains and especially for resource-poor languages like Urdu. The lack of aspect mining studies in Urdu literature further exacerbates the inapplicability of existing methods for Urdu language. The primary challenge lies in the preprocessing of data to ensure its suitability for language comprehension by the model, as well as the availability of appropriate pre-trained models, domain embeddings, and tools. This paper implements an ABSA model Huang et al. (2020) for unlabeled Urdu tweets with minimal user guidance, utilizing a small set of seed words for each aspect and sentiment class. The model first learns sentiment and aspect joint topic embeddings in the word embedding space with regularization to encourage topic distinctiveness. Afterwards, it employs deep neural models for pre-training with embedding-based predictions and self-training on unlabeled data. Furthermore, we optimize the model for improved performance by substituting the CNN with the BiLSTM classifier for sentence-level sentiment and aspect classification. Our optimized model achieves significant improvements over baselines in aspect and sentiment classification for Urdu tweets with accuracy of 64.8% and 72.8% respectively, demonstrating its effectiveness in generating joint topics and addressing existing limitations in Urdu ABSA.

1 Introduction

Opinion mining and sentiment analysis have gained significant importance in analyzing user-generated content for various applications. However, the vast volume of textual content on numerous platforms like social media makes manual analysis impractical. Hence, there is a need for automatic computational frameworks to extract opinions from unstructured texts, leading to the development of sentiment analysis and opinion mining as a research field.

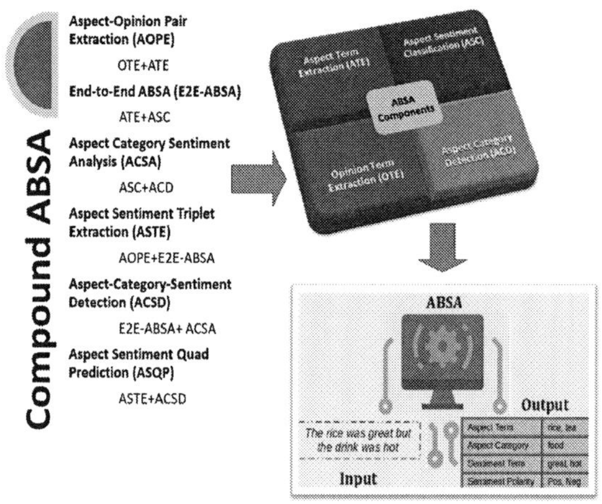

Figure 1: ABSA Individual vs. Compound Elements

Conventional sentiment analysis studies mainly perform prediction at the sentence or document level Yu and Hatzivassiloglou (2003); Pang et al. (2002), identifying the overall sentiment towards the whole sentence or document. However, ABSA (Cai et al., 2021) surpasses traditional sentiment analysis by incorporating finer granularity and enabling the identification of two crucial components: target aspect and sentiment in a given sentence or document. The target represents an entity or aspect of an entity, while the sentiment signifies an expression of opinion. For instance, consider sentences from restaurant reviews "The rice was great" and "The drink was hot". Both sentences convey sentiments but the term 'great' in the first sentence represents a positive sentiment related to the rice aspect, whereas the term 'hot' in the second sen-

Proceedings of the Student Research Workshop associated with RANLP-2023, pages 78–86, Varna, Bulgaria, Sep 4–6, 2023.
https://doi.org/10.26615/issn.2603-2821.2023_009

tence signifies a negative sentiment associated with the drink aspect. ABSA primarily revolves around four target components: aspect category, aspect term, sentiment term, and sentiment polarity Hemmatian and Sohrabi (2019). A comprehensive understanding of opinions at the aspect level requires considering multiple combinations of these components in different scenarios, generally referred to as compound ABSA. However, early ABSA research focused on individual components, such as capturing aspect terms while ignoring terms related to opinions like Aspect Term Extraction (ATE) Yang et al. (2020). Nowadays, various frameworks have been proposed to tackle such compound ABSA tasks that aim to extract and link individual elements Zhao et al. (2020); Cai et al. (2021). Such tasks are further denoted with several abbreviations, based on the specific combinations they address in compound ABSA. Figure 1 illustrates these tasks with their underlying combinations of ABSA individual components, as well as a complete ABSA of an opinion.

Most of the research in ABSA has been conducted in resource-rich languages, primarily English. Recent studies generally adopt supervised frameworks Hu et al. (2021); Yang et al. (2020) that require a large number of labeled sentences for training. Some studies leverage word embeddings in unsupervised He et al. (2017a) or weakly supervised settings Wu et al. (2020); Wang et al. (2021) for aspect extraction without annotated documents. These methods often rely on external language resources or syntactic structures such as POS tags or lexicons. Nevertheless, opinions are expressed in multiple languages in real-world scenarios. Acquiring large annotated data and accurate language resources for new domains or low-resource languages is challenging and expensive. Cross-lingual and cross-domain transfer requires language-specific knowledge of the target language and domain. Besides, previous methods relying on translation systems are limited by translation quality Zhang et al. (2021).

Alike other low-resource languages, Urdu also encounters difficulties in terms of data availability, language tools, and research resources. Additionally, Urdu is a comparatively complex language holding characteristics of multiple languages that pose troubles in minor processing tasks Khattak et al. (2021). Besides, the use of informal language on social media platforms further complicates the preparation of suitable datasets for machine learning models. As a result, ABSA tasks have been largely overlooked in the Urdu language and pretrained models developed for other languages may not generalize effectively. Due to limited literature, many approaches and difficulties as discussed for English need to be explored for the applicability of ABSA in the Urdu language. Meanwhile, the popularity and widespread usage of Urdu on online platforms demand sincere efforts to address these challenges for the advancement of Urdu technologies.

This paper presents a significant contribution to ABSA in Urdu by addressing its unique facets and challenges for Urdu texts. We adopt a pioneering step by employing a weakly-supervised model Huang et al. (2020) developed for English ABSA to unlabeled Urdu tweets on the budget topic. Our methodology involves rigorous pre-processing to ensure data quality and model compatibility to avoid memory leakage, training disruptions caused by invalid tokens, and out-of-vocabulary issues. Moreover, tokenization tools are deeply analyzed to determine the optimal approach for token formation in Urdu, taking into account their pivotal role in comprehending language context and optimizing resource utilization. We evaluate the model with vanilla settings and conduct experiments with architecture modifications specifically replacing CNN with BiLSTM and utilizing Fasttext embeddings. Clustering techniques and graph network analysis are applied to enhance seed words selection rather than manually.

2 Literature Review

Several approaches have been proposed for aspect extraction and sentiment classification in ABSA. Some methods focus on independently addressing these two sub-tasks, while others adopt a joint approach to simultaneously solve them.

2.1 Isolated Extraction of Aspect and Sentiment

The literature review covers various methods for individual element extraction of ABSA. Supervised methods use token-level classification and multi-label classification for ATE and Aspect Category Detection (ACD) Yang et al. (2020); Yin et al. (2020); Hu et al. (2021) respectively. Different techniques such as sequence labeling, dependency paths, and word embeddings have been employed for ATE, while ACD studies use word co-occurrence patterns, hybrid features, and neural models. Opinion Term Extraction (OTE) includes aspect opinion co-extraction (AOCE) and target-oriented opinion word extraction (TOWE) using sequence labeling, dependency-tree, attention-based models, and those considering syntactic structures and positional embeddings with various encoder structuresWang et al. (2016); Li and Lam (2017); Wu et al. (2020). Deep learning-based Aspect Sentiment Classification (ASC) models Zhou et al. (2019); Liu et al. (2020) have shown performance improvements, especially using pre-trained language models and neural network-based dependency parsing. Contrarily, Weakly-supervised methods use few keywords for aspect guidance and data augmentation for self-training Chen and Qian (2020); Wang et al. (2021), while unsupervised methods He et al. (2017b); Luo et al. (2019) use contrastive learning and autoencoder models for aspect extraction and ACD.

The aforementioned methods primarily target the extraction of aspect or opinion words in isolation, which may not fully capture the comprehensive aspect-level opinion. To achieve a deeper understanding, extracting multiple sentiment elements and recognizing their relationships by incorporating their semantic meanings is crucial.

2.2 Joint Extraction of Aspect and Sentiment

Recent research has focused on joint ABSA tasks involving multiple sentiment elements and can be further divided into sub-tasks such as ATE, ACD (presented in Figure 1) aim to extract individual elements. Regardless of the method used, OTE is commonly viewed as an auxiliary task, as it provides valuable insights into the existence of aspect terms and sentiment orientation Liang et al. (2021). Several modeling paradigms like pipeline, joint, and unified have been explored for these tasks. Mao et al. (2021) employed a joint method for the End-to-End ABSA task, which trains the subtasks jointly and uses two label sets to predict the aspect boundaries and sentiment labels, and the final prediction is derived by combining the outputs of the two subtasks. Another approach dismisses the boundary between the subtasks and employs a unified tagging scheme, where both sentiment elements are denoted in the tag of each token Li et al. (2019). In the context of Aspect-Opinion Pair Extraction(AOPE), early studies have employed a pipeline approach to extract aspect and opinion terms in pairs Chen et al. (2020). An alternative method is to extract aspects first and then identify corresponding opinion terms Gao et al. (2021). Unified approaches to address AOPE aim to mitigate potential error propagation from the pipeline method by considering joint term and relation extraction Zhao et al. (2020).

Aspect Category Sentiment Analysis (ACSA) is commonly solved by pipeline approach Hu et al. (2019), where aspect categories are detected first and then sentiment polarities are predicted for those categories. Huang et al. (2020) learns joint topic embeddings for sentiment and aspect pairs and aims to enhance topic distinctiveness as compared to existing models primarily based on conventional topic models LDA often resulting in topic overlapping. The Aspect Sentiment Triplet Extraction (ASTE) task Peng et al. (2020) proposes a two-stage pipeline method for extracting the triplets. In the first stage, two sequence tagging models extract aspects, sentiments, and opinion terms separately. In the second stage, a classifier is employed to identify valid aspect-opinion pairs from the predicted aspects and opinions, thereby constructing the triplet prediction. To better capture the relationships between multiple sentiment elements, several unified methods have been proposed for ASTE, such as multi-task learning frameworks Zhang et al. (2020). The recently proposed Aspect Sentiment Quad Prediction (ASQP) task Cai et al. (2021) focuses on predicting all four sentiment elements in a quadruplet form for a given text item.

Researchers have explored the use of pre-trained language models (PLMs) for different ABSA tasks Mao et al. (2021); Chen et al. (2021). They have found that a simple linear classification layer combined with PLMs can outperform complex neural ABSA models. However, relying solely on PLMs as context-aware embeddings may not be sufficient, as ABSA tasks require capturing dependency relations. Additional designs are needed to fully utilize contextualized embeddings from PLMs and improve the robustness of PLM-based ABSA models Xing et al. (2020).

Early works such as Mitchell et al. (2013) favor the pipeline method, while Li et al. (2019) illustrates that using a tailor-made neural model alongside the unified tagging scheme yields better performance. Hence, research works based on either method can achieved good performance, making it challenging to compare and determine the superiority of one method over the others. Further exploration is needed in this regard. Moreover, many ABSA tasks have been solved by supervised approaches and others are weakly-supervised approaches. However, weakly supervised models trained on a specific dataset or domain may struggle to generalize well to new or diverse data. They may not effectively capture the nuances and variations in sentiment expressions across different contexts and complex languages. These models may produce suboptimal results when faced with such linguistic challenges. Manually selected seed words or heuristics to guide the learning can limit the model's ability to adapt to new domains or capture emerging sentiment patterns that are not covered by the seed words. It can be challenging to establish precise correspondences between aspect terms and sentiment expressions, especially when multiple aspect terms or sentiments coexist within a sentence. This ambiguity can result in noisy or incorrect predictions.

2.3 ABSA in Urdu Language

Existing studies primarily focus on a document or sentence-level labeling and employ machine-learning techniques for binary classification Amjad et al. (2021); Rani and Anwar (2020). Lexicon and rule-based methods are commonly used for opinion mining in Urdu due to limited labeled data and resources required for advanced techniques Khattak et al. (2021). As supervised and weakly-supervised methods requiring large labeled datasets or relying on other linguistic resources are less applicable to Urdu. Therefore, fine-grained ABSA remains unexplored even at its basic level.

3 Methodology

Our methodology consists of three main stages: pre-processing, seed word selection, and model implementation. Figure 2 illustrates the entire process.

3.1 Dataset

We used the Twitter API to extract approximately 100 Urdu tweets daily from each trending topic in Pakistan. Our dataset consists of around 5 million tweets covering diverse subjects from April 2020 to August 2020. We filtered out non-Urdu tweets, truncated tweets, and retweets. The dataset is based on generic query terms and encompasses all topics discussed during that period.

3.2 Pre-processing

Urdu language processing involves several pre-processing steps to structure the input text and reduce noise. These steps enhance the overall data quality and improve the accuracy for further linguistic and computational analysis. We have categorized them into three levels: tweet, token, and character.

3.2.1 Tweet Pre-processing-Level I

This involves cleaning the tweets by normalizing Unicode, punctuation marks, diacritics, hashtags, URLs, emojis, white spaces, hyperlinks, email addresses, phone numbers, mentions, and special characters like currency symbols. Regular expressions and Urdu-specific libraries are used for this purpose.

Unicode Normalization: Urdu text normalization is crucial due to its inclusion in the Arabic Unicode block, which can lead to multiple Unicode representations for Urdu alphabets. This step addresses variations in Unicode values caused by Arabic Unicode or orthographic changes and ensures accuracy in language models.

Stopwords Removal: insignificant words with minimal impact on the model, are removed to reduce vocabulary size. Urdu Language Processing (ULP) categorizes them as generic (applicable to all domains e.g. prepositions) and specific (domain-specific). A total of 1264 stopwords from various sources are collected and removed from the dataset.

Duplicate and Null Removal: Duplicate tweets resulting from related hashtags are eliminated to ensure dataset uniqueness. Additionally, tweets with no useful information like tweets that fell below a specified length threshold or null text are excluded, resulting in a reduced dataset size of approximately 1.2 million tweets.

Consecutive Words & Sentences Removal: We conducted an analysis of consecutive words and sentences within tweets and eliminated any repetitive instances to a certain limit, thus reducing the unnecessary length in the tweets e.g. سلیکٹڈ بجٹ سلیکٹڈ بجٹ... (selected budget selected budget...) or چور چور چور چور... (thief thief thief thief...). This step ensure that the tweets were concise and free from redundant content, resulting in more streamlined and focused text for further analysis

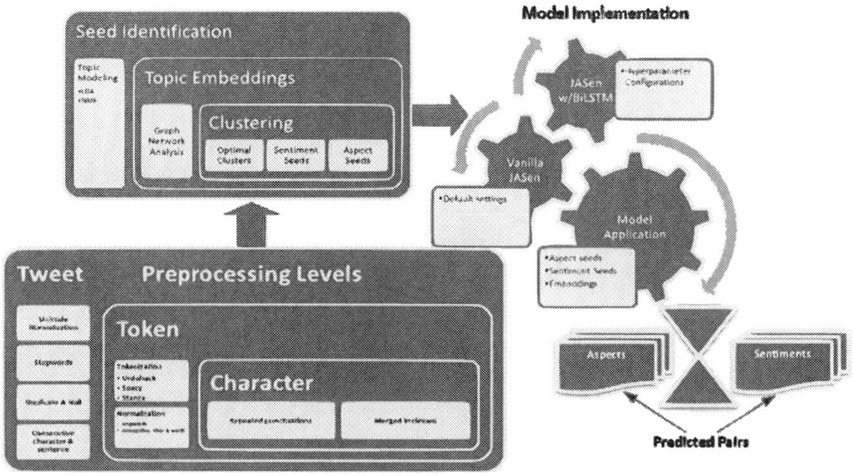

Figure 2: Methodology

3.2.2 Token Pre-processing-Level II

At this level of processing, tokens were formed from the input tweet and their correctness was observed for accuracy and consistency ensuring that they corresponded to the intended linguistic units and were free from errors or irregularities.

Tokenization: We compared multiple linguistic tools such as Qi et al. (2020), ALi (2020), and Vasiliev (2020) with the traditional space-based method to determine the most effective tokenization strategy for the Urdu language that yielded the lowest error rate and produced accurate tokenization results. To assess the performance, we provided a test set containing different forms of incorrect tokens caused by the absence of spaces or the use of informal language on the Twitter platform. Among the various options, we found that Urduhack ALi (2020) performed relatively better demonstrating a better level of accuracy. As a result, we selected Urduhack as the preferred library for tokenizing our dataset.

Normalization: Misspelled words that were joined together in tweets were normalized to their standard form at various levels of processing. *Stopwords Normalization:* Consecutive stopwords merged due to the absence of spaces at various levels like تھیاک (wasone) two stopwords forming incorrect word corrected to تھی اک (was one). Additionally, prior to normalization, these joined words were checked against a list of valid frequent words in Urdu to ensure that they do not form any other correct word.*Consecutive Characters & Words Normalization:* We noticed consecutive irrelevant characters within a token as well as the repetition of words without spaces often resulted in incorrect and lengthy tokens e.g.پاکسسستان,فریفریفری (Pakisssstan, freefreefree) and rectified them.

3.2.3 Character Pre-processing-Level III

This level of pre-processing involved dividing the token further into individual units such as characters and compared with valid Urdu alphabets to facilitate further analysis.*Repeated punctuations removal:* We discovered the missed tokens in the cleaning process consisting of consecutive punctuation marks due to the absence of space and rectified them e.g.'****'.*Merged irrelevant character removal:* We identified and corrected instances where punctuation, digits, alphabets, or misprinted strings were merged inside a token, leading to incorrect formations like نوازc002u ھوئے کا (Nawaz'sbecomingu200c).

3.3 Optimal Seed Words Selection

We employed topic modeling to identify the general topics within our dataset of tweets using conventional topic models like LDA & NMF Jelodar et al. (2019). Specifically, we focused on the topic of 'budget', which yielded approximately 10K related tweets. To analyze this topic further, we generated tweet embeddings using vanilla multilingual SBERT Reimers and Gurevych (2019). To ensure the accuracy of our methodology, we recognized the significance of seeding aspects and sentiment words. As a result, we utilized various techniques and clustering algorithms to obtain reliable seed words for each sub-topic under the 'budget' category. These techniques involved determining the optimal number of clusters as aspect categories through distance-driven clustering or other cluster validation metrics. Our experiments indicated that on average 3-9 clusters provided optimal results (as depicted in Figure 3), and we ultimately selected 9 clusters as our final choice. However, we encountered overlapping words across different clusters, which presented challenges in finalizing the aspect categories. To address this, we performed graph analysis where edges represented cosine similarities between embeddings. We set edge weights to 0 for values below a threshold of 0.7. This approach allowed us to group the most similar tweets within each cluster while obtaining distinct terms across the clusters. The predicted aspect categories and their corresponding aspect terms are presented in Table 1.

3.4 Model Application & Analysis

We experimented with the weakly-supervised JASen model as our baseline, developed for the English language, for Urdu tweets related to budget topic. We analyze its performance under various experimental configurations involving modifications to the dataset, embeddings, model architecture, and hyperparameters. Our dataset consists of approximately 10194 tweets of which we labeled 194 tweets as our test dataset and the remaining 10000 tweets as our unlabeled training dataset. Initially, we applied this model with default settings on our tweets dataset and compared it with the originally reported results on restaurant and laptop reviews to establish a performance benchmark. However, we employed FastText embeddings for representing the tweets, considering their effectiveness in capturing subword information. Though, we did not achieve up to mark results on these experiments for Urdu dataset but the reason could be the chosen seeded words as all sentiment words did not fit well for every aspect category. Subsequently, we made architectural modifications by replacing the CNN component with a BiLSTM layer to capture temporal dependencies in the tweet data. We tested the model with different hyperparameter settings and identified the best-performing configuration like alpha=0.05, hidden size=300, embedding size=100. The modified JASen model with BiLSTM and FastText embeddings outperformed the vanilla settings and showed improved accuracy and sentiment analysis results on Urdu tweets presented in Tables 2, 3, 4 and 5. However, there were no significant improvements observed on the benchmark datasets. These findings emphasize the importance of model modifications and the choice of embeddings for enhancing ABSA in Urdu. The limitations encountered during experimentation, such as memory leakage and out-of-vocabulary words, model disruption due to bad token as highlighted in section 3.2, were addressed through enhanced pre-processing of Urdu text.

Aspect Category	Aspect Terms
Govt. Spending	Expenditure (خرچ), Salary (تنخواہ), Pension (پنشن), Poor (غریب), Loans (قرضوں)
Subsidy & Grant	Subsidy (سبسڈی), Project (پروجیکٹ), Plans (منصوبے), Specific (مختص), Funds (فنڈز)
Social Welfare	Employees (ملازمین), Agriculture (زراعت), Reforms (اصلاحات), Education (تعلیم), Health (صحت)
Defense Spending	War (جنگ), Armed Forces (افواج), Defense (دفاع), Enemy (دشمن), Terrorism (دہشت)
Economic Policy	Financial (مالی), Policy (پالیسی), Crisis (بحران), Economic (اقتصادی), Livelihood (معیشت)
Corruption & Taxation	Corruption (کرپشن), Mafia (مافیا), Wealth (مال), Thieves (چوروں), Taxes (ٹیکس)
Media Coverage	Press (پریس), Report (رپورٹ), Media (میڈیا), Journalist (صحافی), News (نیوز)
Regional Policy	Regions (اضلاع), Areas (علاقوں), Sindh (سندھ), Provinces (صوبے), Limited (محدود)
Politics	Pakistan (پاکستان), Cabinet (کابینہ), State (ریاست), Assembly (اسمبلی), Politics (سیاست)

Table 1: Aspect seed words on tweets of budget topic

Method	Accuracy	Precision	Recall	macro-F1	Dataset
JASen	83.83	64.73	72.95	66.28	Restaurant reviews
JASen	71.01	69.55	71.31	69.69	Laptop reviews
JASen	54.6	46.63	44.19	41.33	Budget tweets
JASen w/BiLSTM	70.3	70.9	71.4	68.7	Laptop reviews
JASen w/BiLSTM	64.8	43.5	45.5	48.8	Budget tweets

Table 2: Aspect identification results (%): English Reviews vs. Urdu Tweets

Method	Accuracy	Precision	Recall	macro-F1	Dataset
JASen	81.96	82.85	78.11	79.44	Restaurant reviews
JASen	74.59	74.69	74.65	74.59	Laptop reviews
JASen	54.2	46.41	50.00	42.14	Budget tweets
JASen w/BiLSTM	75.2	75.7	75.4	75.2	Laptop reviews
JASen w/BiLSTM	72.8	54.6	51.3	52.4	Budget tweets

Table 3: Sentiment identification results (%): English Reviews vs. Urdu Tweets

4 Conclusion

We propose an approach to introduce joint aspect-based sentiment analysis in the Urdu language using advanced techniques with minimal guidance. The weakly-supervised JASen model, originally developed for English, is applied to Urdu tweets to capture fine-grained information. Fasttext embeddings and the vanilla settings of the model are leveraged to establish a benchmark, followed by experiments with modifications in the model architecture and default settings. Extensive pre-processing is performed to prepare the dataset due to the complexity and informality of the language used in tweets, making it compatible with model training and resource utilization. The results demonstrate improvements in the model's performance on the Urdu dataset, attributed to the enhancements in pre-processing and model architecture modifications.

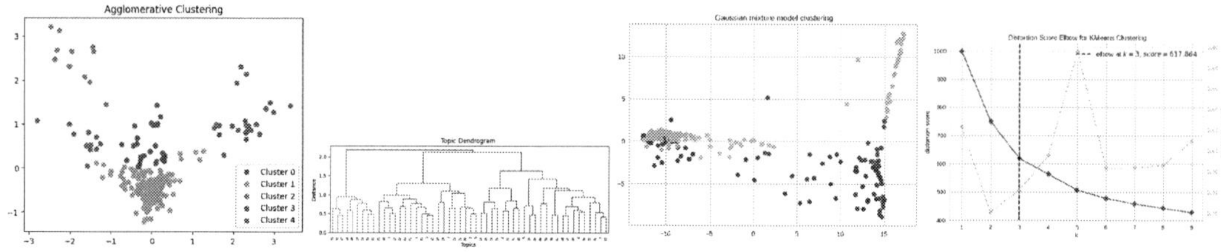

Figure 3: Inspecting optimal number of clusters

	Govt. Spending	Subsidy & Grant	Social Welfare	Defense	Economy	Corruption & Tax.	Media	Regional Policy	Politics
Positive	روزگاری اعتماد اشرافیہ انتخاب ایمانداروں Expenditure Elite Confidence Trustworthy Elections	منصوبہ جامع بندی صنعتوں مختص اسکیموں Comprehensive Projects Industry Specific Schemes	معیار ضروریات کسان ترجیحات اضافے Standards Essential for Farmers Additional Preferences	قربان مضبوط پڑوسی قوت سلامتی Strong Sacrifice Neighbors Health Power	معاشی تجارتی بہتری استحکام موزوں اقدامات Economic Trade Better Strengthening Appropriate Initiatives	نیاٹیکس بزنس فرینڈلی سرپرائز ورثے New tax Business Friendly Surprises Legacies	تبصرے تجزیے ماہرانہ اینکرز معلومات Comments Expert Analysis Anchors' Knowledge	سہولیات کالج اسکولز پختون مطالبہ College Facilities Schools of Khyber Demand	پارلیمانی ووٹنگ بجٹ اتحادیوں اعتماد Parliamentary Voting Coalition Budget Confidence
Negative	خودکشی گزارہ کٹھپتلی ظالمانہ تنگ Suicidal Brutal Oppression Narrow	اندھاباٹے ہولڈنگ بیکار مذموم مسخرے Indebted Holdings Useless Condemned Mockeries	بیرزگاری پیناڈول کارتوس نقصانات غربت Poverty Pinadole Cartouches Losses Poverty	ماتم خطرہ حملہ دھمکی موت Mourning Threat Attack Threat Death	دیوالیہ بدحالی بیروزگاری سود سختیاں Disaster Desolation Unemployment Profit Hardships	نقصان آٹا ذخیرہ سکینڈل ناقص Flawed Flour Hoarding Scandal Incomplete	جوا ئنٹ سربراہی شکار مذمت تقریر Joint Leadership Condemned Hunting Speech	غیرمناسب ناانصافی کٹوتی قبائل دشمنی Inappropriate Unfair Katoori Tribal Enmity	گونج خطرات دستور حکومتی اپوزیشن Roar Threats Government Orders Opposition

Table 4: Aspect terms retrieved by joint topics

Tweet	Ground Truth	Prediction
انشاء اللہ بجٹ عوام دوست خان امید (Inshallah budget people's friend Khan hope)	(politics, pos)	(govt. spending, pos)
عوام دشمن بجٹ غریبوں محنت کشوں سرکاری ملازمین (People's enemy budget poor laborers government employees)	(govt. spending, neg)	(govt.spending, neg)
کٹھ پتلی حکومت کٹھ پتلی بجٹ نامنظور (Puppet government Puppet budget unacceptable)	(politics, neg)	(politics, neg)
عوام معاشی قتل عام پاکستان بدترین انسان دشمن وفاقی بجٹ (People economic massacre common Pakistan worse human enemy federal budget)	(economy, neg)	(politics, neg)

Table 5: Comparison of Model Predictions with Ground Truth

In future work, we intend to conduct additional experiments involving variations in hyperparameter settings, embeddings, seeded knowledge, and architectural changes to further explore advanced approaches for ABSA in the Urdu language. We also aim to identify any limitations these approaches may have when applied to Urdu. Another promising direction is the development of annotated datasets to leverage state-of-the-art deep learning methods and enhance the performance of ABSA in Urdu.

Limitations

Our experimentation focused only on the "budget" topic in the ABSA domain, leaving the other topics largely unexplored with a large dataset. Additionally, we did not explore the use of other embeddings such as sentence BERT embeddings, transformer architectures with multi-head attention, and pre-trained language models with varying hyper-parameter settings. Furthermore, the current methodology does not enable the prediction of multiple aspects in a sentence along with their associated sentiments.

References

Ikram ALi. 2020. Urduhack: A python library for urdu language processing. `https://docs.urduhack.com/en/stable/#urduhack`.

Maaz Amjad, Noman Ashraf, Alisa Zhila, Grigori Sidorov, Arkaitz Zubiaga, and Alexander Gelbukh. 2021. Threatening language detection and target identification in urdu tweets. *IEEE Access*, 9:128302–128313.

Hongjie Cai, Rui Xia, and Jianfei Yu. 2021. Aspect-category-opinion-sentiment quadruple extraction with implicit aspects and opinions. In *Proceedings of the 59th Annual Meeting of the Association for Computational Linguistics and the 11th International Joint Conference on Natural Language Processing (Volume 1: Long Papers)*, pages 340–350.

Shaowei Chen, Jie Liu, Yu Wang, Wenzheng Zhang, and Ziming Chi. 2020. Synchronous double-channel recurrent network for aspect-opinion pair extraction. In *Proceedings of the 58th annual meeting of the association for computational linguistics*, pages 6515–6524.

Shaowei Chen, Yu Wang, Jie Liu, and Yuelin Wang. 2021. Bidirectional machine reading comprehension for aspect sentiment triplet extraction. In *Proceed-*

ings of the AAAI conference on artificial intelligence, volume 35, pages 12666–12674.

Zhuang Chen and Tieyun Qian. 2020. Enhancing aspect term extraction with soft prototypes. In *Proceedings of the 2020 Conference on Empirical Methods in Natural Language Processing (EMNLP)*, pages 2107–2117, Online. Association for Computational Linguistics.

Lei Gao, Yulong Wang, Tongcun Liu, Jingyu Wang, Lei Zhang, and Jianxin Liao. 2021. Question-driven span labeling model for aspect–opinion pair extraction. In *Proceedings of the AAAI conference on artificial intelligence*, volume 35, pages 12875–12883.

Ruidan He, Wee Sun Lee, Hwee Tou Ng, and Daniel Dahlmeier. 2017a. An unsupervised neural attention model for aspect extraction. In *Proceedings of the 55th Annual Meeting of the Association for Computational Linguistics (Volume 1: Long Papers)*, pages 388–397.

Ruidan He, Wee Sun Lee, Hwee Tou Ng, and Daniel Dahlmeier. 2017b. An unsupervised neural attention model for aspect extraction. In *Proceedings of the 55th Annual Meeting of the Association for Computational Linguistics (Volume 1: Long Papers)*, pages 388–397, Vancouver, Canada. Association for Computational Linguistics.

Fatemeh Hemmatian and Mohammad Karim Sohrabi. 2019. A survey on classification techniques for opinion mining and sentiment analysis. *Artificial intelligence review*, 52(3):1495–1545.

Mengting Hu, Shiwan Zhao, Honglei Guo, Chao Xue, Hang Gao, Tiegang Gao, Renhong Cheng, and Zhong Su. 2021. Multi-label few-shot learning for aspect category detection. In *Proceedings of the 59th Annual Meeting of the Association for Computational Linguistics and the 11th International Joint Conference on Natural Language Processing (Volume 1: Long Papers)*, pages 6330–6340, Online. Association for Computational Linguistics.

Mengting Hu, Shiwan Zhao, Li Zhang, Keke Cai, Zhong Su, Renhong Cheng, and Xiaowei Shen. 2019. CAN: Constrained attention networks for multi-aspect sentiment analysis. In *Proceedings of the 2019 Conference on Empirical Methods in Natural Language Processing and the 9th International Joint Conference on Natural Language Processing (EMNLP-IJCNLP)*, pages 4601–4610, Hong Kong, China. Association for Computational Linguistics.

Jiaxin Huang, Yu Meng, Fang Guo, Heng Ji, and Jiawei Han. 2020. Weakly-supervised aspect-based sentiment analysis via joint aspect-sentiment topic embedding. In *Proceedings of the 2020 Conference on Empirical Methods in Natural Language Processing (EMNLP)*, pages 6989–6999, Online. Association for Computational Linguistics.

Hamed Jelodar, Yongli Wang, Chi Yuan, Xia Feng, Xiahui Jiang, Yanchao Li, and Liang Zhao. 2019. Latent dirichlet allocation (lda) and topic modeling: models, applications, a survey. *Multimedia Tools and Applications*, 78:15169–15211.

Asad Khattak, Muhammad Zubair Asghar, Anam Saeed, Ibrahim A Hameed, Syed Asif Hassan, and Shakeel Ahmad. 2021. A survey on sentiment analysis in urdu: A resource-poor language. *Egyptian Informatics Journal*, 22(1):53–74.

Xin Li, Lidong Bing, Piji Li, and Wai Lam. 2019. A unified model for opinion target extraction and target sentiment prediction. In *Proceedings of the AAAI conference on artificial intelligence*, volume 33, pages 6714–6721.

Xin Li and Wai Lam. 2017. Deep multi-task learning for aspect term extraction with memory interaction. In *Proceedings of the 2017 conference on empirical methods in natural language processing*, pages 2886–2892.

Yunlong Liang, Fandong Meng, Jinchao Zhang, Yufeng Chen, Jinan Xu, and Jie Zhou. 2021. An iterative multi-knowledge transfer network for aspect-based sentiment analysis. In *Findings of the Association for Computational Linguistics: EMNLP 2021*, pages 1768–1780, Punta Cana, Dominican Republic. Association for Computational Linguistics.

Haoyue Liu, Ishani Chatterjee, MengChu Zhou, Xiaoyu Sean Lu, and Abdullah Abusorrah. 2020. Aspect-based sentiment analysis: A survey of deep learning methods. *IEEE Transactions on Computational Social Systems*, 7(6):1358–1375.

Ling Luo, Xiang Ao, Yan Song, Jinyao Li, Xiaopeng Yang, Qing He, and Dong Yu. 2019. Unsupervised neural aspect extraction with sememes. In *IJCAI*, pages 5123–5129.

Yue Mao, Yi Shen, Chao Yu, and Longjun Cai. 2021. A joint training dual-mrc framework for aspect based sentiment analysis. In *Proceedings of the AAAI conference on artificial intelligence*, volume 35, pages 13543–13551.

Margaret Mitchell, Jacqui Aguilar, Theresa Wilson, and Benjamin Van Durme. 2013. Open domain targeted sentiment. In *Proceedings of the 2013 conference on empirical methods in natural language processing*, pages 1643–1654.

Bo Pang, Lillian Lee, and Shivakumar Vaithyanathan. 2002. Thumbs up? sentiment classification using machine learning techniques. *arXiv preprint cs/0205070*.

Haiyun Peng, Lu Xu, Lidong Bing, Fei Huang, Wei Lu, and Luo Si. 2020. Knowing what, how and why: A near complete solution for aspect-based sentiment analysis. In *Proceedings of the AAAI Conference on Artificial Intelligence*, volume 34, pages 8600–8607.

Peng Qi, Yuhao Zhang, Yuhui Zhang, Jason Bolton, and Christopher D Manning. 2020. Stanza: A python natural language processing toolkit for many human languages. *arXiv preprint arXiv:2003.07082*.

Sadaf Rani and Waqas Anwar. 2020. Resource creation and evaluation of aspect based sentiment analysis in urdu. In *Proceedings of the 1st Conference of the Asia-Pacific Chapter of the Association for Computational Linguistics and the 10th International Joint Conference on Natural Language Processing: Student Research Workshop*, pages 79–84.

Nils Reimers and Iryna Gurevych. 2019. Sentence-bert: Sentence embeddings using siamese bert-networks. In *Proceedings of the 2019 Conference on Empirical Methods in Natural Language Processing*. Association for Computational Linguistics.

Yuli Vasiliev. 2020. *Natural Language Processing with Python and SpaCy: A Practical Introduction*. No Starch Press.

Qianlong Wang, Zhiyuan Wen, Qin Zhao, Min Yang, and Ruifeng Xu. 2021. Progressive self-training with discriminator for aspect term extraction. In *Proceedings of the 2021 Conference on Empirical Methods in Natural Language Processing*, pages 257–268, Online and Punta Cana, Dominican Republic. Association for Computational Linguistics.

Wenya Wang, Sinno Jialin Pan, Daniel Dahlmeier, and Xiaokui Xiao. 2016. Recursive neural conditional random fields for aspect-based sentiment analysis. page 616626.

Meixi Wu, Wenya Wang, and Sinno Jialin Pan. 2020. Deep weighted maxsat for aspect-based opinion extraction. In *Proceedings of the 2020 Conference on Empirical Methods in Natural Language Processing (EMNLP)*, pages 5618–5628.

Xiaoyu Xing, Zhijing Jin, Di Jin, Bingning Wang, Qi Zhang, and Xuanjing Huang. 2020. Tasty burgers, soggy fries: Probing aspect robustness in aspect-based sentiment analysis. In *Proceedings of the 2020 Conference on Empirical Methods in Natural Language Processing (EMNLP)*, pages 3594–3605, Online. Association for Computational Linguistics.

Yunyi Yang, Kun Li, Xiaojun Quan, Weizhou Shen, and Qinliang Su. 2020. Constituency lattice encoding for aspect term extraction. In *Proceedings of the 28th international conference on computational linguistics*, pages 844–855.

Yichun Yin, Chenguang Wang, and Ming Zhang. 2020. PoD: Positional dependency-based word embedding for aspect term extraction. In *Proceedings of the 28th International Conference on Computational Linguistics*, pages 1714–1719, Barcelona, Spain (Online). International Committee on Computational Linguistics.

Hong Yu and Vasileios Hatzivassiloglou. 2003. Towards answering opinion questions: Separating facts from opinions and identifying the polarity of opinion sentences. In *Proceedings of the 2003 conference on Empirical methods in natural language processing*, pages 129–136.

Chen Zhang, Qiuchi Li, Dawei Song, and Benyou Wang. 2020. A multi-task learning framework for opinion triplet extraction. In *Findings of the Association for Computational Linguistics: EMNLP 2020*, pages 819–828, Online. Association for Computational Linguistics.

Wenxuan Zhang, Ruidan He, Haiyun Peng, Lidong Bing, and Wai Lam. 2021. Cross-lingual aspect-based sentiment analysis with aspect term code-switching. In *Proceedings of the 2021 Conference on Empirical Methods in Natural Language Processing*, pages 9220–9230.

He Zhao, Longtao Huang, Rong Zhang, Quan Lu, and Hui Xue. 2020. Spanmlt: A span-based multi-task learning framework for pair-wise aspect and opinion terms extraction. In *Proceedings of the 58th annual meeting of the association for computational linguistics*, pages 3239–3248.

Jie Zhou, Jimmy Xiangji Huang, Qin Chen, Qinmin Vivian Hu, Tingting Wang, and Liang He. 2019. Deep learning for aspect-level sentiment classification: survey, vision, and challenges. *IEEE access*, 7:78454–78483.

Exploring Low-resource Neural Machine Translation for Sinhala-Tamil Language Pair

Ashmari Pramodya

University of Colombo School of Computing, Sri Lanka
ash@ucsc.cmb.ac.lk

Abstract

At present, Neural Machine Translation has become a promising strategy for machine translation. Transformer-based deep learning architectures in particular show a substantial performance increase in translating between various language pairs. However, many low-resource language pairs still struggle to lend themselves to Neural Machine Translation due to their data-hungry nature. In this article, we investigate methods of expanding the parallel corpus to enhance translation quality within a model training pipeline, starting from the initial collection of parallel data to the training process of baseline models. Grounded on state-of-the-art Neural Machine Translation approaches such as hyper-parameter tuning, and data augmentation with forward and backward translation, we define a set of best practices for improving Tamil-to-Sinhala machine translation and empirically validate our methods using standard evaluation metrics. Our results demonstrate that the Neural Machine Translation models trained on larger amounts of back-translated data outperform other synthetic data generation approaches in Transformer base training settings. We further demonstrate that, even for language pairs with limited resources, Transformer models are able to tune to outperform existing state-of-the-art Statistical Machine Translation models by as much as 3.28 BLEU points in the Tamil to Sinhala translation scenarios.

1 Introduction

Since 1949, when machine translation was initially proposed (Hutchins, 1995), Statistical Machine Translation (SMT) models dominated the machine translation field for decades. However, the advent of Neural Machine Translation (NMT) using deep learning (Bahdanau et al., 2014; Cho et al., 2014; Sutskever et al., 2014) has revolutionized the field, enabling superior performance in translation tasks. Recently, NMT tends to employ Transformer (Vaswani et al., 2017) architecture which is a novel architecture grounded only on attention mechanisms. While it has shown remarkable results for high-resource languages, such as English, it struggles with low-resource languages like Sinhala and Tamil, which are morphologically rich and low-resourced languages. Despite the existence of the best open-source Sinhala-Tamil translator using SMT, NMT has not been widely experimented on in an open-domain setting. Hence, improving NMT for low-resourced languages remains an open research problem with proven success.

In this paper we aims to investigate the performance of Transformer models on Tamil and Sinhala machine translation, with the goal of establishing best practices for low-resource NMT. We explore various model architectures and hyperparameter tuning methods to develop an accurate model for these languages. To address the issue of insufficient parallel data, we expand the corpus size and evaluate the impact of data size on NMT for low-resource languages. We also examine the effects of back translation and forward translation mechanisms for machine translation. Finally, we compare the performance of our Transformer models with SMT. Our research represents a novel contribution, as there is currently an absence of exploration into the best practices for Transformer-based models in Sinhala and Tamil Neural Machine Translation (NMT) within low-resource contexts.

The rest of the paper is structured as follows: the state-of-the-art studies are critically analyzed in Section 2, Section 3 describes the methodology, and Section 4 presents the detailed experimental settings, including the utilised data sets, tools, and training protocol of MT. In Section 5 we present the experimental results. Finally, Section 6 presents the future works and concludes the paper.

Proceedings of the Student Research Workshop associated with RANLP-2023, pages 87–97, Varna, Bulgaria, Sep 4–6, 2023.
https://doi.org/10.26615/issn.2603-2821.2023_010

2 Literature Review

2.1 Low Resourced Machine Translation

Bilingual sentence pairs are a large collection of annotated data that is essential for training a model with adequate translation quality. However, for numerous languages, we are unable to access large parallel data sets. As a result, numerous research attempts have been made to incorporate monolingual corpora into machine translation (Haddow et al., 2022; Ranathunga et al., 2023).

One of the techniques to improve NMT for low-resource languages is back translation (Sennrich et al., 2015). This involves training a target-to-source (backward) model on the parallel data available and using that model to construct synthetic translations in the monolingual sentences of the targeted language. To train the final source-to-target (forward) model, the existing authentic parallel data are combined with the newly created synthetic parallel data without differentiating between the two (Sennrich et al., 2015). The authentic parallel data provided for NMT isn't large enough to train a backward model that produces qualitative synthetic data. As a result, giving priority to the issue of the lack of parallel data, numerous methods have been proposed to improve the efficiency of the backward model.

Park et al. (2017) solely used synthetic parallel data from both the source and target sides to create the NMT model. Further, according to the Sennrich et al. (2015) the amount of monolingual data only increases the quality of translation to a certain extent, and then it begins to degrade. This phenomenon allows to impose constraints on the amount of monolingual data that can be employed in translation tasks. Moreover, as a result of low-quality synthetic data, the back-translated data may face numerous issues and long-term negative impacts on translation efficiency. Hoang et al. (2018) propose an iterative back-translation approach to address this issue and improve the performance, by using the monolingual data more than once. Additionally, Xu et al. (2019) suggested a method based on sentence similarity score to filter quality synthetic data utilizing bilingual word embeddings (Xu et al., 2019) and sentence similarity metrics (Imankulova et al., 2017). Further, there are a few possible methods of incorporating the monolingual corpora into machine translation, including Dual learning (Xia et al., 2016) and unsupervised machine translation using monolingual corpora alone for both sides (Lample et al., 2017).

2.2 Hyper-Parameter Exploration

Knowing which hyper-parameters to select while training a model is crucial. The parameters chosen prior to the start of training are referred to as hyper-parameters. The optimization of hyper-parameters basically referred to as finding the most optimal tuple that will minimize the predefined loss function on a given set of data.

The difference between low and high-resource NMT is not limited to having more parallel data. It has been shown that in bilingual low-resource scenarios, Phrase-Based Statistical Machine Translation (PBSMT) models outperform NMT models. However, in high-resource scenarios, NMT outperforms PBSMT models (Koehn and Knowles, 2017). Moreover, Sennrich and Zhang (2019) study on low-resource NMT, shows that it is extremely sensitive to hyper-parameters, architectural design, and other design considerations. Unfortunately, their outcomes are limited to a recurrent NMT architecture. Recently, Duh et al. (2020) show that SMT and NMT Transformers work similarly in low-resource scenarios, but the NMT systems require more careful tuning to achieve the same performance as SMT. Most recently, Araabi and Monz (2020) researched the effects of hyper-parameter settings for the Transformer architecture under various low-resource data conditions. Their experiments demonstrate that compared to a Transformer system with default settings for all low-resource data sizes, the appropriate combination of Transformer configurations and regularization algorithms yields significant improvements.

There are numerous ways to choose hyper-parameters, most often with manual tuning and random search or grid search (Bergstra and Bengio, 2012). Apart from that, other methods, such as Bayesian optimization (Bergstra et al., 2011), genetic algorithms (Chapelle et al., 2002), and gradient updates (Maclaurin et al., 2015) direct the hyperparameter selection based on the objective function. However, in order to get accurate performance, all of these approaches require the training of several networks with different hyper-parameter settings.

2.3 Research in Sinhala-Tamil Language Pair

Sinhala and Tamil are the national languages of Sri Lanka. Sinhala belongs to the Indo-Aryan language family, while Tamil is a member of the Dravidian language family (Pushpananda et al., 2014). Both Sinhala and Tamil have a broad morphological vocabulary, Sinhala has up to 110 noun word forms and up to 282 verb word forms (Welgama et al., 2011) and Tamil has around 40 noun word forms and up to 240 verb word forms (Pushpananda et al., 2014). Moreover, syntactically, both Sinhala and Tamil are also close. As a result, the SMT method was able to produce a superior performance in Tamil to Sinhala translation (Pushpananda and Weerasinghe, 2015).

However, Only a few research studies have examined NMT in the Sinhala-Tamil language pairs. Research by Arukgoda et al. (2019) on improving Sinhala–Tamil translation through deep learning techniques provides a prominent foundation for Sinhala and Tamil machine translation in a semi-supervised manner using bidirectional recurrent neural networks. This study has been undertaken for the open-domain context whereas Tennage et al. (2017) also report studies for the NMT using recurrent neural networks for a specific domain. Moreover, recently (Nissanka et al., 2020) explored the use of a monolingual word embedding approach for developing the translations between Sinhala and Tamil language pairs just utilizing monolingual corpora. Additionally, in the context of Tamil to Sinhala machine translation, Pramodya et al. (2020) contrasted Transformers, Recurrent Neural Networks, and SMT with default parameter settings.

3 Methodology

In this article, we concentrate on two primary research directions to address the low-resource problem: (1) exploring hyper parameters with available parallel data (25k), and (2) devise methods to exploit additional opportunistic data sources.

3.1 Hyper-parameter Exploration

Transformer, like all NMT models, involves the setting of different hyper-parameters, but researchers often use the default values, even though their data conditions differ significantly from those used to evaluate the default values (Gu et al., 2018). Computing the full set of possible values for several hyper-parameters at once is computationally intensive. Hence, we will adjust the hyper-parameters that come under vocabulary representation, architecture tuning and regularization settings.

Text-To-Text Transfer Transformer (T5) : At present, with the burgeoning of Transfer Learning, Deep Learning has excelled in various complex tasks. Specifically, in NLP, we leverage transfer learning by pre-training on a task-agnostic objective and then fine-tuning it on particular downstream problems. By leveraging a unified text-to-text format and a massive training data-set (C4 : Colossal Clean Crawled Corpus), the original T5 (Raffel et al., 2019) model achieved state-of-the-art results on a variety of NLP benchmarks. Moreover, the mT5 (Xue et al., 2020) model is a multilingual variant of the original T5 model, aimed at remedying this problem. Although the mT5 model was trained on mC4 (about 26 Terabytes), a multilingual variation of the C4 data set, it closely follows the architecture and training process of T5. Because of this, it still has all the benefits of the T5 model and supports a total of 101 distinct languages.

3.2 Exploring Additional Data with Different Domains

We explored several resources to collect parallel sentences such as crawling the web to mine parallel sentences that already exist and to mine completely novel parallel sentences.

3.3 Exploring Synthetic Data

Here we applied Back Translation (Sennrich et al., 2015), which involve creating artificial source-side sentences by translating a monolingual set in the target language. Further, we employed synthetic data on the target side (Zhang and Zong, 2016). Specifically, the synthetic data was generated through two sources namely 1) Using Transformer-base, and 2) Google translate (GNMT).

Back Translation: Back-translation is a popular method in state-of-the-art machine translation tasks (Edunov et al., 2018). It has shown superior performance compared to other translation approaches in high-resource language settings, and it has also been proven to be effective in low-resource language situations (Cho et al., 2014). This technique involves building a backward model from parallel data, which is used to generate synthetic translations of monolingual sentences in the target language. The produced synthetic parallel data is mixed with the real parallel data to train a final source-to-target (forward) model.

Forward Translation: Forward translation (Zhang and Zong, 2016) improves NMT efficiency by using source-side monolingual data to generate synthetic translations and create a synthetic parallel data set. This leads to a better source-to-target translation model trained with a massive amount of data, while also allowing the target side to learn from synthetic data for improved grammatical correctness

Synthetic Data through Google translate: In order to maximize the use of Google Translate, the back-translation method and Google Translate are used to generate a parallel corpus for training our translation model. This is an approach that is close to the one suggested by (Pham and Nguyen, 2019). However, we had to do some post-processing to the synthetic data as it contains English words in between the words.

4 Experimental Setup

4.1 Hyper-parameter Exploration

Dataset : Our baseline training data comprises around 25000 phrases with a length between 8 and 12 words which was used in the SMT collected by Pushpananda and Weerasinghe (2015). They have used two approaches to collect these parallel data. The first approach was identifying Sinhala-Tamil parallel documents such as magazines, books, articles and the second approach was translating Sinhala sentences to Tamil with the help of professional translators. The corpus statistics for the parallel corpus is given in Table 7 in appendix. We investigated the hyper-parameters for the Tamil to Sinhala translation direction. We were able to fairly compare SMT and NMT in the setting of Tamil and Sinhala because our baseline SMT study (Pushpananda and Weerasinghe, 2015) employed the same corpora (25k).

BPE Effect: In order to improve the translation of rare words, word segmentation approaches such as Byte-Pair-Encoding (BPE) (Sennrich et al., 2016) have become standard practice in NMT.

For Tamil to Sinhala translation, we used BPE merge values of 1k, 2k, 5k, and 10k. The BPE model was trained on the complete training corpus, enabling us to assess the influence of various levels of BPE segmentation on translation performance Here, we selected the merge values by training the models on default parameter settings, and we used smaller numbers of merging operations since we were dealing with smaller training data conditions.

Architecture and Regularization: All the research experiments were carried on openNMT toolkit (Klein et al., 2017). For our experiments, we reduced the number of attention heads in encoder and decoder layers as well as the model dimension. Moreover, we sampled the size of the feed-forward network and also the batch size. Further, we conducted experiments with different values for the learning rate (1,2) and warm-up steps (8000,4000) using the learning rate scheduler, as implemented within OpenNMT-py (Klein et al., 2017). Regularization is used to increase generalization ability and minimize over-fitting in neural networks. Thus, in our experiments, we employed Dropout, one of most effective regularization strategy introduced by (Srivastava et al., 2014). Following (Sennrich and Zhang, 2019), we investigated the impact of regularization by applying dropouts to Transformer. Moreover, we also experimented with larger label-smoothing factors. The selected hyper-parameters for our experiments, and their values are presented in Table 1. Notably, these hyper-parameters and their values depend on preliminary experiments and previous findings (Sennrich and Zhang, 2019; Fonseka et al., 2020; Duh et al., 2020) that identify the hyper-parameters that have the greatest impact on translation efficiency.

Hyper-parameter	Values
Number of Layers in encoder/decoder	5,6
Attention Heads	2, 4
Embedding dimension	256, 512
Feed Forward dimension	1024, 2048
Drop Out	0.2, 0.3, 0.4
Label smoothing	0.1, 0.2
Batch size	2048, 4096
Warm-up steps	8000, 4000
Learning rate(define by OpenNMT (Klein et al., 2017))	1, 2

Table 1: Hyper-parameters considered during the tuning of Transformer with 25k parallel data.

Furthermore, we fine tuned the mT5 model with our data and used it for evaluation of Tamil to Sinhala Translation tasks. To train the mT5 model, we used the Simple Transformers library[1] (based on the Huggingface Transformers library) and the training and testing data will be the same as earlier experiments. For the experiments, we used a training/evaluation batch size of 20 and a maximum sequence length (max seq length) of 96. In our initial experiments, the model worked with relatively long text due to the maximum sequence length of 96. However, we ran out of GPU memory (CUDA

[1] https://github.com/ThilinaRajapakse/simpleTransformers

memory error), and then we decided to reduce the batch size to 4 instead of reducing the maximum sequence length.

4.2 Exploring Additional Data

Previous studies have been conducted (Arukgoda et al., 2019; Nissanka et al., 2020) using only 25k parallel data. In this, we aimed to determine the impact of corpus size on the quality of Tamil to Sinhala translation by expanding the parallel dataset with additional bi-text data. We investigated various resources to collect parallel sentences, including those that already exist and those that can be mined by crawling web pages(refer to the Appendix for more details). Sinhala and Tamil sentence tokenization was done using indicNLP library [2]. Further, models were trained using the default parameters of the Transformer-based architecture and the BPE merge operation value was set to 5k. In order to fairly assess the translation, we employed the BLEU score metric (Bi-Lingual Assessment Understudy) (Papineni et al., 2002).

Before merging the collected parallel datasets, we performed additional cleaning and deduplication. Only after this step, we trained the datasets independently. Initially, we trained the datasets separately and evaluated their performance. However, the BLEU scores did not show any significant improvement in the entire corpus of the bible. This could be attributed to the fact that the bible was aligned by verse, rather than by sentences.

Further, it contains sentences that are too long and need to be split, which is challenging due to irregular usage of splitting punctuations. Therefore, we reduced the corpus by taking the sentences which have sentence length between 1 and 20. The used test set consists of 10% of the training data set which are mutually exclusive. We show the BLEU scores on both Test sets. When compared to Test set A, Test set B does not contain any bible sentences in the evaluation set. Basically, it only contains News Crawl as same as the test set used in section 5.1. The two test sets used in our experiments can be summarized as follows:

i. Test A: 10% of the training data (Eval contains domain-specific data).
ii. Test B: 1000 news sentences (This test set is used for evaluating the baseline systems presented in Table 3).

[2] https://github.com/anoopkunchukuttan/indic_nlp_library

4.3 Exploring Synthetic Data

Monolingual Corpus: For our experiments, we used a Sinhala monolingual corpus with 10M words and a Tamil monolingual corpus with 400,000 words (Pushpananda and Weerasinghe, 2015). Both of these corpora are ideal for an open-domain translation as they have been collected from sentences from different domains such as newspaper articles, technical writing and creative writing.

We conducted experiments to evaluate synthetic data in both source and target sides for the machine translation. In addition, we also examined, how the models perform when training data is augmented with synthetic data which was generated using various MT approaches. In particular, we investigated generated synthetic data not only by Transformer base methods (our NMT model) but also by Google neural Machine translate (GNMT) model.

In addition to backward translation where monolingual corpora were used in the target language, we also also looked at forward translation where monolingual corpora were used in the source language.

Inspired by Poncelas et al. (2019), we continued to create NMT models with increasing sizes of data to assess the effects of synthetic data. Here we used the same default training settings for Transformer-base architecture in order to evaluate how much synthetic data is required to switch back to the commonly used Transformer configurations. Moreover, by employing a random search of hyper parameters we tuned the models at different data-sets only in Tamil $\rightarrow$ Sinhala translation direction, and those configurations were subsequently utilized to train Sinhala $\rightarrow$ Tamil translation direction models. We demonstrate those results in T-tuned columns in Table 6 and Table 7.

5 Results

This section presents the results obtained from the experiments conducted on the Tamil and Sinhala language pairs.

5.1 Hyper Parameter Exploration

We used Transformer-base and SMT (Pushpananda and Weerasinghe, 2015) as our baselines. It took approximately 10-12hrs time to train our models for 15k train steps. For different selected subsets, we obtained significant improvements over Transformer-base. The best results obtained so far from tuning are presented in the Table 2. The re-

	A	B	C	D	E
Layers	5	5	5	5	5
Embedding dimension	512	512	512	512	512
Heads	4	2	2	4	2
Feed-forward dimension	2048	2048	2048	2048	2048
Dropout	0.4	0.3	0.4	0.4	0.3
Label smoothing	0.2	0.2	0.2	0.2	0.2
Batch-size	2048	2048	2048	4096	2048
Warm-up steps	8000	4000	8000	8000	4000
Learning rate (define by OpenNMT)	2	1	2	2	1
BLEU	**16.39**	16.13	16.11	15.83	15.60

Table 2: The best hyper-parameter configurations obtained

sults demonstrate that, reducing the Transformer attention heads, and the number of layers, along with increasing the rate of different regularization techniques are highly effective (+5 BLEU) for the 25k data-set.

Test	இந்த வரலாற்று கதையுடன் வெளிப்படும் மேலும் முக்கியமான பாடமொன்று இருக்கின்றது
English	There is one more important lesson that emerges with this historical story
Reference	මේ ඉතිහාස කතාවත් සමඟ මතුවන තවත් වැදගත් පාඩමක් තිබේ
SMT	මෙම ඓතිහාසික කතා න්ද රය කින් මතුවන තවත් වැදගත් පාඩමක් තිබේ.
Transformer-B	මෙම ඓතිහාසික කතාවලට බලපාන තවත් වැදගත් පාඩමක් තිබේ.
Transformer-T	එම ඓතිහාසික කතාවෙන් හෙළි වන තවත් වැදගත් පාඩමක් තිබේ
mT5_TA-SI	මේ ඉතිහාසය තුළින් පැහැදිලි වනතවත් වැදගත් පාඩමක් තිබේ.

Figure 1: Tamil Sinhala translation example with SMT and NMT systems trained on 25k parallel data on Transformer-B(base),Transformer-T(tuned)(gray color highlighted words give semantically correct meaning)

As Sennrich and Zhang (2019) report reducing the batch size is effective. We also demonstrated that setting the batch size to 2048 performs better than when the batch size is 4096. We were able to outperform SMT results by 3.28 BLEU points with our optimized Transformer. The BLEU scores obtained by our optimized Transformer model were compared with the baseline models presented in Table 3. We also compared the translation quality with that of Google Translate on the same test data set. Examples of translations between SMT and NMT systems can be seen in Figure 1. In summary, our Transformer-T model provided more semantically accurate translations compared to the other models.

5.1.1 Human Evaluation

We utilized the Human ranking of translation scores at the sentence level strategy to compare the performance of the models listed in the Table 3. The models were trained using an equivalent volume (25k) of parallel data. For the human evaluation, ten final-year undergraduates from the translation studies department at the University of Kelaniya, Sri Lanka, participated. Ten sentences from the test set were randomly selected and distributed among the participants, who were subsequently tasked with ranking the translated output. Participants were provided with reference sentences and translated sentences from the four different systems. Furthermore, we instructed them to rank the sentences based on quality, arranging them from best to worst. Throughout this process, we ensured that no ties were permitted and that we adhered to the established guidelines in (Narayan et al., 2017). Table 4 shows the findings of our human evaluation study. We compared our tuned Transformer, mT5_TA-SI, Transformer base, with SMT to determine how much each system is rated as the best, second best, and so on. According to the participants' rankings presented in Table 4, Transformer-Tuned got the highest ranking percentage (43%). Moreover, the mT5_TA-SI was the second-highest-ranked approach by 32%. However, Transformer-Base and SMT, are the least ranked methods respectively. Moreover, evaluating the Transformer-Tuned, mT5_TA-SI and Transformer-Base using the BLEU score also gives the same results. However, BLEU evaluation scores are different when evaluating all four models. Notably, synonyms and paraphrases are only taken into account by the BLEU metric only if they are in the set of multiple reference translations. Further, NMT systems capture the similarity of words which may results in having synonyms in translation outputs. However,

Model	**BLEU**
	Tamil - Sinhala
SMT (Pushpananda and Weerasinghe, 2015)	13.11
Transformer-Base	11.49
Transformer-Tuned	16.39
mT5_TA-SI	11.56

Table 3: Comparison of BLEU score against baseline models for Tamil to Sinhala

Model	1st	2nd	3rd	4th
SMT	0.11	0.25	0.37	0.27
Transformer-Base	0.14	0.22	0.34	0.30
Transformer-Tuned	0.43	0.35	0.10	0.12
mT5_TA-SI	0.32	0.18	0.19	0.31

Table 4: Ranking of various systems. Rank 1st is best and rank 4th, worst. Numbers show the percentage of times a system gets ranked at a certain position.

due to the limited resources, Sinhala and Tamil language pairs do not have the luxury of having multiple references. Hence, we are able to assume that this would be the reason why the Ranking and BLEU metrics calculations produced different results.

5.2 Exploring additional Data

	Data size	Tamil- Sinhala		Sinhala - Tamil	
		Test A	Test B	Test A	Test B
baseline	25k	11.49	11.49	4.98	4.98
+ Bible	45k	13.48	9.38	7.82	4.28
+ Bible + found bitext	55k	14.22	13.25	9.89	6.87
+ Bible + found bitext + Text extracted	65k	15.61	14.48	11.10	6.99

Table 5: The effect of additional resource types for NMT. We observed that adding Bible, Text extracted and found-bitext to baseline tends to improve the performance for NMT, with NMT gaining significant benefits. Models are trained with Transformer-base configurations.

5.2.1 Analysis

The impact of different data types on the model's quality is systematically assessed in the following section.

Effectiveness of additional data

Table 5 shows the performance impact of found Bitext, Paracrawl, and the Bible datasets when combined with our initial training set. We observed noticeable improvement of translation for both directions. For example, on Test Set A, the BLEU points were improved from 11.49 to 15.61 by 4.12 points for Tamil to Sinhala direction and for Sinhala to Tamil direction there was a 6.12 BLEU points improvement from 4.98 to 11.10. The trend is observed in the Test set B as well but only after adding biblical corpus. As depicted in the second row of 5, we observed a significant drop in performance for the parallel training data that differ from the evaluation domain in Test set B. However, in order to improve performance and robustness, we might need to create a validation set that is better matched or use a domain adaptation technique for different domains. We conclude that employing additional data types is a promising research direction, particularly for NMTs with limited resources like Tamil and Sinhala languages.

Figure 2 shows an example sentence from a Bible corpus that has been translated. The resulting translation accurately conveys the intended meaning of the target sentence. It's worth noting that the writing style of Bible verses differs from that of typical news articles sentences, which presents a unique challenge for machine translation.

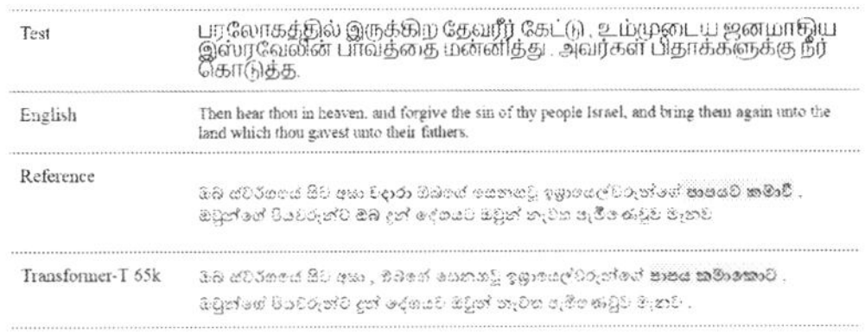

Figure 2: Sample Translation example of Bible verse From Transformer 65k (gray color highlighted words give semantically correct meaning)

Effect of various synthetic data

The experimental results for the analysis of diverse synthetic data are shown in Table 6 and Table 7. We can see from the findings in Table 6 and Table 7 that adding synthetic data on both sides can enhance the performance in the translation from Tamil $\rightarrow$ Sinhala direction. Moreover, all BLEU scores are also higher when compared to the networks built only using authentic data. Surprisingly, in opposite translation direction (Sinhala $\rightarrow$ Tamil) synthetic data has a significant negative impact on results when the data size is increased. Although BLEU scores are dropping when the synthetic data amount is 75k in Tamil $\rightarrow$ Sinhala direction, they are still higher than the baseline and this phenomenon can be observed in both synthetic data generation approaches we used to generate synthetic data.

Particularly, based on the outcomes shown in Table 7, models developed with synthetic data produced by GNMT outperform those developed with data produced by Transformer-Base (*NMT_syn_ta*). Here NMT models are trained with default configurations of Transformer base architecture in both translation directions When comparing models trained on Transformer base architecture, with an equal amount of GNMT (*GNMT_syn_ta*, *GNMT_syn_si*) or Transformer-Base (*NMT_syn_sin*, *NMT_syn_ta*) synthetic data, we find that the GNMT one outperforms the Transformer-Base by around 2.0 BLEU points. However, the difference is only 0.01 BLEU points when the GNMT and Transformer base models' (100k) hyper-parameters are tuned.

As depict in the Table 6 and Table 7, synthetic data have opposite effects on the two translation directions. Specifically, when translating Tamil to Sinhala direction, the monolingual synthetic data from both sides have positive effects. Moreover, the back translation with both approaches, Transformer-base (*NMT_syn*) and Google Translate (*GNMT_syn*) have nearly same performance when the NMT models are tuned with correct hyper parameters. Moreover, forward translation under performs back translation in both synthetic data generation methods we used.

Direction	Tamil → Sinhala		Sinhala → Tamil	
	T-base	T-tuned	T-base	T-tuned
baseline	11.46	16.39	4.89	8.08
+ Synthetic Tamil data *(NMT_syn_ta)*				
25k	12.32	14.42	5.97	7.52
50k	13.03	14.12	**7.12**	**8.10**
75k	15.12	17.74	6.54	6.95
100k	**16.46**	**19.00**	6.65	6.96
+ Synthetic Sinhala data *(NMT_syn_sin)*				
25k	11.74	14.03	6.05	6.81
50k	13.64	13.54	**6.34**	7.14
75k	13.69	14.13	6.12	**8.26**
100k	**13.71**	**14.42**	5.39	6.56

Table 6: Results of corpus extension by using synthetic data generated by Transformer-base model

How much synthetic data do we need for Sinhala-Tamil language pair models to reach reasonable translation quality ?

Direction	Tamil → Sinhala		Sinhala → Tamil	
	T-base	T-tuned	T-base	T-tuned
Baseline	11.46	16.39	4.89	8.08
+ google Synthetic Tamil data *(GNMT_syn_ta)*				
25k	13.25	14.85	5.30	7.86
50k	15.84	18.05	**6.29**	8.49
75k	17.32	18.26	6.09	6.25
100k	**18.44**	**19.01**	5.89	6.84
+ google Synthetic Sinhala data *(GNMT_syn_sin)*				
25k	14.89	17.42	7.14	7.28
50k	15.75	17.89	**8.08**	**8.80**
75k	16.26	18.42	7.20	8.12
100k	**17.78**	**18.69**	7.39	**8.26**

Table 7: Results of corpus extension by using synthetic data generated by Google translate

We conduct a separate set of experiments to study the impact of the amount of synthetic data, for both the source and target sides. From these experiments, we discovered that having more synthetic data does not always increase translation accuracy in Sinhala to Tamil direction. We empirically demonstrate how crucial it is to choose a high-quality NMT system for generating synthetic parallel corpus. For Tamil to Sinhala translation direction, when the ratio between authentic to synthetic parallel sentences were increased, translation performance has continuously improved. However, unlike the Tamil to Sinhala translation, we were unable to obtain a proper translation performance in the opposite direction.

When using higher morphologically rich language as the source language, the NMT architecture encoder performed well. As a result when the source side is more morphologically rich than the target side, the encoder encodes more detail about the sentence, resulting in better decoding by the decoder. The encoded sentences lack sufficient information for the decoder to deduce a successful translation when the source language is less morphologically complex than the target language. We argue that this would be the reason why translations from Tamil to Sinhala are more accurate than translations from Sinhala to Tamil. Additionally, the impact of synthetic data can vary depending on various factors such as the languages involved, data size, and translation direction. In comparison to using only a parallel corpus, incorporating synthetic target data leads to an improvement in source-to-target translation performance. However, the improvement is relatively smaller compared to using source side synthetic data (back translated).

6 Conclusion

We performed an empirical comparison of SMT and NMT in low-resource settings: Tamil-to-Sinhala. Benchmarking common models and establishing best practises are our objectives. This study has demonstrated that, for low-resource data sizes, a proper combination of Transformer configurations together with regularization techniques (Araabi and Monz, 2020) and also with proper vocabulary selection, results in significant improvements when compared with the Transformer system with default settings. Moreover, this research proved the fact suggested by (Duh et al., 2020), in low-resource scenarios, both statistical machine translation (SMT) and neural machine translation (NMT) can work similarly, but in order to get better performance, the neural systems require more careful tuning.

Developing machine translation models for low-resource languages with limited online presence can be challenging, but our preliminary results suggest that even a small amount of parallel data (a few hundred thousand example translations) can make a significant difference when using current neural architectures. Therefore, we believe it is essential to continue pushing the boundaries of finding and curating exploitable parallel text for low-resource languages. In future, NMT system can be improved for low-resource scenarios by experimenting with transfer-learning approaches.

7 Acknowledgement

I would like to express my gratitude to my research supervisors Dr. Randil Pushpananda and Dr. Ruvan Weerasinghe (University of Colombo School of Computing) for their encouragement, support, and valuable feedback. Additionally, I would also like to thank K.T Yasas Mahima for the invaluable assistance provided in structuring the paper.

References

Ali Araabi and Christof Monz. 2020. Optimizing transformer for low-resource neural machine translation. *arXiv preprint arXiv:2011.02266*.

Anupama Arukgoda, A. Weerasinghe, and Randil Pushpananda. 2019. Improving sinhala-tamil translation through deep learning techniques. In *NL4AI@AI*IA*.

Dzmitry Bahdanau, Kyunghyun Cho, and Yoshua Bengio. 2014. Neural machine translation by jointly learning to align and translate. *arXiv preprint arXiv:1409.0473*.

James Bergstra, Rémi Bardenet, Yoshua Bengio, and Balázs Kégl. 2011. Algorithms for hyper-parameter optimization. In *25th annual conference on neural information processing systems (NIPS 2011)*, volume 24. Neural Information Processing Systems Foundation.

James Bergstra and Yoshua Bengio. 2012. Random search for hyper-parameter optimization. *Journal of machine learning research*, 13(2).

Olivier Chapelle, Vladimir Vapnik, Olivier Bousquet, and Sayan Mukherjee. 2002. Choosing multiple parameters for support vector machines. *Machine learning*, 46(1):131–159.

Kyunghyun Cho, Bart Van Merriënboer, Caglar Gulcehre, Dzmitry Bahdanau, Fethi Bougares, Holger Schwenk, and Yoshua Bengio. 2014. Learning phrase representations using rnn encoder-decoder for statistical machine translation. *arXiv preprint arXiv:1406.1078*.

Kevin Duh, Paul McNamee, Matt Post, and Brian Thompson. 2020. Benchmarking neural and statistical machine translation on low-resource african languages. In *Proceedings of The 12th Language Resources and Evaluation Conference*, pages 2667–2675.

Sergey Edunov, Myle Ott, Michael Auli, and David Grangier. 2018. Understanding back-translation at scale. *arXiv preprint arXiv:1808.09381*.

Thilakshi Fonseka, Rashmini Naranpanawa, Ravinga Perera, and Uthayasanker Thayasivam. 2020. English to sinhala neural machine translation. In *2020 International Conference on Asian Language Processing (IALP)*, pages 305–309. IEEE.

Jiatao Gu, Hany Hassan, Jacob Devlin, and Victor O.K. Li. 2018. Universal neural machine translation for extremely low resource languages. In *Proceedings of the 2018 Conference of the North American Chapter of the Association for Computational Linguistics: Human Language Technologies, Volume 1 (Long Papers)*, pages 344–354, New Orleans, Louisiana. Association for Computational Linguistics.

Francisco Guzmán, Peng-Jen Chen, Myle Ott, Juan Pino, Guillaume Lample, Philipp Koehn, Vishrav Chaudhary, and Marc'Aurelio Ranzato. 2019. The flores evaluation datasets for low-resource machine translation: Nepali-english and sinhala-english. *arXiv preprint arXiv:1902.01382*.

Barry Haddow, Rachel Bawden, Antonio Valerio Miceli Barone, Jindřich Helcl, and Alexandra Birch. 2022. Survey of low-resource machine translation. *Computational Linguistics*, 48(3):673–732.

Vu Cong Duy Hoang, Philipp Koehn, Gholamreza Haffari, and Trevor Cohn. 2018. Iterative back-translation for neural machine translation. In *Proceedings of the 2nd Workshop on Neural Machine Translation and Generation*, pages 18–24.

W John Hutchins. 1995. Machine translation: A brief history. In *Concise history of the language sciences*, pages 431–445. Elsevier.

Aizhan Imankulova, Takayuki Sato, and Mamoru Komachi. 2017. Improving low-resource neural machine translation with filtered pseudo-parallel corpus. In *Proceedings of the 4th Workshop on Asian Translation (WAT2017)*, pages 70–78.

Guillaume Klein, Yoon Kim, Yuntian Deng, Jean Senellart, and Alexander M Rush. 2017. Opennmt: Open-source toolkit for neural machine translation. *arXiv preprint arXiv:1701.02810*.

Philipp Koehn and Rebecca Knowles. 2017. Six challenges for neural machine translation. In *Proceedings of the First Workshop on Neural Machine Translation*, pages 28–39, Vancouver. Association for Computational Linguistics.

Guillaume Lample, Alexis Conneau, Ludovic Denoyer, and Marc'Aurelio Ranzato. 2017. Unsupervised machine translation using monolingual corpora only. *arXiv preprint arXiv:1711.00043*.

Dougal Maclaurin, David Duvenaud, and Ryan Adams. 2015. Gradient-based hyperparameter optimization through reversible learning. In *International conference on machine learning*, pages 2113–2122. PMLR.

Shashi Narayan, Nikos Papasarantopoulos, Shay B Cohen, and Mirella Lapata. 2017. Neural extractive summarization with side information. *arXiv preprint arXiv:1704.04530*.

LNASH Nissanka, BHR Pushpananda, and AR Weerasinghe. 2020. Exploring neural machine translation for sinhala-tamil languages pair. In *2020 20th International Conference on Advances in ICT for Emerging Regions (ICTer)*, pages 202–207. IEEE.

Kishore Papineni, Salim Roukos, Todd Ward, and Wei-Jing Zhu. 2002. Bleu: a method for automatic evaluation of machine translation. In *Proceedings of the 40th annual meeting of the Association for Computational Linguistics*, pages 311–318.

Jaehong Park, Jongyoon Song, and Sungroh Yoon. 2017. Building a neural machine translation system using only synthetic parallel data. *arXiv preprint arXiv:1704.00253*.

Nghia Luan Pham and Van Vinh Nguyen. 2019. Adapting neural machine translation for english-vietnamese using google translate system for back-translation.

Alberto Poncelas, Maja Popovic, Dimitar Shterionov, Gideon Maillette de Buy Wenniger, and Andy Way. 2019. Combining smt and nmt back-translated data for efficient nmt. *arXiv preprint arXiv:1909.03750*.

Ashmari Pramodya, Randil Pushpananda, and Ruvan Weerasinghe. 2020. A comparison of transformer, recurrent neural networks and smt in tamil to sinhala mt. In *2020 20th International Conference on Advances in ICT for Emerging Regions (ICTer)*, pages 155–160. IEEE.

Randil Pushpananda and Ruvan Weerasinghe. 2015. Statistical machine translation from and into morphologically rich and low resourced languages. In *International Conference on Intelligent Text Processing and Computational Linguistics*, pages 545–556. Springer.

Randil Pushpananda, Ruvan Weerasinghe, and Mahesan Niranjan. 2014. Sinhala-tamil machine translation: Towards better translation quality. In *Proceedings of the Australasian Language Technology Association Workshop 2014*, pages 129–133.

Colin Raffel, Noam Shazeer, Adam Roberts, Katherine Lee, Sharan Narang, Michael Matena, Yanqi Zhou, Wei Li, and Peter J Liu. 2019. Exploring the limits of transfer learning with a unified text-to-text transformer. *arXiv preprint arXiv:1910.10683*.

Surangika Ranathunga, En-Shiun Annie Lee, Marjana Prifti Skenduli, Ravi Shekhar, Mehreen Alam, and Rishemjit Kaur. 2023. Neural machine translation for low-resource languages: A survey. *ACM Computing Surveys*, 55(11):1–37.

Rico Sennrich, Barry Haddow, and Alexandra Birch. 2015. Improving neural machine translation models with monolingual data. *arXiv preprint arXiv:1511.06709*.

Rico Sennrich, Barry Haddow, and Alexandra Birch. 2016. Edinburgh neural machine translation systems for wmt 16. *arXiv preprint arXiv:1606.02891*.

Rico Sennrich and Biao Zhang. 2019. Revisiting low-resource neural machine translation: A case study. *arXiv preprint arXiv:1905.11901*.

Nitish Srivastava, Geoffrey Hinton, Alex Krizhevsky, Ilya Sutskever, and Ruslan Salakhutdinov. 2014. Dropout: a simple way to prevent neural networks from overfitting. *The journal of machine learning research*, 15(1):1929–1958.

Ilya Sutskever, Oriol Vinyals, and Quoc V Le. 2014. Sequence to sequence learning with neural networks. In *Advances in neural information processing systems*, pages 3104–3112.

Pasindu Tennage, Prabath Sandaruwan, Malith Thilakarathne, Achini Herath, Surangika Ranathunga, Sanath Jayasena, and Gihan Dias. 2017. Neural machine translation for sinhala and tamil languages. In *2017 International Conference on Asian Language Processing (IALP)*, pages 189–192. IEEE.

Jörg Tiedemann. 2012. Parallel data, tools and interfaces in opus. In *Lrec*, volume 2012, pages 2214–2218.

Ashish Vaswani, Noam Shazeer, Niki Parmar, Jakob Uszkoreit, Llion Jones, Aidan N Gomez, Lukasz Kaiser, and Illia Polosukhin. 2017. Attention is all you need. *arXiv preprint arXiv:1706.03762*.

Viraj Welgama, Dulip Lakmal Herath, Chamila Liyanage, Namal Udalamatta, Ruvan Weerasinghe, and Tissa Jayawardana. 2011. Towards a sinhala wordnet. In *Proceedings of the Conference on Human Language Technology for Development*.

Yingce Xia, Di He, Tao Qin, Liwei Wang, Nenghai Yu, Tie-Yan Liu, and Wei-Ying Ma. 2016. Dual learning for machine translation. *arXiv preprint arXiv:1611.00179*.

Guanghao Xu, Youngjoong Ko, and Jungyun Seo. 2019. Improving neural machine translation by filtering synthetic parallel data. *Entropy*, 21(12):1213.

Linting Xue, Noah Constant, Adam Roberts, Mihir Kale, Rami Al-Rfou, Aditya Siddhant, Aditya Barua, and Colin Raffel. 2020. mT5: A massively multilingual pre-trained text-to-text transformer.

Jiajun Zhang and Chengqing Zong. 2016. Exploiting source-side monolingual data in neural machine translation. In *Proceedings of the 2016 Conference on Empirical Methods in Natural Language Processing*, pages 1535–1545.

A Appendix

A.1 Corpus Statistics

A.1.1 Parallel Corpus Statistics

The corpus statistics for the parallel corpus we used in section 4.1 is given in Table 8.

Corpus Statistics	Sinhala	Tamil
Sentence Pairs	26,187	26,187
Vocabulary Size (V)	38,203	54,543
Total number of words (T)	262,082	227,486
V/T %	14.58	23.98

Table 8: Parallel corpus statistics

The various types of resources we investigated for gathering online parallel data, as detailed in Section 4.2, are outlined below:

- **Found Bitext**: Pre-existing parallel sentences could found via various sources such as Opus [3], JW300 [4].
- **Mined Bitext**: Parallel sentences can be mined by crawling the web, for example via Paracrawl [5]. We exploit the fact that various websites exist in multiple languages and devise methods to discover and extract these parallel sentences. We basically focus into Government websites [6] and, online newspapers.
- **Bible**: Studies (Guzmán et al., 2019) have used Bible as a corpus for natural language processing and also for NMT for low resource languages. A parallel corpus of the bible in 100 languages (Tiedemann, 2012) is available online[7]. However, for Sinhala and Tamil it is not available. So we scraped the online bible found in Wordproject Bibles Index[8] which uses the KJV version of English and other languages.
- Text Extraction from sources like Textbooks (provided by educational publications).

[3]http://opus.nlpl.eu/
[4]http://opus.nlpl.eu/JW300.php
[5]https://paracrawl.eu/
[6]https://www.mohe.gov.lk
[7]https://github.com/christos-c/bible-corpus/
[8]https://www.wordproject.org/bibles/index.htm
[9]https://github.com/nlpc-uom/Sinhala-Tamil-Aligned-Parallel-Corpus
[10]https://tico-19.github.io

Corpus	Sentence pairs
Bible	31k
GNOME	8.4k
Ubuntu	4.9k
Open Subtitles	8k
JW300	4M
TextBooks	1.2k
Sinhala Tamil aligned [9]	0.9k
Translation data related to the COVID-19 [10]	0.3k

Table 9: The parallel corpora available online.

A.1.2 Monolingual Corpus Statistics

Corpus Statistics	Sinhala	Tamil
Number of sentence pairs	1,067,173	407,578
Total words	13,158,152	4,178,440
Vocabulary size	933,153	301,251

Table 10: Monolingual Corpus Statistics

A.2 Transformer-base settings

	Transformer-base default parameters
Layers	6
Embedding dimension	512
Heads	8
Feed-forward dimension	2048
Dropout	0.3
Label smoothing	0.1
Batch-size	4096
Warm-up steps	8000
Learning rate	2
BLEU	11.49

Table 11: Default hyper parameters used in Transformer-base

Prompting *ChatGPT* to Draw Morphological Connections for New Word Comprehension

Bianca-Madalina Zgreaban and **Rishabh Suresh**
Institute for Language Sciences, Utrecht University, Utrecht, Netherlands
madalinazgreaban0@gmail.com and r.suresh@students.uu.nl

Abstract

Though more powerful, Large Language Models need to be periodically retrained for updated information, consuming resources and energy. In this respect, prompt engineering can prove a possible solution to re-training. To explore this line of research, this paper uses a case study, namely, finding the best prompting strategy for asking ChatGPT to define new words based on morphological connections. To determine the best prompting strategy, each definition provided by the prompt was ranked in terms of plausibility and humanlikeness criteria. The findings of this paper show that adding contextual information, operationalised as the keywords 'new' and 'morpheme', significantly improve the performance of the model for any prompt. While no single prompt significantly outperformed all others, there were differences between performances on the two criteria for most prompts. ChatGPT also provided the most correct definitions with a *persona*-type prompt.

1 Introduction

In recent years, *Large Language Models* (henceforth LLMs) have become increasingly more powerful (Bender et al., 2021). However, in terms of training, LLMs have large power consumption (Bender et al., 2021). This results in large expenditures of energy and resources if the models are periodically re-trained to have updated information, such as an updated vocabulary. A potential alternative to re-training is prompt engineering, namely designing better input prompts to get heightened performance (Ekin, 2023; Zhao et al., 2021). Through prompt engineering, considered even a programming method by Zhao et al. (2021), a model applies previous acquired knowledge to new tasks, thereby increasing its performance.

To research the advantages of prompt engineering in terms of updating vocabulary, the current study looks for the best prompting strategy in a case study, namely employing morphological connections for new word comprehension. We define morphological connections as extrapolating the definition of unfamiliar words by use of morphological knowledge, i.e. morphemes.

Thus, our research question is "What prompting strategy best allows an LLM to make correct morphological connections in a context of zero-shot learning?".

This study is not relevant only for novel word comprehension, but also for the task of morphological decomposition. For example, Kim and Smolensky (2021) showed evidence that BERT can abstract over grammatical categorisations, while McCoy et al. (2023) showed some models, such as GPT-2, use derivational morphemes in the generation of novel words, being able to generalise and use morphemes in a compositional manner. However, though LLMs might hold knowledge on abstract morphological categories, they might not always exploit this knowledge (Mahowald et al., 2023), given such models are not task-specific like decompositional models (for a systematic review on unsupervised learning in morphology, see Hammarström and Borin, 2011).

Thus, the current article specifically concerns prompting agnostic-task models to exploit morphological knowledge, i.e. individual morphemes and their functional roles, for morphological connection.

The chosen model was ChatGPT (OpenAI, 2021), a GPT-3.5 fine-tuned model. We compared statistically how the model performed given different types of prompts, and varying amounts of contextual information. Here, 'context' was operationalised in terms of keywords (i.e. 'new' or 'morpheme') or information about the task the model needed to perform. Given the model's training to avoid hallucinations, we expected it to classify new words as non-existent in the absence of context. We also used English as our test case, primarily due

Proceedings of the Student Research Workshop associated with RANLP-2023, pages 98–107, Varna, Bulgaria, Sep 4–6, 2023.
https://doi.org/10.26615/issn.2603-2821.2023_011

to being one of the languages for which ChatGPT performs the best in various tasks (Lai et al., 2023).

We show that depending on the criteria considered (i.e. plausibility or humanlikeness) different prompting strategies were better. Additionally, in line with our expectations, regardless of the criteria used, adding more contextual information increases the model's chance of offering a correct word definition.

Our results prove useful specifically for the users of ChatGPT, as despite the spread in its use, limited studies have been conducted on ChatGPT's neologism comprehension (Lenci, 2023). Even more, our results also prove important for research on novelty and LLMs, especially given this is overall a neglected research topic according to (McCoy et al., 2023). Moreover, this study presents a systematic methodology to test an LLM's ability to identify morphological connections or decompositions, which can be applied in the future to investigate other languages and language models as well.

The article is organized as follows: Section 2 outlines out methods, including the materials, procedure, scoring, and analysis, Section 3 describes our results, and Sections 4 and 5 include our discussion and conclusions.

2 Methods

2.1 Prompts

We adopted an approach advocated by White et al. (2023) in defining six basic prompts to be tested. We also manipulated the amount of contextual information in each prompt by designing four conditions: -morpheme, -new, as in (1); -morpheme, +new, as in (2); +morpheme, -new, as in (3); and +morpheme, +new, as in (4).

(1) Define...
(2) Define the *new* word ...
(3) Define the word ... considering its *morphemes*.
(4) Define the *new* word ... considering its *morphemes*.

Table 1: 'Define' prompt pattern in all four conditions

White et al.'s (2023) paper proved useful not only in offering examples of prompts, but also in presenting them systematically through what they call *prompt patterns*. They argue that when defining a prompt, it is important to specify its intent, motivation, structure, key ideas and consequences, along with an example of it. Such characteristics might help users design better prompts in view of their expectations, what they predict to be necessary information for the task, and possible consequences. An illustration of the prompt pattern for the prompt 'Define' can be seen in the following sentences:

> **Name**: Define
>
> **Intent:** Make morphological connections.
>
> **Motivation**: In case of use of novel word outside training data, the user needs to prompt the model for the new word.
>
> **Structure and key ideas**:
>
> Define **[word]**.
>
> Define **[the new word]**.
>
> Define **[the word]** considering its morphemes.
>
> Define **[the new word]**, considering its morphemes.
>
> **An example**: Define signatorily.
>
> **Consequences**: The model can generate hallucinations as it accepts the 'new word' as truly existent.

We adopted four prompts directly from White et al. (2023) with two variants of one pattern (i.e. the 'Persona' pattern), and defined one of our own (i.e. the 'Define' pattern presented above).

In another paper (Ekin, 2023), efficient prompt engineering entails, among other things, clear instructions, explicit constraints, varying contexts or examples, but also considering the type of task the system has to achieve (i.e. based on analysis or recall). The same paper also recommends other practices such as testing iteratively more prompts and designing prompts for specific domains. The chosen prompts from White et al.'s (2023) paper achieve these recommendations to various degrees. For example, the prompts' instructions vary in detail ('define words' vs. 'define new words'), have different contexts (e.g.. with or without 'new'), and various constraints (i.e. no constraints vs. following a pattern). Though the prompts do not provide any examples, given our zero-shot learning task, some of them can be regarded as domain-specific. For example, the *persona*-type prompt (see Appendix) by default restrains the domain of the output.

2.2 Test Items

For the words to test the model on, we decided to create a set of non-existent, but plausible English words, comprised of an existing English word, with a derivational affix. In making this choice, we followed McCoy et al. (2023) to ensure that we were testing the capacity of morphological connection, and not just recall of the model. In a previous study on the role of derivational morphology in lexical acquisition by Scandinavian children (Bertram et al., 2000), the authors found that the productivity of a given affix was strongly predictive of how well the participants performed on new word comprehension. They argued that more productive affixes were acquired earlier because they are used more regularly, and the form-meaning mapping may thus be easier to learn for children. In the case of LLMs, in may be argued analogously that the less productive a derivational affix is, the less is recombined with different lexical roots. As a consequence, the chances the model considers that affix as an independent meaningful unit are lower.

Thus, the novel words were created with either productive or unproductive suffixes to see if productivity had any systematic influence on the model's performance. The specific suffixes were selected from a paper by Ford et al. (2010) who tested word recognition by human participants based on morpheme frequency and productivity. They provide a list of derivational suffixes which are classified as either productive or unproductive based on three criteria: "hapax legommena of an affix, the type and token frequency of an affix and dictionary citation dates for neologisms" (Ford et al., 2010, p.120). Five productive suffixes: *-ly*, *-less*, *-ish*, *-able*, and *-ify*, and five unproductive suffixes: *-ise*, *-ous*, *-some*, *-ary*, and *-en* were selected from that paper to create the non-words.

In total, 10 new words were created with an equal number of productive and unproductive suffixes: *signatorily*, *assemblyless*, *benchish*, *delveable*, *lunchify*, *palatialise*, *violinous*, *musksome*, *containary*, *shallowen*. The complete list included nouns, verbs, adjectives, and adverbs, though adjectives were the most frequent. It was important to ensure that all test words were absent from the model's training data, so for every word, a browser search using *Microsoft Bing* was carried out to make sure that there were no matching hits. Additionally, we also verified that the words differed from a familiar word by a maximum of one derivational morpheme, in order to limit the number of morphological connections that the model would have to draw.

2.3 Procedure

The testing was conducted on three separate occasions within a two-week period on two separate devices, due to the number of prompts per hour per user. For each of the 24 prompts, a single attempt to define each word was given for the model. Additionally, a new chat was used for each word, given that Ortega-Martín et al. (2023) showed that repeated use of the same chat leads to lack of inference from the model due to its cache memory. In this way, we ensured wrong answers are not generated due to lack of inference, while we also ruled out the possibility that ChatGPT could improve its performance as it "learns" what is expected of it. The total number of trials was 240, and for each trial the output was saved for coding and analysis.

2.4 Scoring and Coding

Every output text produced by the model was scored on two criteria, *plausibility* and *humanlikeness*, being coded a 1 if the given definition was a 'success' (i.e. was plausible or humanlike) or 0 otherwise. If the model failed to provide any definition at all, this was coded as 0.

The need for two criteria was based on the understanding that expectations of the model may differ based on the downstream task. For example, if morphological connection is used in sentiment analysis of perfume reviews, we would prefer the model to make more humanlike inferences about one of our fictional words, i.e. *musksome*, has more on earthy, strong smell.

A definition was deemed plausible if it specified the correct word class of the derived word, and if it was related to the definition of the root word.

To score the output on humanlikeness, we conducted a survey with a sample of 11 native English-speakers, asking participants to provide hypothetical definitions for our words. In this survey, participants were asked to provide an intuitive definition of words taking advantage of the fact that the non-words were related to existing words. It was assumed that participants would not have knowledge of the linguistic definition of a *morpheme*. The participants were also requested to provide a words class for the words, along with hypothetical example sentences. The 11 definitions for each word were then analysed to identify a set of common characteristics based on which to define *human-likeness*. An example of such characteristics is provided below for the word *violinous*.

> **violinous**: Adjective, violin-like quality in sound or appearance, of music/of an object/of a composition.

In general, definitions provided by human participants were assumed to be plausible themselves as long as they involved correct identification of the component morphemes. Human definitions that were not based on the morphological structure of a word were not used in formulating the criteria for humanlikeness. For example, one definition of the word *shallowen* provided by a participant was a "shallow Halloween", which clearly did relate to the meaning of the morpheme *-en*. In sum, a definition was considered humanlike if it had the common characteristics of the definitions in our survey.

2.5 Analysis

Two generalised linear mixed-effect regression models were created for humanlikeness and plausibility using R (Team, 2021), in RStudio (RStudio Team, 2020). The models contained a three-way interaction between the presence in the prompt of the word *new*, that of the word *morpheme* (both coded as binary variables), and the productivity of the suffixes. By-type (prompt type) random intercepts were also included in the models. The type of the prompt was left out of the model given it did not improve its fit. The effects *new*, *morpheme*, and *productive* had orthogonal contrasts set.

3 Results

The descriptive statistics for the number of plausible and humanlike definitions provided by the model for any given prompt are shown in table 2 below. In principle, a prompt could score anywhere between 0 and 10 on each criterion.

Plausibility			
Mean	*SD*	*Min.*	*Max.*
6.58	2.89	1	10
Humanlikeness			
Mean	*SD*	*Min.*	*Max.*
5.38	2.70	0	9

Table 2: Descriptive statistics for plausibility and humanlikeness scores for the model across prompts.

3.1 Plausibility

In terms of plausibility, two tested prompts offered plausible definitions for all words, such as the 'Persona' prompt word generator, conditions +new, +morpheme and -new, +morpheme, and the 'Context manager' prompt, condition +new, +morpheme.

From the model we built, we found significant main effects of adding the word *new* (β = 1.5645, z-score = 4.47, p-value < 0.05), and the word *morpheme* (β = 1.3083, z-score = 3.76, p-value < 0.05), as well as a significant main effect of suffix productivity (β = 1.1030, z-score = 3.18, p-value < 0.05). Thus, ChatGPT was over four and a half times more likely to provide a plausible definition if the prompt included the word *new*, over three and a half times more likely if the prompt included the word *morpheme*, and performed approximately three times better for words with a productive suffix than an unproductive one.

3.2 Humanlikeness

Considering humanlikeness, no prompt achieved correct definitions for all words. However, the 'Persona' prompt word generator, in condition -new, -morpheme and condition +new, +morpheme had 9 out of 10 correct definitions. Note that that the 'Persona' prompt word generator, condition +new, +morpheme, scores high for both measurements.

We found significant main effects of adding the word *new* (β = 1.81369, z-score = 5.92, p-value < 0.05), and the word *morpheme* (β = 0.78839, z-score = 2.60, p-value < 0.05), and a significant interaction effect of *new* with the productivity of the suffix (β = -1.39553, z-score = -2.3, p-value < 0.05). Thus, ChatGPT was approximately six times more likely to provide a humanlike definition if the prompt included the word *new*, approximately twice as likely to provide a humanlike definition if the prompt included the word *morpheme*, and the effect of adding the word *new* was almost four times greater for words with an unproductive suffix, than for words with productive suffixes.

4 Discussion

While our analysis did not identify one prompt that was significantly better than all others in humanlikenss or plausibility, we found that the model always performed better when the prompt provided additional contextual information in the form of the words *new* and *morpheme*. As expected, the more specific the task is for the language model, the better it performs. Thus, our results also reinforce Ekin's (2023) suggestions on giving specific details about the task.

Better performance on plausibility for words with a productive affix suggests that ChatGPT may be better at identifying form-meaning mappings for productive suffixes than for unproductive ones. This finding is in line with what authors like Bertram et al. (2000) found for language acquisition in children, and might be, similarly, caused by frequency of the affix. For example, the more productive the morpheme, the more often it may occur in the training data, and the more information the model could have regarding the contexts it appears in. Eventually this might result in a more accurate representation of the meaning of the morpheme.

In contrast, productivity had no significant effect on humanlike outputs of the models, which might indicate that high probabilities counts of productive morphemes do not encompass characteristics of human definitions. This might be because human definitions rely often on aspects that cannot be inferred from probabilities counts, such as personal experience or world knowledge when defining new words, e.g. defining *musksome* as having a certain kind of smell.

However, though productivity had no effect on humanlike definitions, there was a significant interaction between productivity and the word *new*. More exactly, adding the word *new* to the prompt always improves it. However, the impact of the word 'new' on the humanlikeness of the generated definition is less strong if the morpheme is productive. Thus, for words with unproductive morphemes, the model may improve more because it may be more likely to "look for" a morphological decomposition as a heuristic when given the additional context.

This interaction effect between productivity and the word 'new' can also be influenced by the root morphemes of the words. This might be because the most salient word meaning differs significantly for humans and ChatGPT: given the model was trained on data for a numerous specialised tasks, it sometimes regards specialised definitions very likely. This was clearly shown for the word *assemblyless*. We found that while almost all human participants defined the word in relation to an *assembly* as a 'group or gathering of people' or 'the process of assembling something', ChatGPT most frequently drew the connection to a programming language called 'assembly'. This resulted in less humanlike definitions for the model, showcasing humanlike definitions were always plausible, but not the other way around, as shown in the example below:

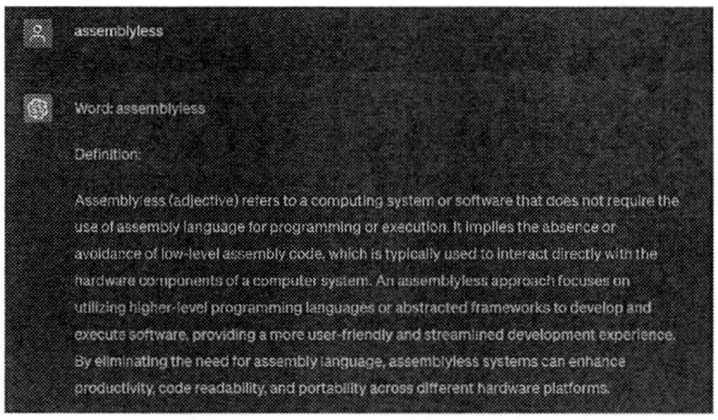

Figure 1: Definition for *assemblyless* provided by ChatGPT using the 'Word generator' prompt template.

Even more, productive morphemes are defined in Ford et al. (2010) in terms of appearance in hapax legomena, which might indicate they form more specialised words. Thus, the probability of generating specialised definitions can increase because our definition of productive suffixes is defined, to some extent, in relation to specialised words. This would overall increase chance of generating specialised word definitions if the root morpheme can also have a specialised meaning, like *assembly*.

Even for words without a root morpheme with specialised meanings, productive derivational morphemes might often be associated with various root morphemes with diverse meanings, which can lead to bigger perplexity and, consequently, less specific or humanlike output. Comparatively, unproductive morphemes have less chances to be associated with more words, which would make the model stick to a few definitions that might also be more specific.

Thus, depending if the user intends to obtain more humanlike or just plausible definitions, the prompt that scored highest in one of the criteria can be used. The statistical results can also be used to further create new prompts by addition of the two contextual words, i.e. 'new' and 'morpheme', depending on the tasks morphological connection will be used in. Note that the both conditions of the best humanlike prompt either have no context, or both context words. This indicates some successful prompts follow an overall opposite effect, i.e. they lack context words but perform well.

Lastly, if the reader wants to achieve a balance in the chosen prompt, i.e. to be as humanlike and as plausible as possible, the 'Persona' word generator prompt, condition + new, + morpheme may be the best choice, given its high scores in both criteria, averaged at 9.5 correct definitions for morphological connection.

5 Conclusion

Our study aimed to identify an optimal prompting strategy for ChatGPT to draw morphological connections while producing word definitions for unfamiliar words. We conducted a word definition task using different prompts, and compared the model's performance on plausibility and humanlikeness for definitions that it provided for a set of morphologically complex nonce words.

We found that irrespective of the prompt template, adding the words *new* and *morpheme* to a prompt, significantly improved the performance of ChatGPT. Thus, the users looking to obtain definitions of unfamiliar morphologically complex words from the model can apply the current findings by including such keywords in their prompts.

In terms of best prompting strategies, our results found two prompts that had the maximal performance on plausibility, i.e. 'Persona' prompt word generator, condition + new, + morpheme and condition - new, + morpheme, and 'Context manager' prompt, condition + new, + morpheme. In terms of humanlikeness, our results show one prompt that had the best performance, i.e. 'Persona' prompt word generator, condition - new, - morpheme, and condition + new, + morpheme. These results also indicate the 'Persona' prompt word generator, condition + new, + morpheme scores, on average, the highest. However, note that the statistical analysis did not point to an overall best prompt.

We found evidence that ChatGPT's response is however also always modulated by factors such as the nature of its training data and world knowledge, which can lead it to produce definitions which while plausible, may not be humanlike. This is something that may be of interest to researchers in the future.

Limitations

The first limitation to our study is small sample sizes in terms of the number of prompting strategies tested, the number of words tested, the number of human participants to define *humanlike* performance, and the number of contextual factors compared. Given that this was designed as a pilot study, we restricted our sample in a number of ways, so expanding the testing material in any direction would be a useful direction for future research.

We also recognise that one prominent difference between the way that we prompted the model and the human participants is that we specifically suggested to the latter that they provide examples with their definitions, and we did not do so for ChatGPT. This meant that especially for humanlikeness, a very brief or vague definition from the model was difficult to categorise, since we would not necessarily obtain direct evidence that the model was exploiting morphological relatedness in a humanlike way. Including a request for examples in the prompt text in future research might help in the coding of outputs.

With regards to the test words, we also wish to point out that for all the nonce words, the lexical root morpheme could always also be used as a free morpheme. That is to say, we did not look at how allomorphy might affect the performance of the model, a point which would be of great interest in the context of the form-meaning mapping question. If we had used a nonce word like *proficiate*, a hypothetical combination of the lexical root in *proficiency*, and the verbalising suffix *-ate*, how successful might the model be at parsing the word into its component morphemes and extrapolating a definition? In addition to that, all the nonce words differed from a familiar word by only a single morpheme, so it would be worth looking at how the model performs when the number of derivational morphemes involved increases. Future studies should also consider controlling for meaning of root morphemes, i.e. for specialised meanings, so as to rule the possibility of the model to choose more unlikely humanlike definitions.

According to previous studies (Ortega-Martín et al., 2023), ChatGPT generalises knowledge with time. To test this, the study initially planned to have prompts run a second time. However, due to limitations of time and because the prompting was done in 3 rounds, testing for generalisation could not be systematic, and therefore, would have not been relevant anymore. It would be interesting in the future to investigate if generalisation exists and if the model can become increasingly specialised on the topic only by prompting. If true, this might be an alternative to fine-tuning to some extent.

Finally, as we pointed out in the introduction, we focused on English as our test case, despite the observation that other languages have far more extensive morphological systems. This reduces the generalisability of our conclusions to the performance of the model with languages with richer morphological systems. Morphological decomposition is especially important for languages with rich or agglutinative morphology. For example, rich morphology has been anticipated to be problematic since Creutz and Lagus (2002), where high morpheme productivity would lead to a irrationally high number of distinct types, which, in turn, would lead to poor comprehension abilities. Languages rich in morphology still raise difficulties today. For example, Belinkov et al. (2017) trained a classifier for morphological prediction on word feature representations from a machine translation model and showed that representations learned in the English model do better when predicting morphology, than those for languages richer in morphology such as Hebrew. As the authors remark, one could expect models for languages with richer morphologies to encode more morphological knowledge. However, the inherent difficult nature of translating into a language with rich morphology might make the model perform overall worse, which would result in weaker features representations. In this respect, future studies might also look to expand the number of test cases to improve the validity of our findings, but to also test if our methodology can improve morphological features of models by forcing better decomposition of words.

Lastly, future work should consider automatic methods in designing prompts too. As Wang et al. (2023) remarks, manually designing prompts is expensive and time-consuming. Thus, future studies in prompting for morphological connection might benefit from deploying models in designing prompts, i.e. seeing the task as sequence-to-sequence generation task (for a better review, see Wang et al., 2023).

Acknowledgements

We would like to thank Dr. Denis Paperno for his supervision and advice during the project, as well as our peers at Utrecht University for their input and feedback. We would also like to acknowledge the contributions of the two anonymous reviewers whose comments helped us refine this article.

References

Yonatan Belinkov, Nadir Durrani, Fahim Dalvi, Hassan Sajjad, and James Glass. 2017. What do neural machine translation models learn about morphology? In *Proceedings of the 55th Annual Meeting of the Association for Computational Linguistics (Volume 1: Long Papers)*, pages 861–872, Vancouver, Canada. Association for Computational Linguistics.

Emily M. Bender, Timnit Gebru, Angelina McMillan-Major, and Shmargaret Shmitchell. 2021. On the dangers of stochastic parrots: Can language models be too big? In *Proceedings of the 2021 ACM Conference on Fairness, Accountability, and Transparency*, FAccT '21, pages 610–623, New York, NY, USA. Association for Computing Machinery.

Raymond Bertram, Matti Laine, and Minna Maria Virkkala. 2000. The role of derivational morphology in vocabulary acquisition: Get by with a little help from my morpheme friends. *Scandinavian Journal of Psychology*, 41(4):287–296.

Mathias Creutz and Krista Lagus. 2002. Unsupervised discovery of morphemes. In *Proceedings of the ACL-02 Workshop on Morphological and Phonological Learning - Volume 6*, MPL '02, pages 21–30, USA. Association for Computational Linguistics.

Sabit Ekin. 2023. Prompt engineering for chatgpt: A quick guide to techniques, tips, and best practices. *TechRxiv*.

Michael A. Ford, Matt H. Davis, and William David Marslen-Wilson. 2010. Derivational morphology and base morpheme frequency. *Journal of Memory and Language*, 63(1):117–130.

Harald Hammarström and Lars Borin. 2011. Unsupervised learning of morphology. *Computational Linguistics*, 37(2):309–350.

Najoung Kim and Paul Smolensky. 2021. Testing for grammatical category abstraction in neural language models. In *Proceedings of the Society for Computation in Linguistics 2021*, pages 467–470, Online. Association for Computational Linguistics.

Viet Dac Lai, Nghia Trung Ngo, Amir Pouran Ben Veyseh, Hieu Man, Franck Dernoncourt, Trung Bui, and Thien Huu Nguyen. 2023. Chatgpt beyond english: Towards a comprehensive evaluation of large language models in multilingual learning.

Alessandro Lenci. 2023. Understanding natural language understanding systems. a critical analysis. *ArXiv*, abs/2303.04229.

Kyle Mahowald, Anna A. Ivanova, Idan A. Blank, Nancy Kanwisher, Joshua B. Tenenbaum, and Evelina Fedorenko. 2023. Dissociating language and thought in large language models: a cognitive perspective.

R. Thomas McCoy, Paul Smolensky, Tal Linzen, Jianfeng Gao, and Asli Celikyilmaz. 2023. How Much Do Language Models Copy From Their Training Data? Evaluating Linguistic Novelty in Text Generation Using RAVEN. *Transactions of the Association for Computational Linguistics*, 11:652–670.

OpenAI. 2021. ChatGPT 3.5. OpenAI Blog. https://openai.com/blog/chatgpt.

Miguel Ortega-Martín, Óscar García-Sierra, Alfonso Ardoiz, Jorge Álvarez, Juan Carlos Armenteros, and Adrián Alonso. 2023. Linguistic ambiguity analysis in chatgpt.

RStudio Team. 2020. *RStudio: Integrated Development Environment for R*. RStudio, PBC., Boston, MA.

R Core Team. 2021. *R: A Language and Environment for Statistical Computing*. R Foundation for Statistical Computing, Vienna, Austria.

Jiaqi Wang, Zhengliang Liu, Lin Zhao, Zihao Wu, Chong Ma, Sigang Yu, Haixing Dai, Qiushi Yang, Yiheng Liu, Songyao Zhang, Enze Shi, Yi Pan, Tuo Zhang, Dajiang Zhu, Xiang Li, Xi Jiang, Bao Ge, Yixuan Yuan, Dinggang Shen, Tianming Liu, and Shu Zhang. 2023. Review of large vision models and visual prompt engineering.

Jules White, Quchen Fu, Sam Hays, Michael Sandborn, Carlos Olea, Henry Gilbert, Ashraf Elnashar, Jesse Spencer-Smith, and Douglas C. Schmidt. 2023. A prompt pattern catalog to enhance prompt engineering with chatgpt.

Tony Z. Zhao, Eric Wallace, Shi Feng, Dan Klein, and Sameer Singh. 2021. Calibrate before use: Improving few-shot performance of language models.

A Appendix A: Prompts

Define Pattern

1. Define...
2. Define the *new* word ...
3. Define the word ... considering its *morphemes*.
4. Define the *new* word ... considering its *morphemes*.

Context Manager Pattern

1. I want you to generate a definition for the word I provide.
2. I want you to generate a definition for the *new* word I provide.
3. I want you to generate a definition for the word I provide. When analysing the word, especially consider its *morphemes*.
4. I want you to generate a definition for the *new* word I provide. When analysing the word, especially consider its *morphemes*.

Template Pattern

1. Provide definitions for words. I am going to provide a template for your output. Everything in all caps is a placeholder. Any time that you generate text, try to fit it into one of the placeholders that I list. Please preserve the formatting and overall template that I provide as WORD, means DEFINITION.
2. Provide definitions for words. I am going to provide a template for your output. Everything in all caps is a placeholder. Any time that you generate text, try to fit it into one of the placeholders that I list. Please preserve the formatting and overall template that I provide as *NEW* WORD, means DEFINITION.
3. Provide definitions for words. I am going to provide a template for your output. Everything in all caps is a placeholder. Any time that you generate text, try to fit it into one of the placeholders that I list. Please preserve the formatting and overall template that I provide as WORD, with *morphemes* MORPHEMES, means DEFINITION.
4. Provide definitions for words. I am going to provide a template for your output. Everything in all caps is a placeholder. Any time that you generate text, try to fit it into one of the placeholders that I list. Please preserve the formatting and overall template that I provide as *NEW* WORD, with *morphemes* MORPHEMES, means DEFINITION.

Word Generator Persona

1. You are going to pretend to be a word generator. When I type in a word, you are going to output the corresponding definition that the word generator would produce.
2. You are going to pretend to be a word generator that can generate *new* words. When I type in a word, you are going to output the corresponding definition that the word generator would produce.
3. You are going to pretend to be a word generator that can generate words only by considering the *morphemes* of words. When I type in a word, you are going to output the corresponding definition that the word generator would produce.
4. You are going to pretend to be a word generator that can generate *new* words only by considering the *morphemes* of words. When I type in a word, you are going to output the corresponding definition that the word generator would produce.

Lexicographer Persona

1. From now on, act as a lexicographer when providing definitions of words. Provide outputs that a lexicographer would regarding words.
2. From now on, act as a lexicographer when providing definitions of *new* words. Provide outputs that a lexicographer would regarding words.
3. From now on, act as a lexicographer when providing definitions of words. Pay close attention to the *morphemes* of any word that we talk about. Provide outputs that a lexicographer would regarding words.
4. From now on, act as a lexicographer when providing definitions of *new* words. Pay close

attention to the *morphemes* of any word that we talk about. Provide outputs that a lexicographer would regarding words.

Infinite Generation Pattern

1. From now on, I want you to generate a definition for the word I provide until I say stop. I am going to provide a template for your output. Everything in all caps is a placeholder. Any time that you generate text, try to fit it into one of the placeholders that I list. Please preserve the formatting and overall template that I provide at WORD, means DEFINITION

2. From now on, I want you to generate a definition for the *new* word I provide until I say stop. I am going to provide a template for your output. Everything in all caps is a placeholder. Any time that you generate text, try to fit it into one of the placeholders that I list. Please preserve the formatting and overall template that I provide at WORD, means DEFINITION.

3. From now on, I want you to generate a definition for the word I provide until I say stop. I am going to provide a template for your output. Everything in all caps is a placeholder. Any time that you generate text, try to fit it into one of the placeholders that I list. Please preserve the formatting and overall template that I provide at WORD, with *morphemes* MORPHEMES, means DEFINITION

4. From now on, I want you to generate a definition for the *new* word I provide until I say stop. I am going to provide a template for your output. Everything in all caps is a placeholder. Any time that you generate text, try to fit it into one of the placeholders that I list. Please preserve the formatting and overall template that I provide at WORD, with *morphemes* MORPHEMES, means DEFINITION.

Author Index

Arora, Adwita, 44

Berbatova, Melania, 55

Chopra, Krish, 44

Dhaini, Mahdi, 1

Erdogan, Ege, 1
Estienne, Lautaro, 13

Jamnicki, Jędrzej, 64

Knappich, Valentin, 23

Maqsood, Zoya, 78
Martín Soeder, Teresa, 68

Poelman, Wessel, 1
Pramodya, Ashmari, 87

Rosario, Charlotte, 33

Salambashev, Yoan, 55
Schrader, Timo Pierre, 23
Suresh, Rishabh, 98
Suri, Manan, 44

Tyagi, Sarthak, 44

Zgreaban, Bianca-Madalina, 98

Association for Computational Linguistics
209 N. Eighth Street
Stroudsburg, Pennsylvania 18360

CURRAN ASSOCIATES INC.
proceedings.com

ISBN 978-1-7138-9041-6